KINSKI

WRITTEN AND DRAWN BY

GABRIEL HARDMAN

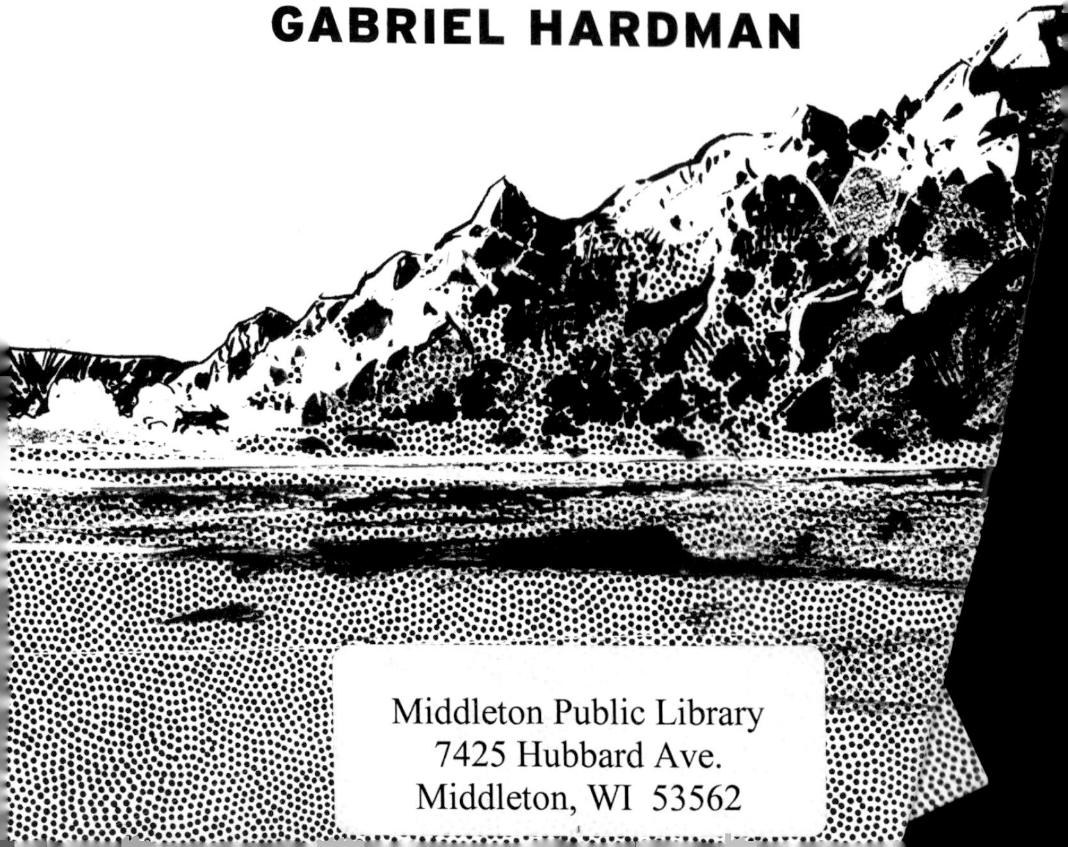

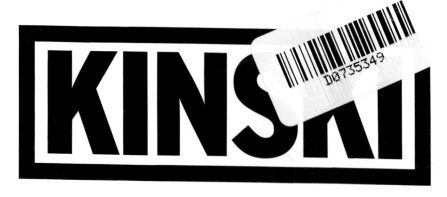

FOR CORINNA, CAMILA AND THE REAL KINSKI.

IMAGE COMICS, INC.
Robert Kirkman – Chief Operating Officer
Erik Larsen – Chief Financial Officer
Todd McFarlane – President
Marc Silvestri – Chief Executive Officer
Jim Valentino – Vice-President

Eric Stephenson – Publisher
Ron Richards – Director of Business Development
Jennifer de Guzman – Director of Trade Book Sales
Kat Salazar – Director of PR & Marketing
Corey Murphy – Director of Retail Sales
Jeremy Sullivan – Director of Digital Sales
Emilio Bautista – Sales Assistant
Branwyn Bigglestone – Senior Accounts Manager
Emily Miller – Accounts Manager
Jessica Ambriz – Administrative Assistant
Tyler Shainline – Events Coordinator
David Brothers – Content Manager
Jonathan Chan – Production Manager
Drew Gill – Art Director
Meredith Wallace – Print Manager
Monica Garcia – Senior Production Artist
Jenna Savage – Production Artist
Addison Duke – Production Artist
Tricia Ramos – Production Assistant
IMAGECOMICS.COM

KINSKI. COPYRIGHT @ 2014 GABRIEL HARDMAN. NOVEMBER 2014.

Published by Image Comics, Inc. Office of publication: 2001 Center Street, 6th Floor, Berkeley, CA 94704. © 2014 Gabriel Hardman. Image Comics® and its logos are registered trademarks of Image Comics, Inc.

Printed in the USA.

For information regarding the CPSIA on this printed material call: 203-595-3636 and provide reference # RICH – 586518
BOOK DESIGN BY DYLAN TODD

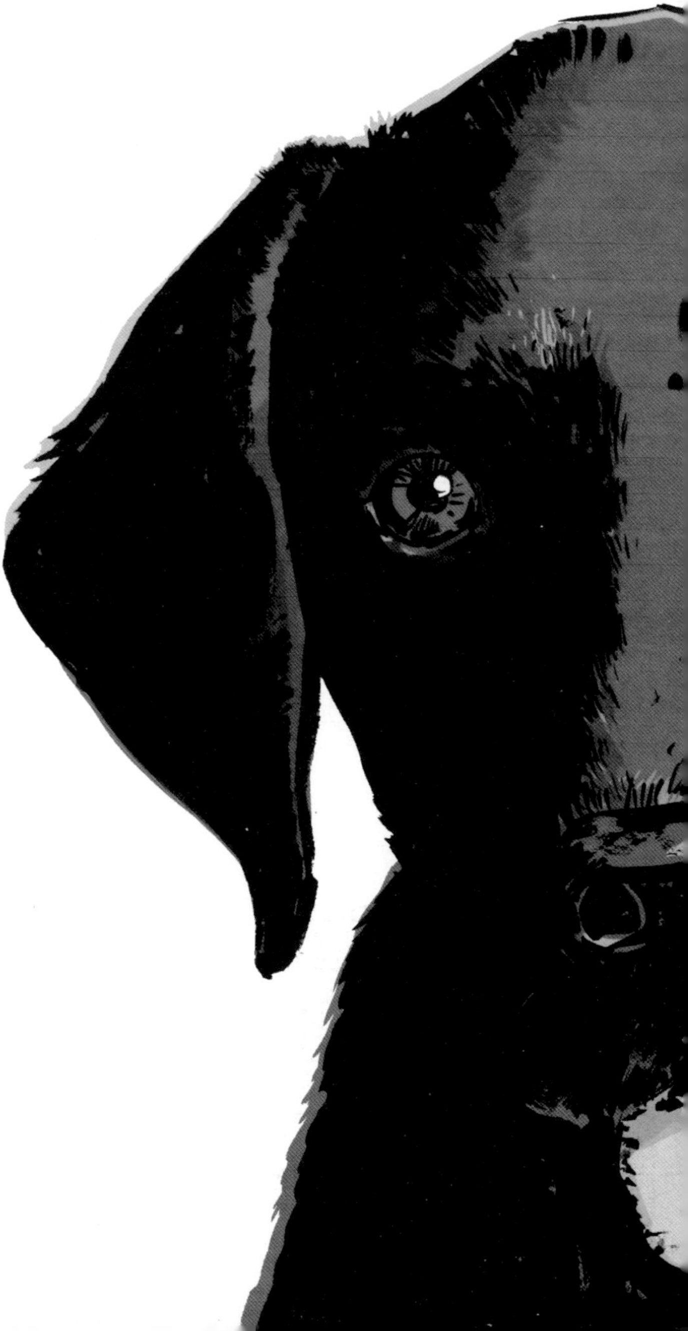

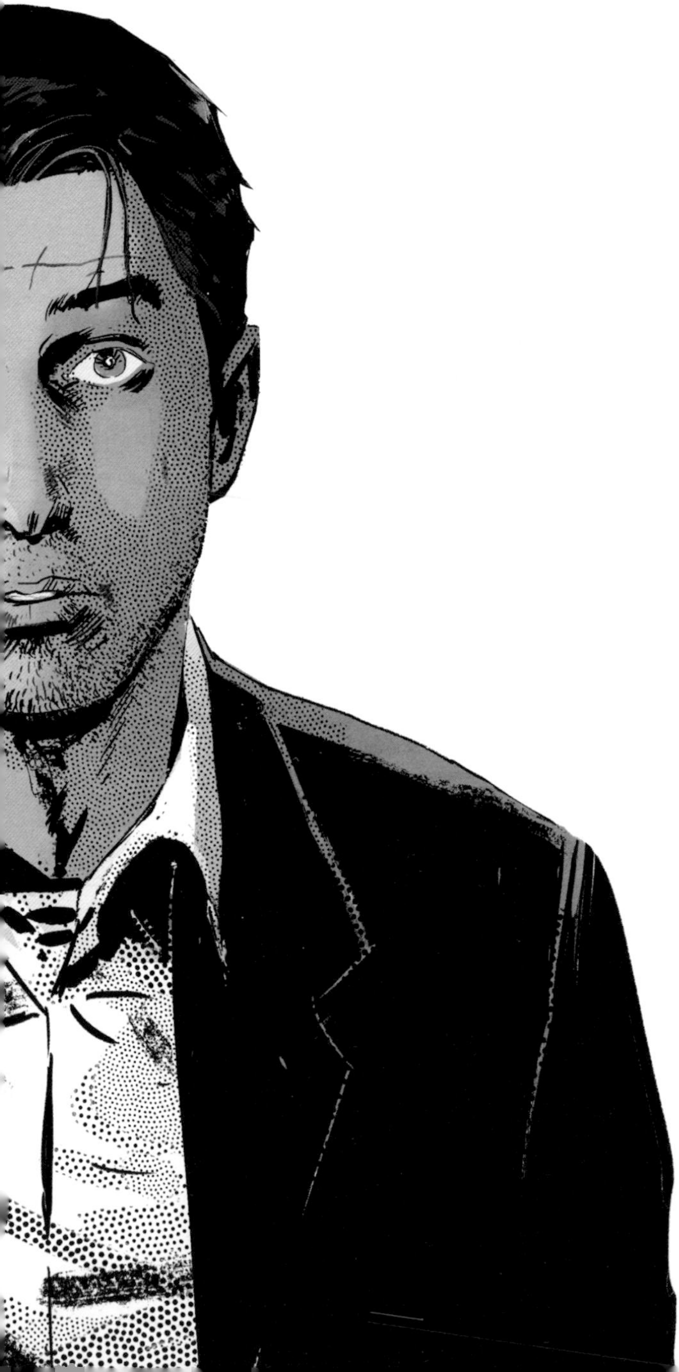

ONE

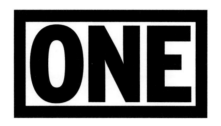

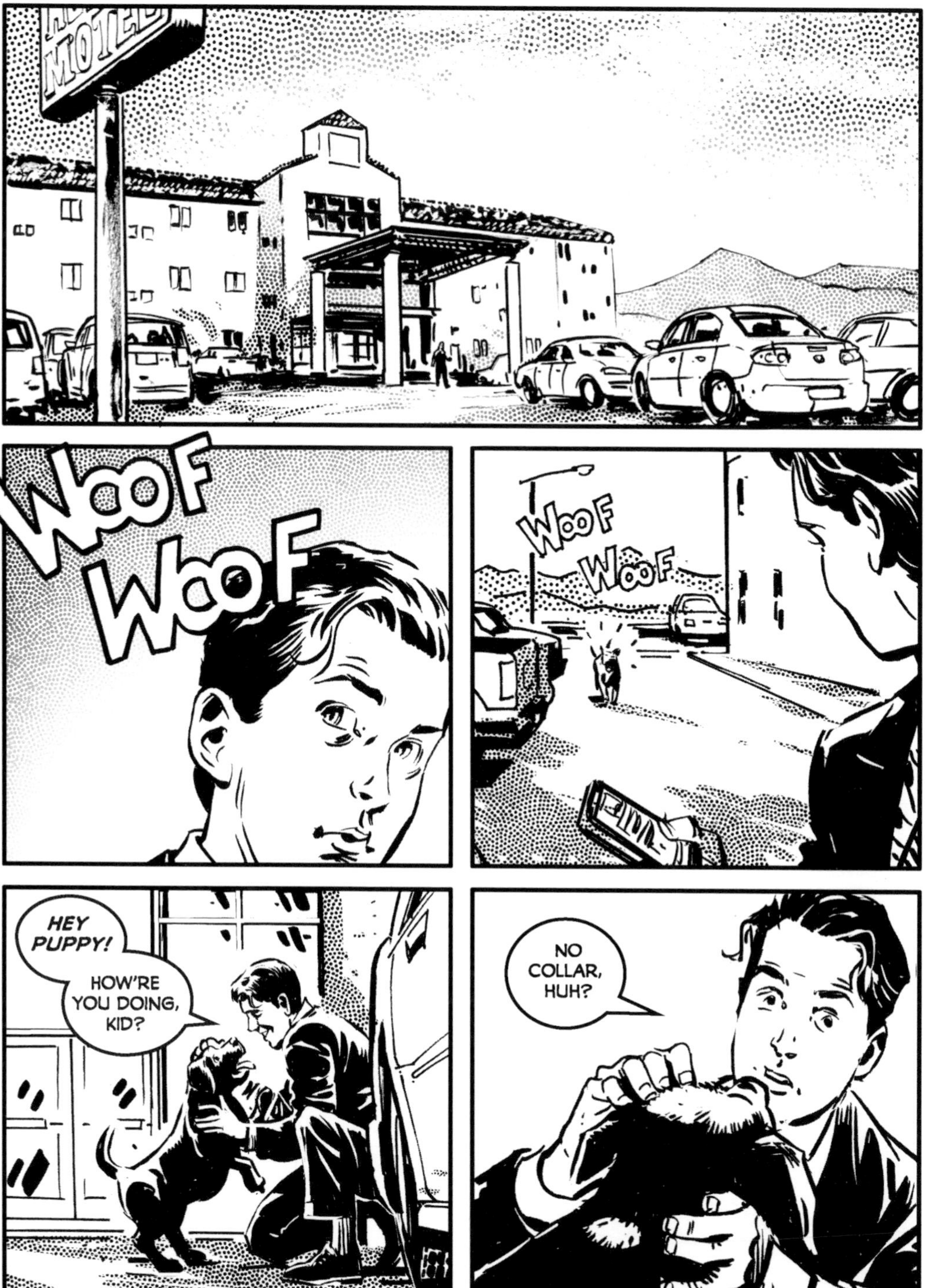
MOTEL
WOOF
WOOF
WOOF
WOOF
HEY PUPPY!
HOW'RE YOU DOING, KID?
NO COLLAR, HUH?

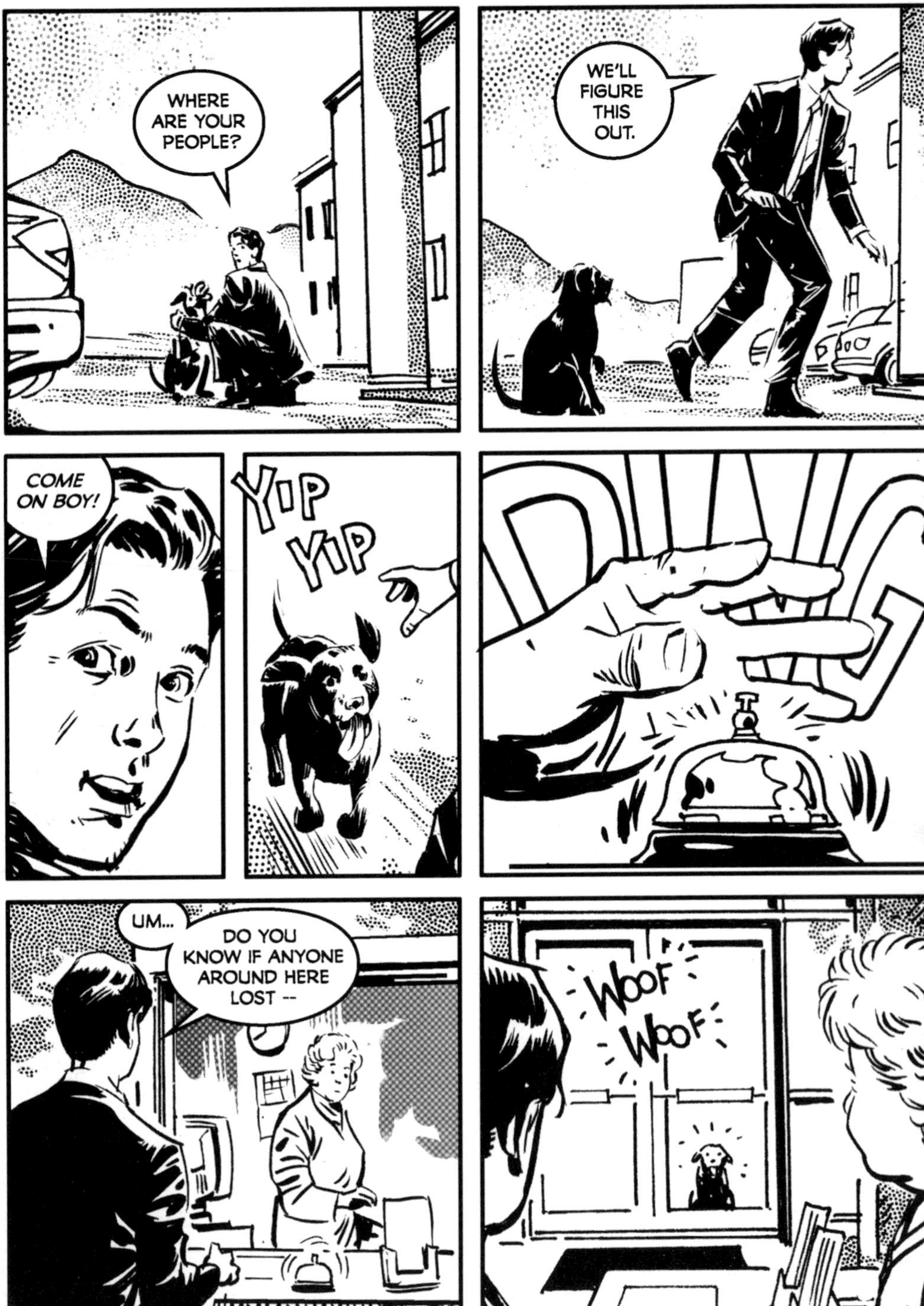
WHERE ARE YOUR PEOPLE?
WE'LL FIGURE THIS OUT.
COME ON BOY!
YIP YIP
UM...
DO YOU KNOW IF ANYONE AROUND HERE LOST --
WOOF WOOF

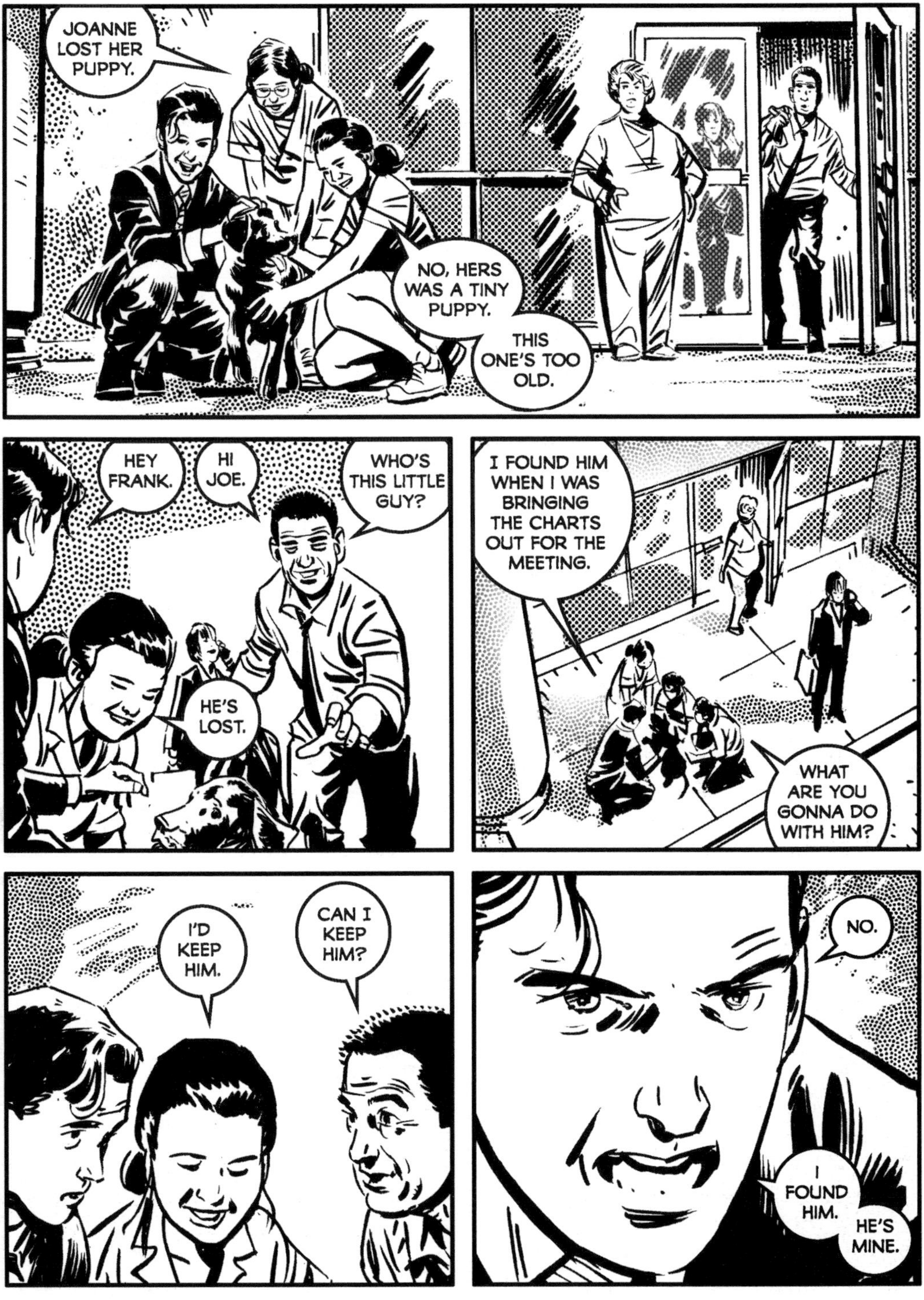
JOANNE LOST HER PUPPY.
NO, HERS WAS A TINY PUPPY.
THIS ONE'S TOO OLD.
HEY FRANK.
HI JOE.
WHO'S THIS LITTLE GUY?
HE'S LOST.
I FOUND HIM WHEN I WAS BRINGING THE CHARTS OUT FOR THE MEETING.
WHAT ARE YOU GONNA DO WITH HIM?
I'D KEEP HIM.
CAN I KEEP HIM?
NO.
I FOUND HIM.
HE'S MINE.

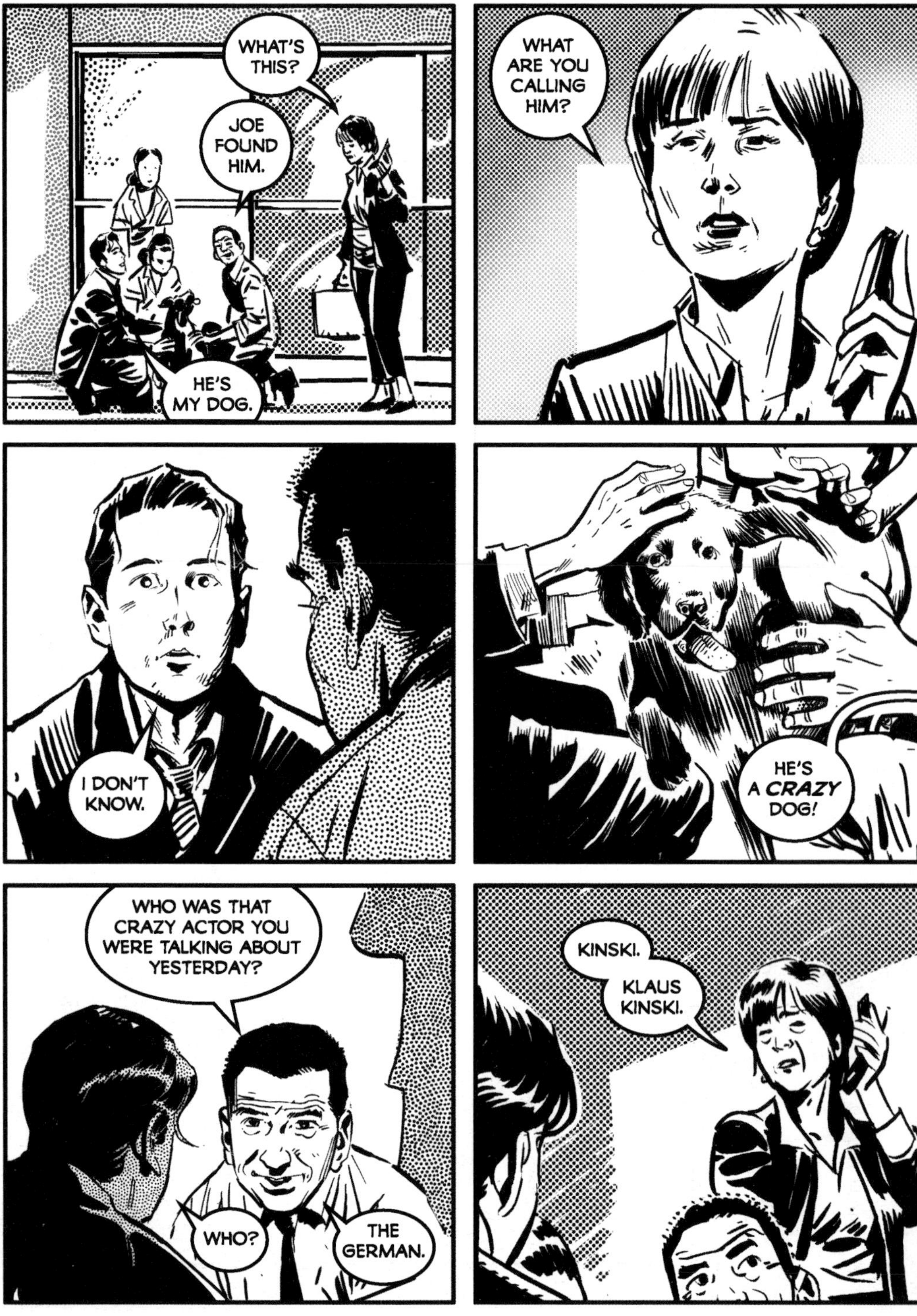
WHAT'S THIS?
JOE FOUND HIM.
HE'S MY DOG.
WHAT ARE YOU CALLING HIM?
I DON'T KNOW.
HE'S A *CRAZY* DOG!
WHO WAS THAT CRAZY ACTOR YOU WERE TALKING ABOUT YESTERDAY?
WHO?
THE GERMAN.
KINSKI.
KLAUS KINSKI.

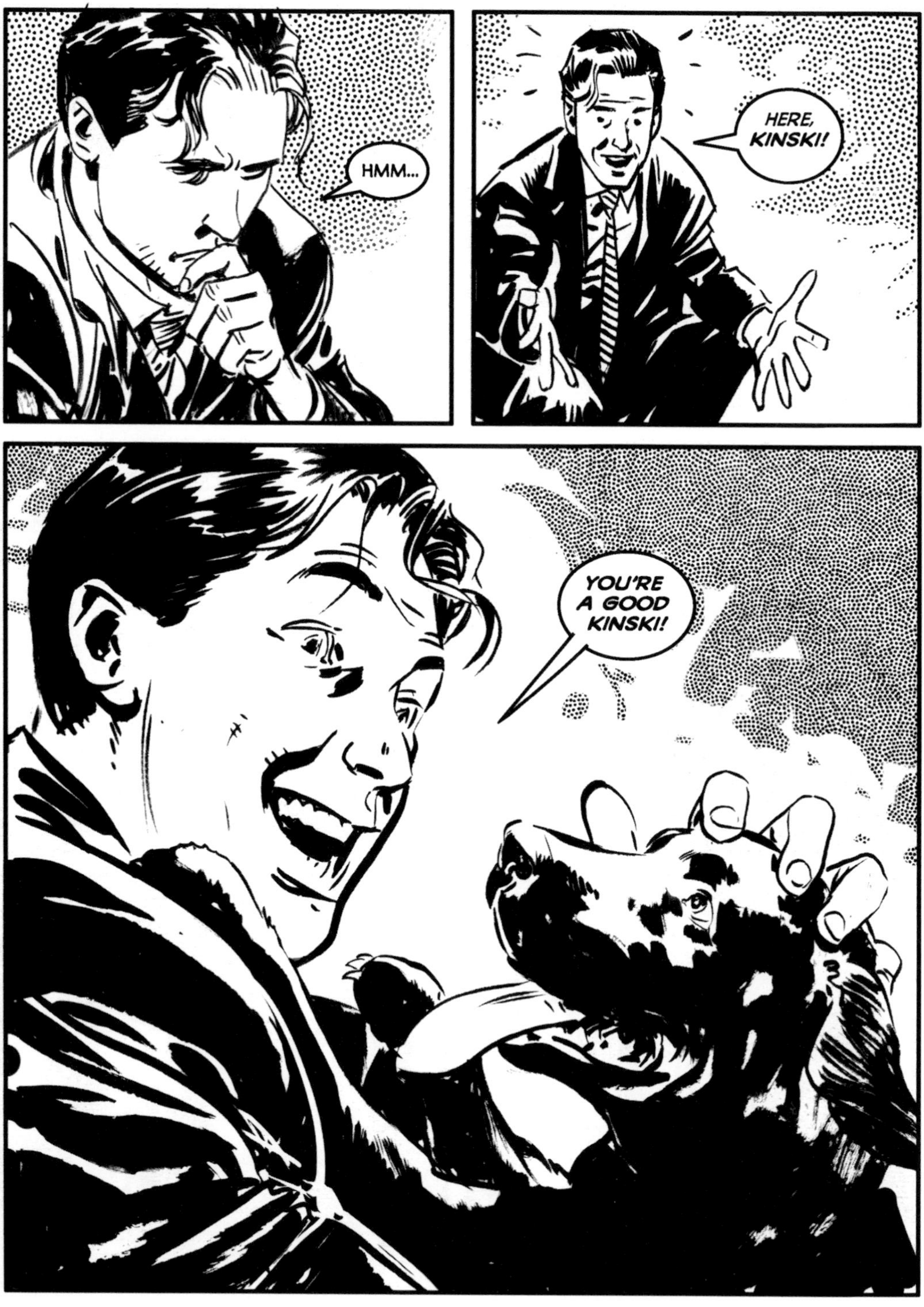
HMM...
HERE, KINSKI!
YOU'RE A GOOD KINSKI!

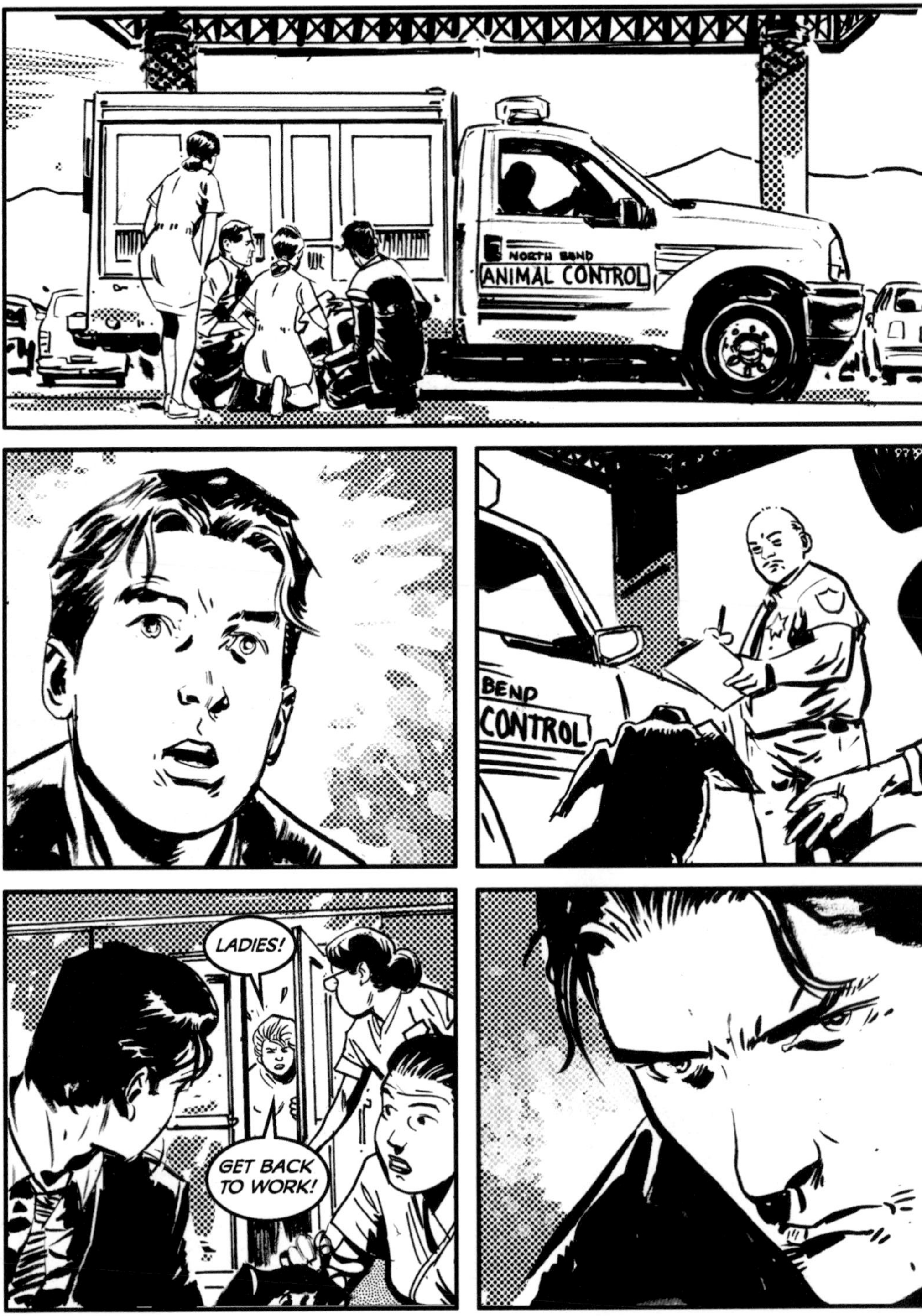
NORTH BEND
ANIMAL CONTROL
BEND
CONTROL
LADIES!
GET BACK TO WORK!

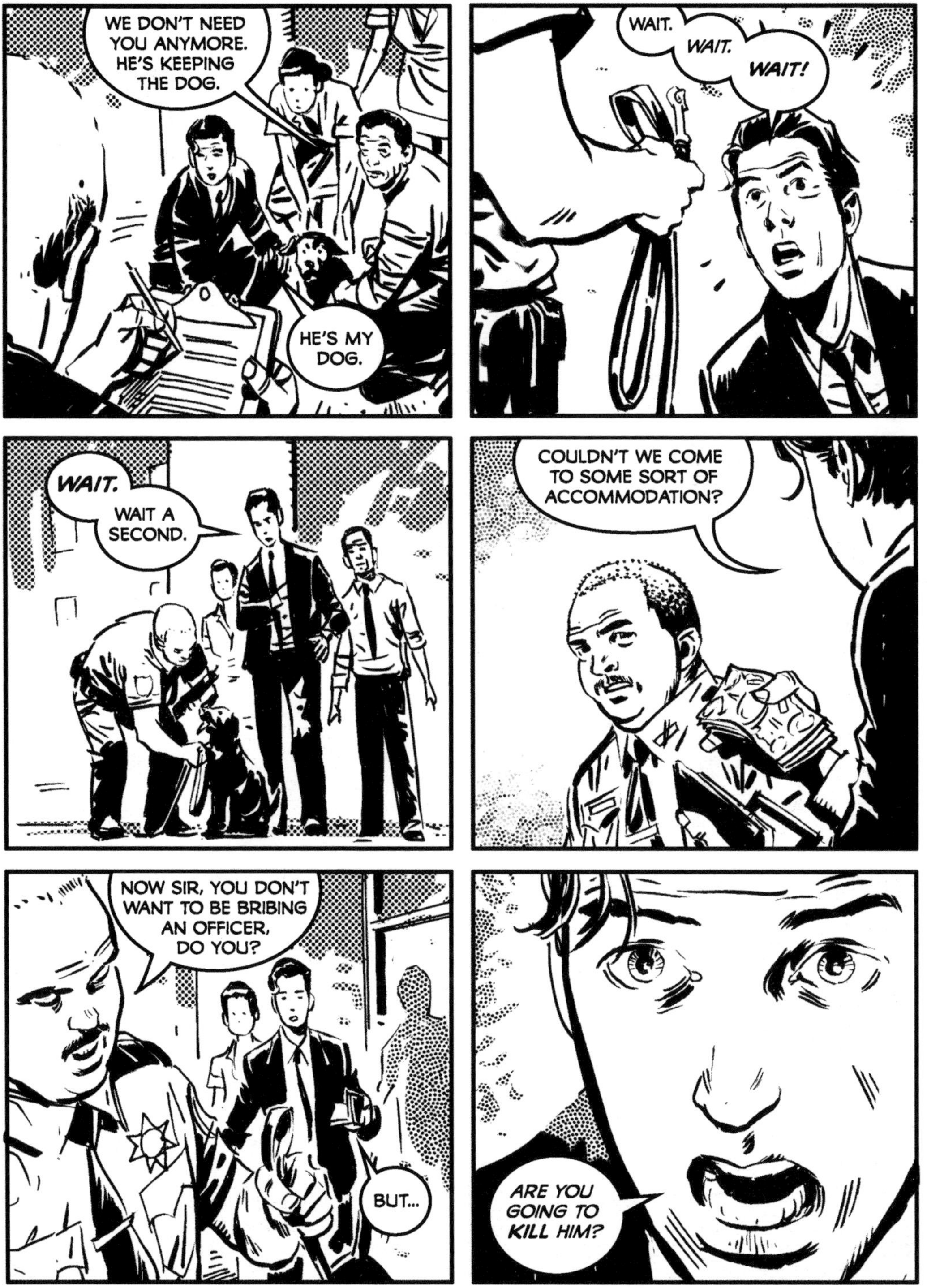
WE DON'T NEED YOU ANYMORE. HE'S KEEPING THE DOG.
HE'S MY DOG.
WAIT.
WAIT.
WAIT!
WAIT.
WAIT A SECOND.
COULDN'T WE COME TO SOME SORT OF ACCOMMODATION?
NOW SIR, YOU DON'T WANT TO BE BRIBING AN OFFICER, DO YOU?
BUT...
ARE YOU GOING TO KILL HIM?

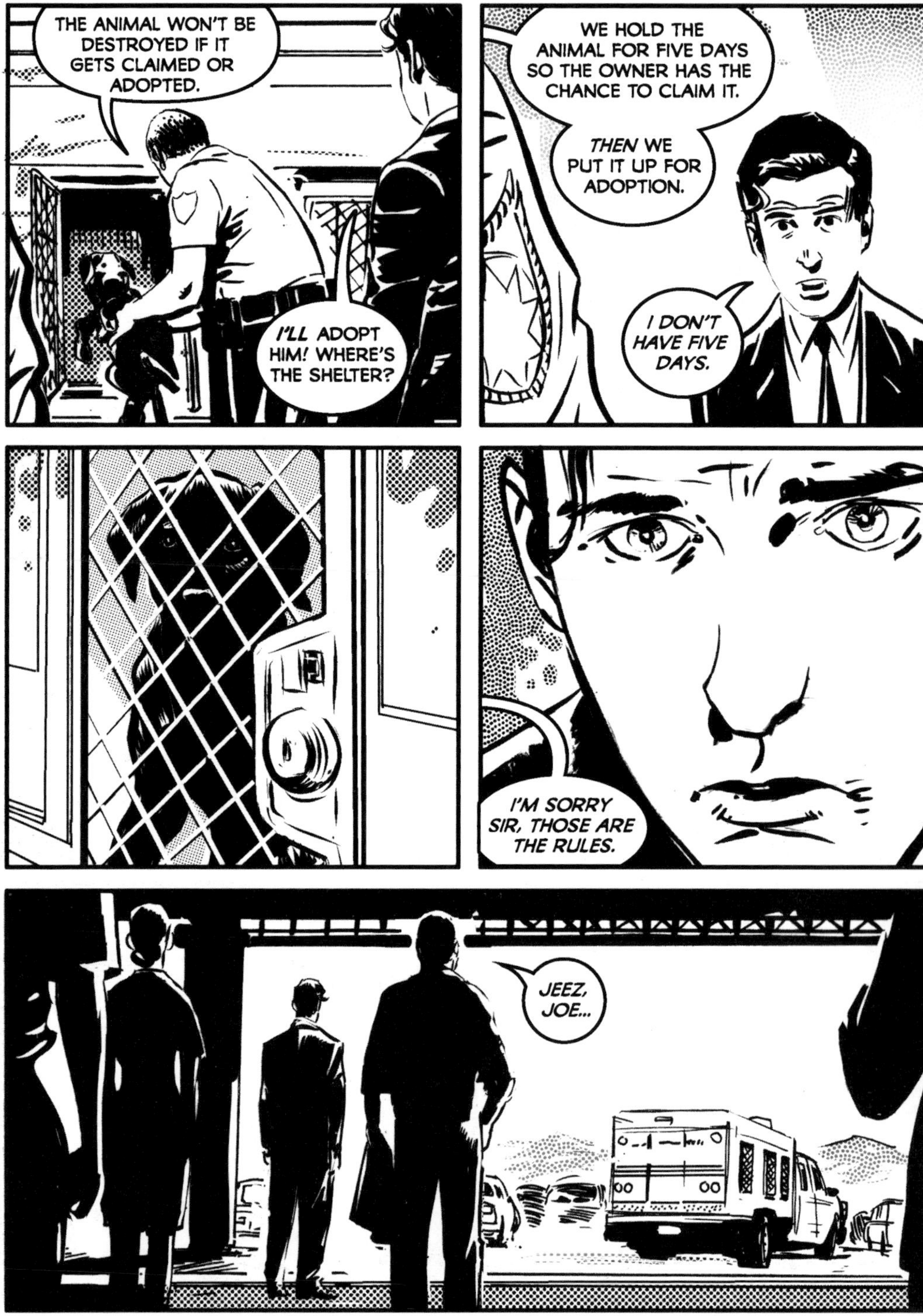
THE ANIMAL WON'T BE DESTROYED IF IT GETS CLAIMED OR ADOPTED.
I'LL ADOPT HIM! WHERE'S THE SHELTER?
WE HOLD THE ANIMAL FOR FIVE DAYS SO THE OWNER HAS THE CHANCE TO CLAIM IT.
THEN WE PUT IT UP FOR ADOPTION.
I DON'T HAVE FIVE DAYS.
I'M SORRY SIR, THOSE ARE THE RULES.
JEEZ, JOE...

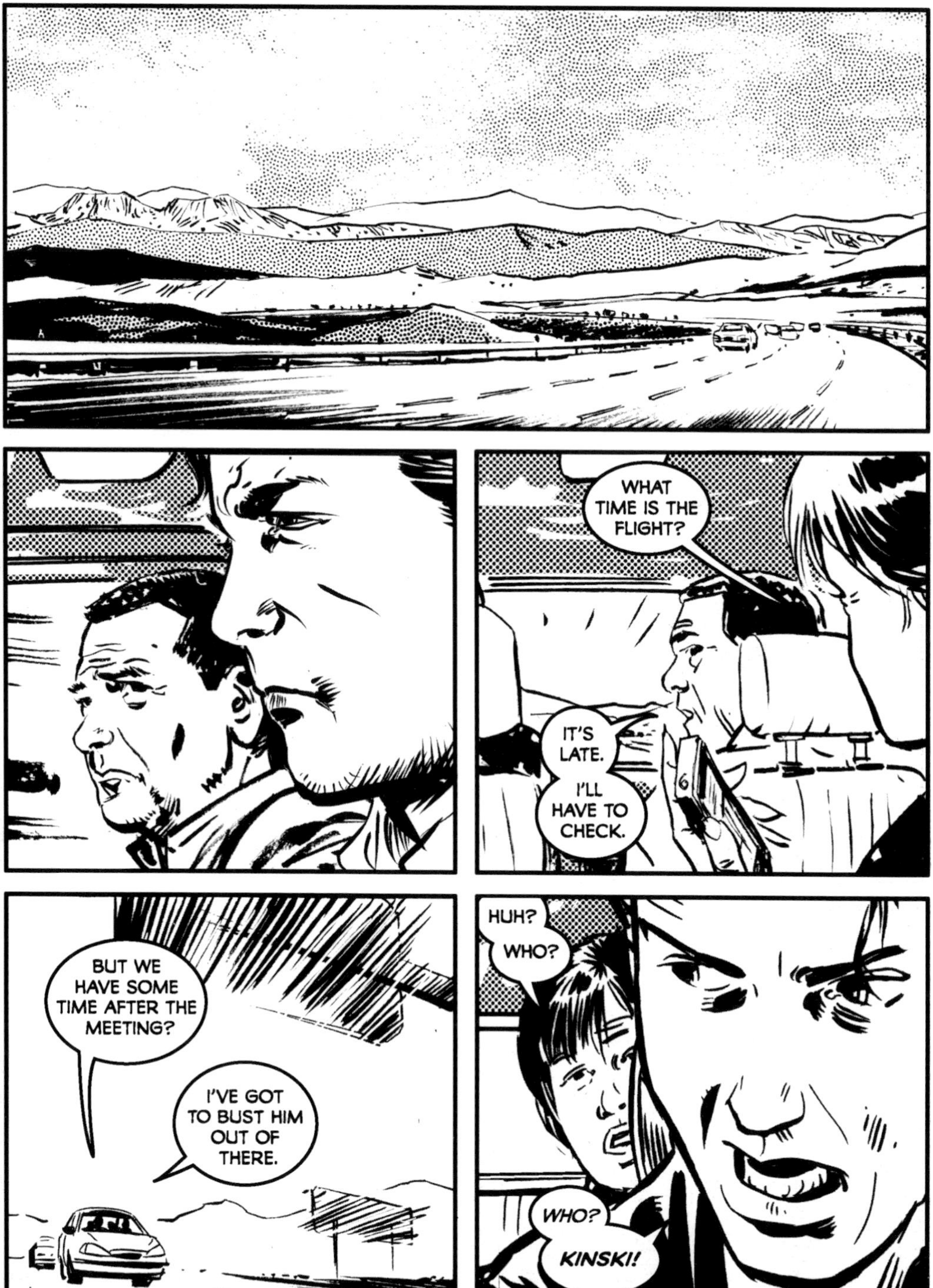
WHAT TIME IS THE FLIGHT?
IT'S LATE.
I'LL HAVE TO CHECK.
BUT WE HAVE SOME TIME AFTER THE MEETING?
I'VE GOT TO BUST HIM OUT OF THERE.
HUH?
WHO?
WHO?
KINSKI!

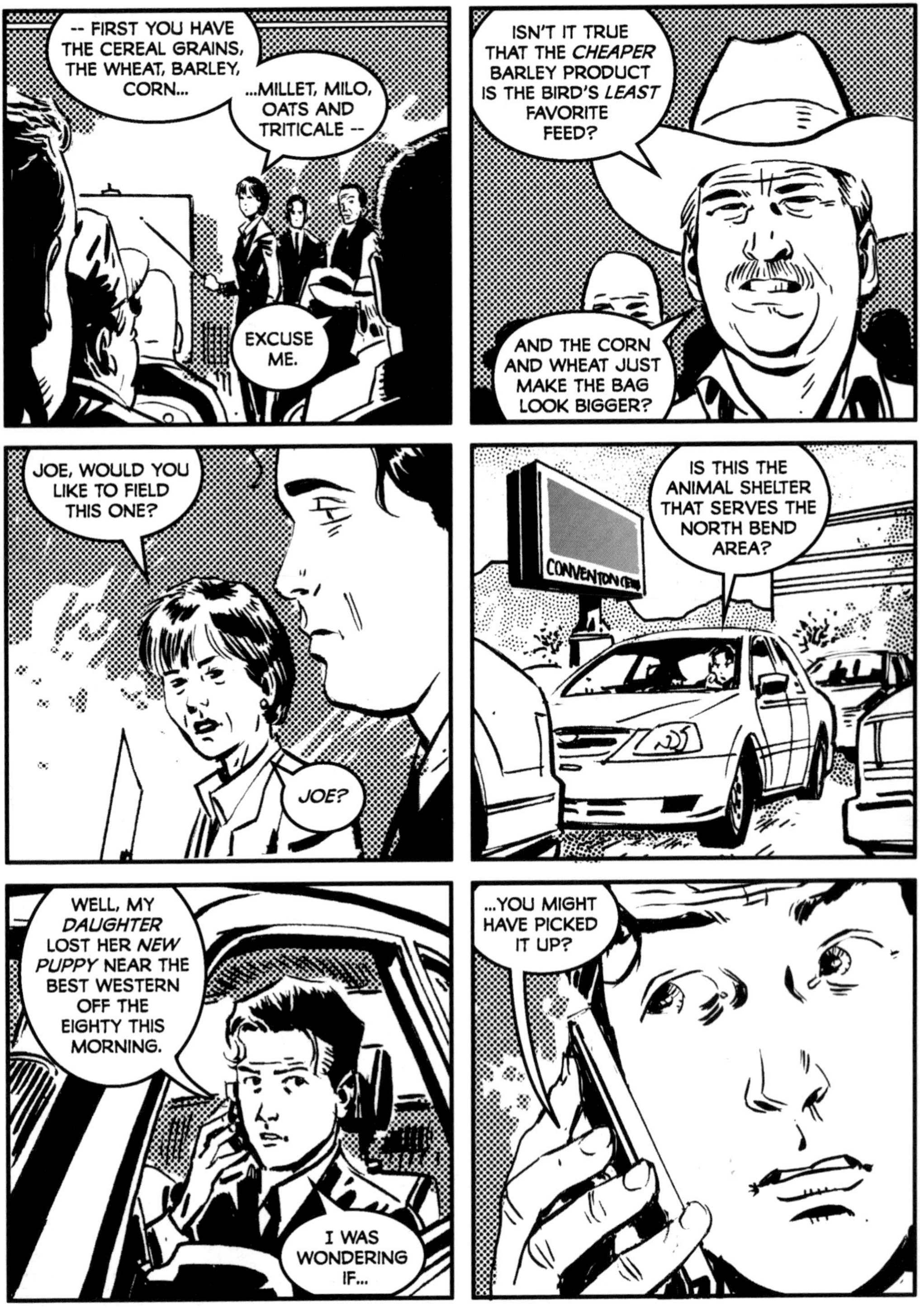
-- FIRST YOU HAVE THE CEREAL GRAINS, THE WHEAT, BARLEY, CORN...
...MILLET, MILO, OATS AND TRITICALE --
EXCUSE ME.
ISN'T IT TRUE THAT THE *CHEAPER* BARLEY PRODUCT IS THE BIRD'S *LEAST* FAVORITE FEED?
AND THE CORN AND WHEAT JUST MAKE THE BAG LOOK BIGGER?
JOE, WOULD YOU LIKE TO FIELD THIS ONE?
JOE?
IS THIS THE ANIMAL SHELTER THAT SERVES THE NORTH BEND AREA?
WELL, MY *DAUGHTER* LOST HER *NEW PUPPY* NEAR THE BEST WESTERN OFF THE EIGHTY THIS MORNING.
I WAS WONDERING IF...
...YOU MIGHT HAVE PICKED IT UP?

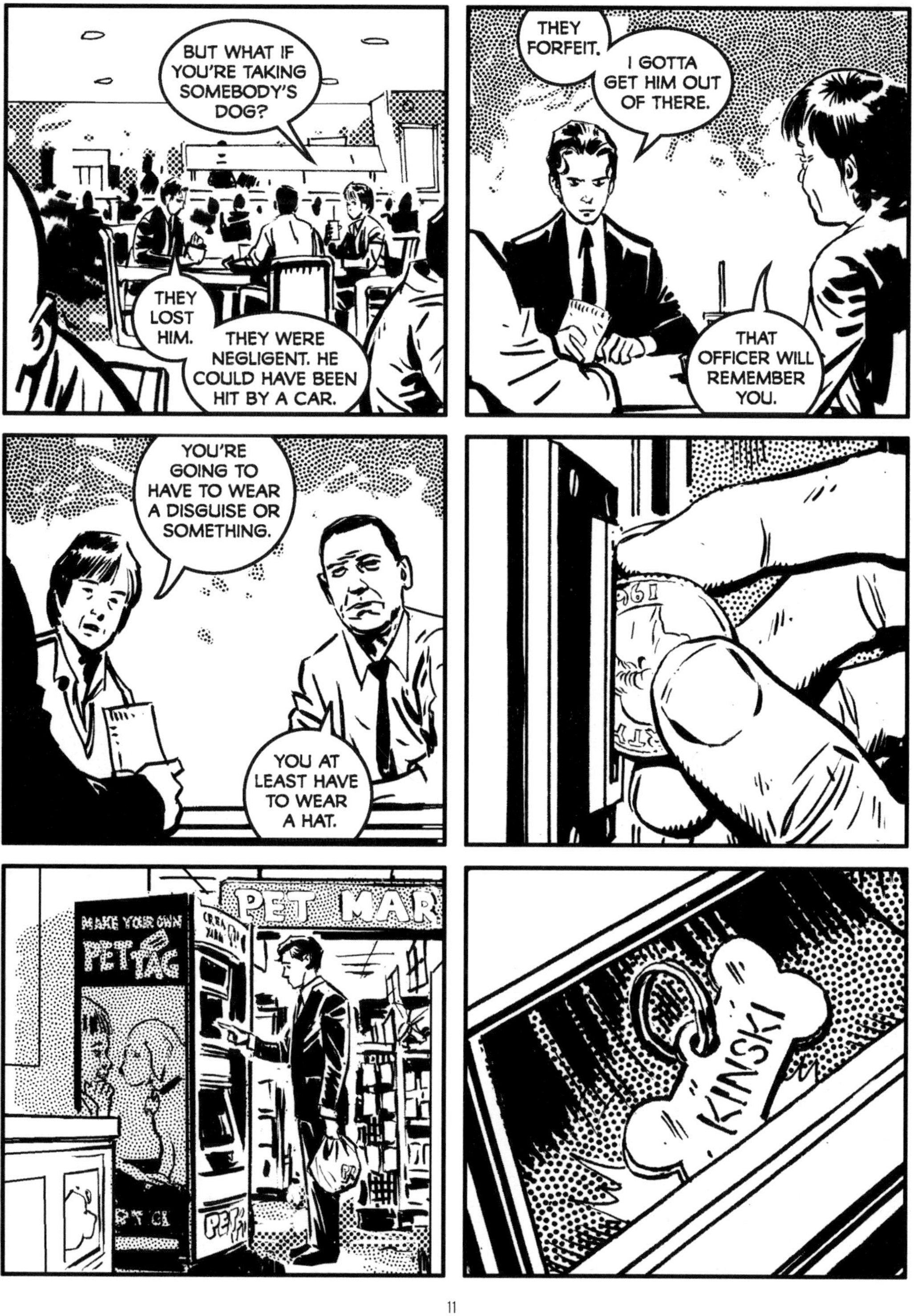
BUT WHAT IF YOU'RE TAKING SOMEBODY'S DOG?
THEY LOST HIM.
THEY WERE NEGLIGENT. HE COULD HAVE BEEN HIT BY A CAR.
THEY FORFEIT.
I GOTTA GET HIM OUT OF THERE.
THAT OFFICER WILL REMEMBER YOU.
YOU'RE GOING TO HAVE TO WEAR A DISGUISE OR SOMETHING.
YOU AT LEAST HAVE TO WEAR A HAT.
PET MAR
MAKE YOUR OWN PET TAG
KINSKI

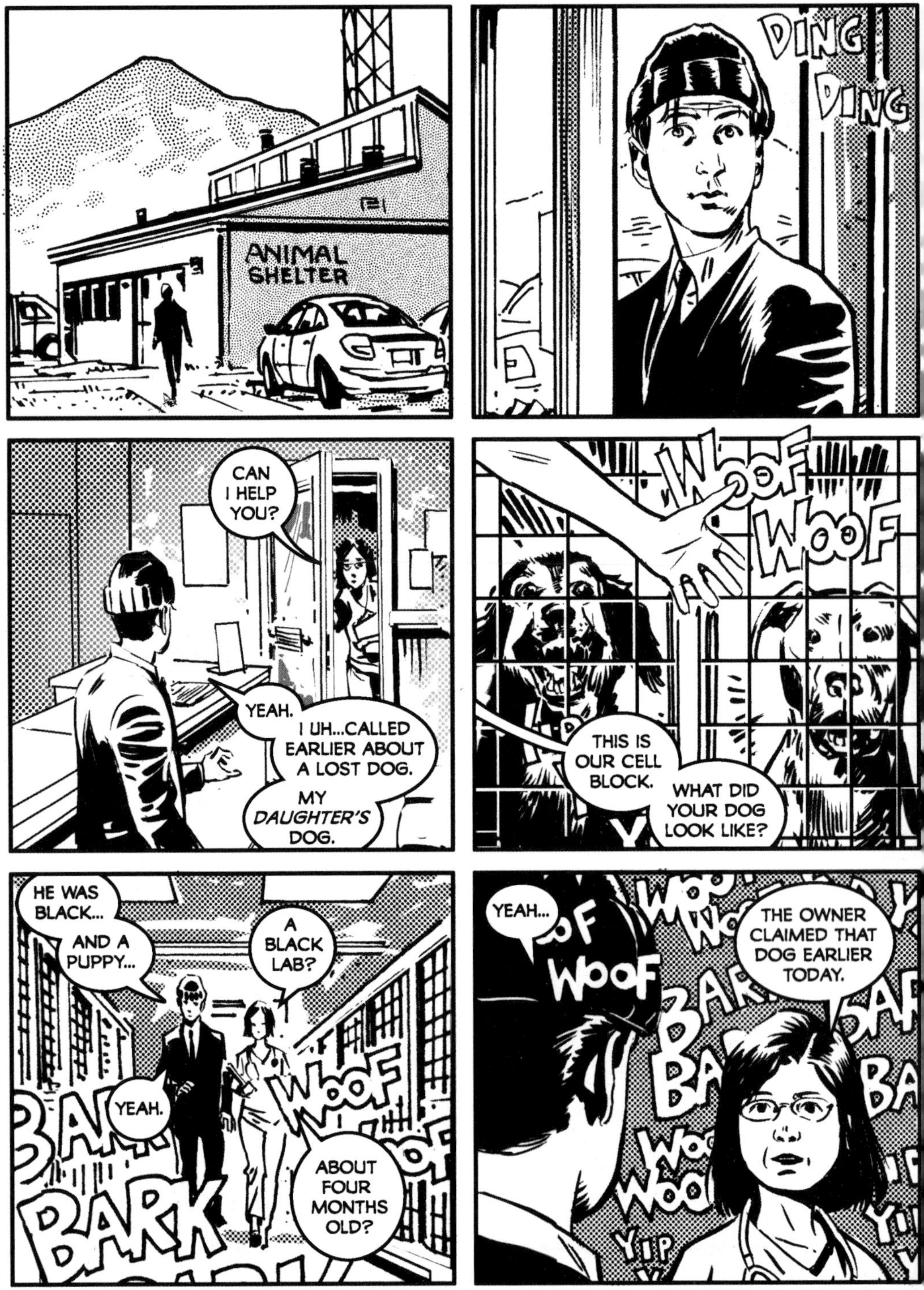
ANIMAL SHELTER
DING
DING
CAN I HELP YOU?
YEAH.
I UH...CALLED EARLIER ABOUT A LOST DOG.
MY *DAUGHTER'S* DOG.
WOOF
WOOF
THIS IS OUR CELL BLOCK.
WHAT DID YOUR DOG LOOK LIKE?
HE WAS BLACK...
AND A PUPPY...
A BLACK LAB?
YEAH.
WOOF
BARK
ABOUT FOUR MONTHS OLD?
YEAH...
WOOF
THE OWNER CLAIMED THAT DOG EARLIER TODAY.
YIP

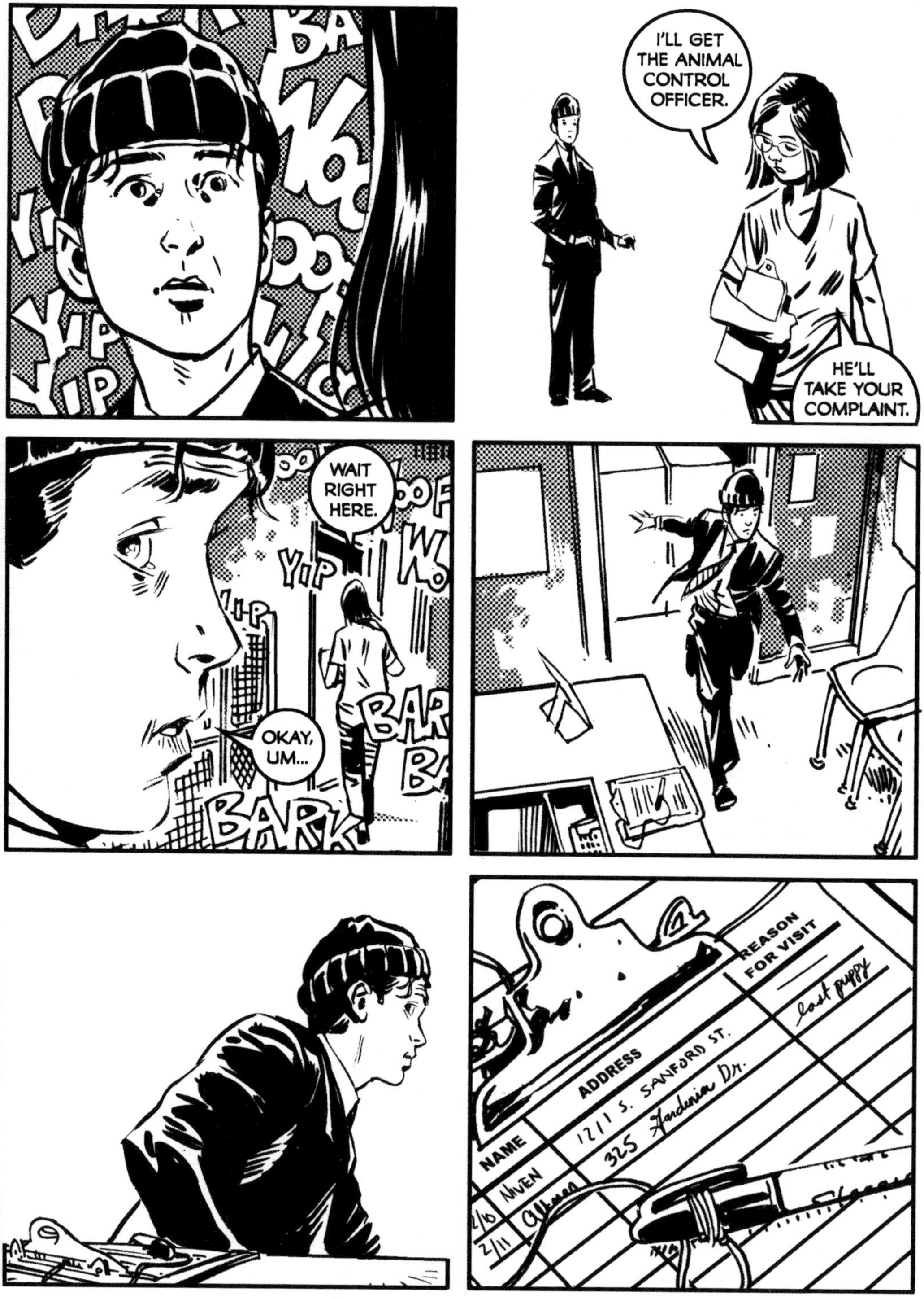
I'LL GET THE ANIMAL CONTROL OFFICER.
HE'LL TAKE YOUR COMPLAINT.
WAIT RIGHT HERE.
YIP
OKAY, UM...
BARK
REASON FOR VISIT
ADDRESS
NAME
NIVEN
1211 S. SANFORD ST.
lost puppy
2/10
2/11

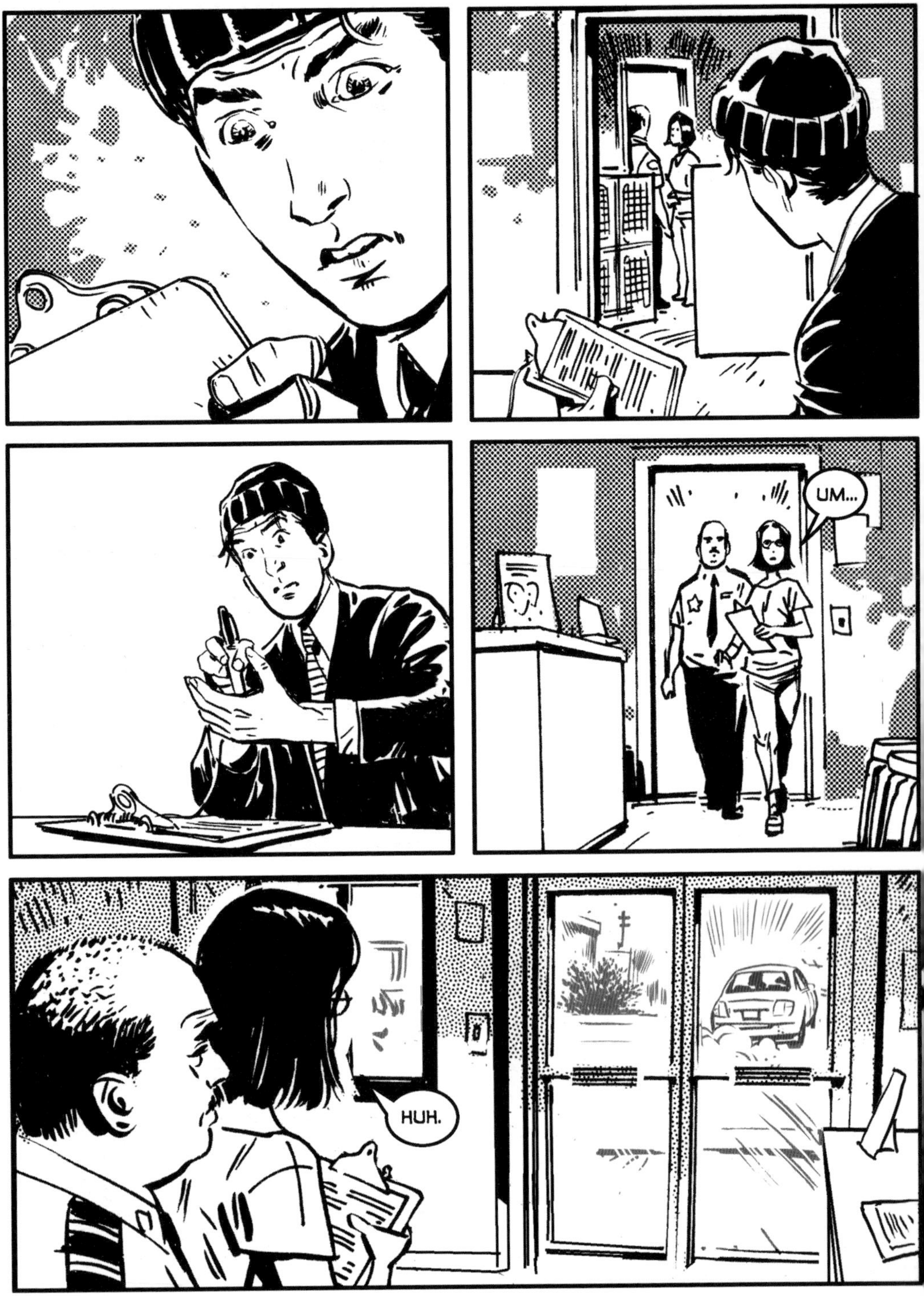
UM...
HUH.

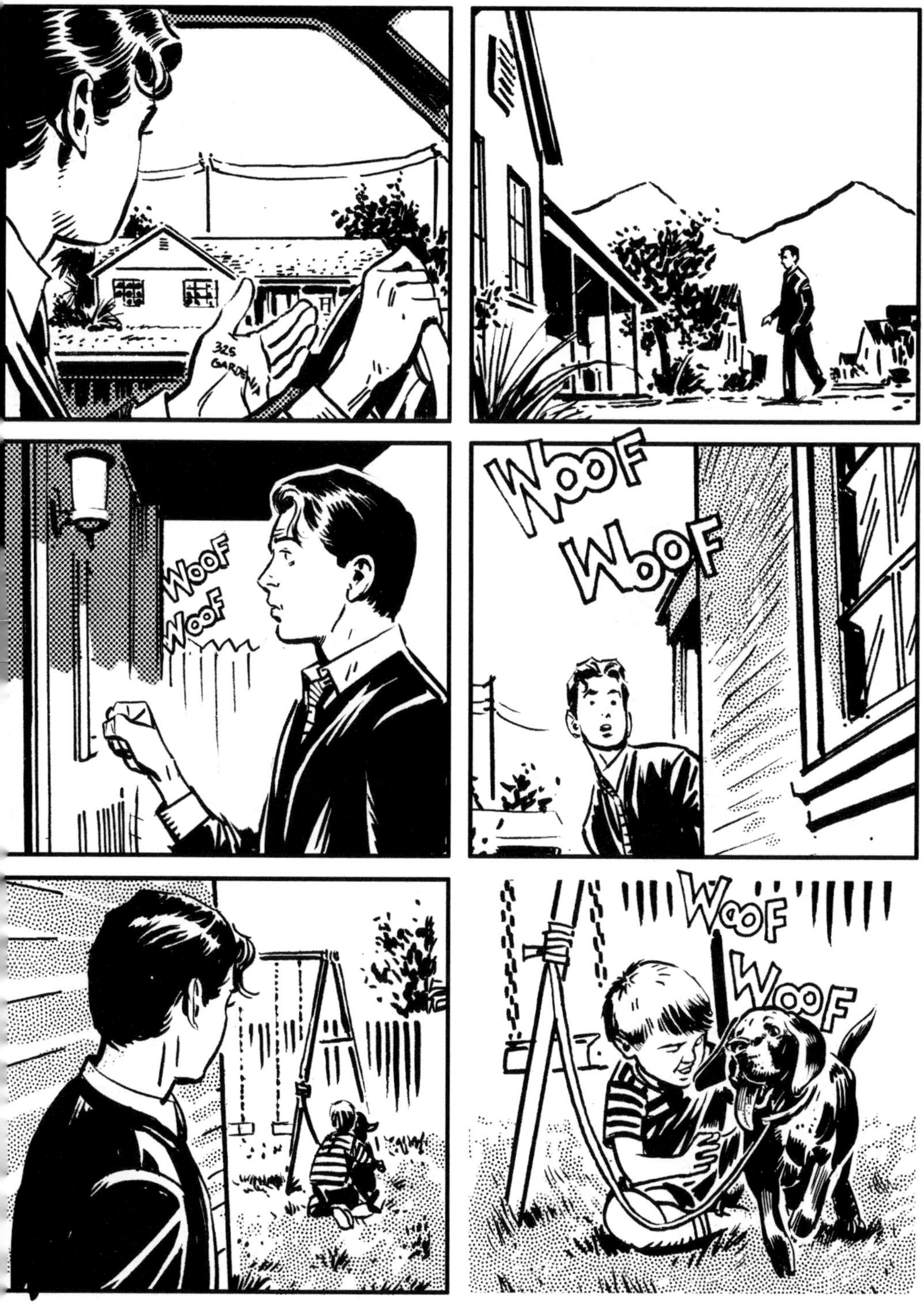
325 GARDENIA
WOOF
WOOF
WOOF
WOOF
WOOF
WOOF

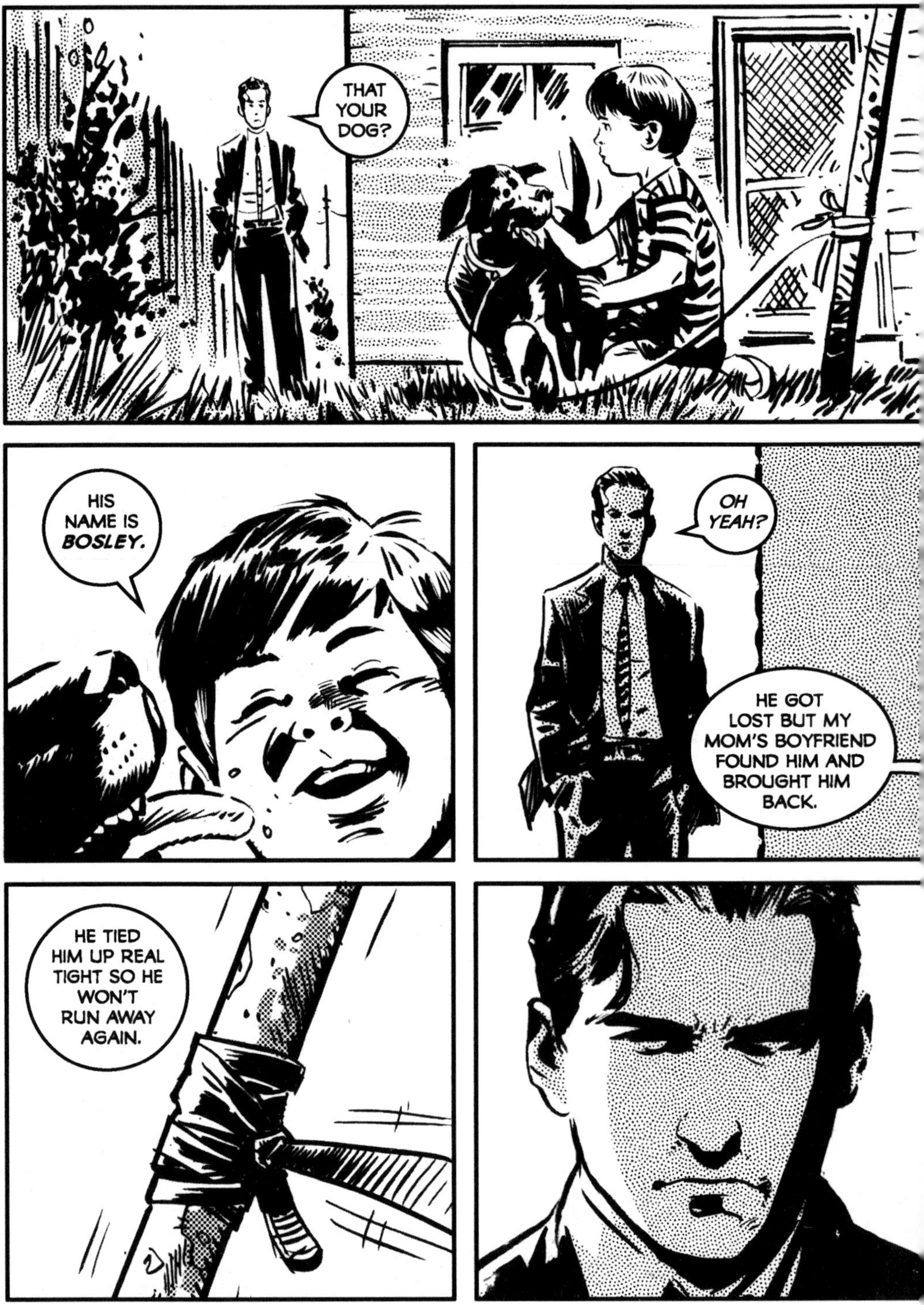
THAT YOUR DOG?
HIS NAME IS BOSLEY.
OH YEAH?
HE GOT LOST BUT MY MOM'S BOYFRIEND FOUND HIM AND BROUGHT HIM BACK.
HE TIED HIM UP REAL TIGHT SO HE WON'T RUN AWAY AGAIN.

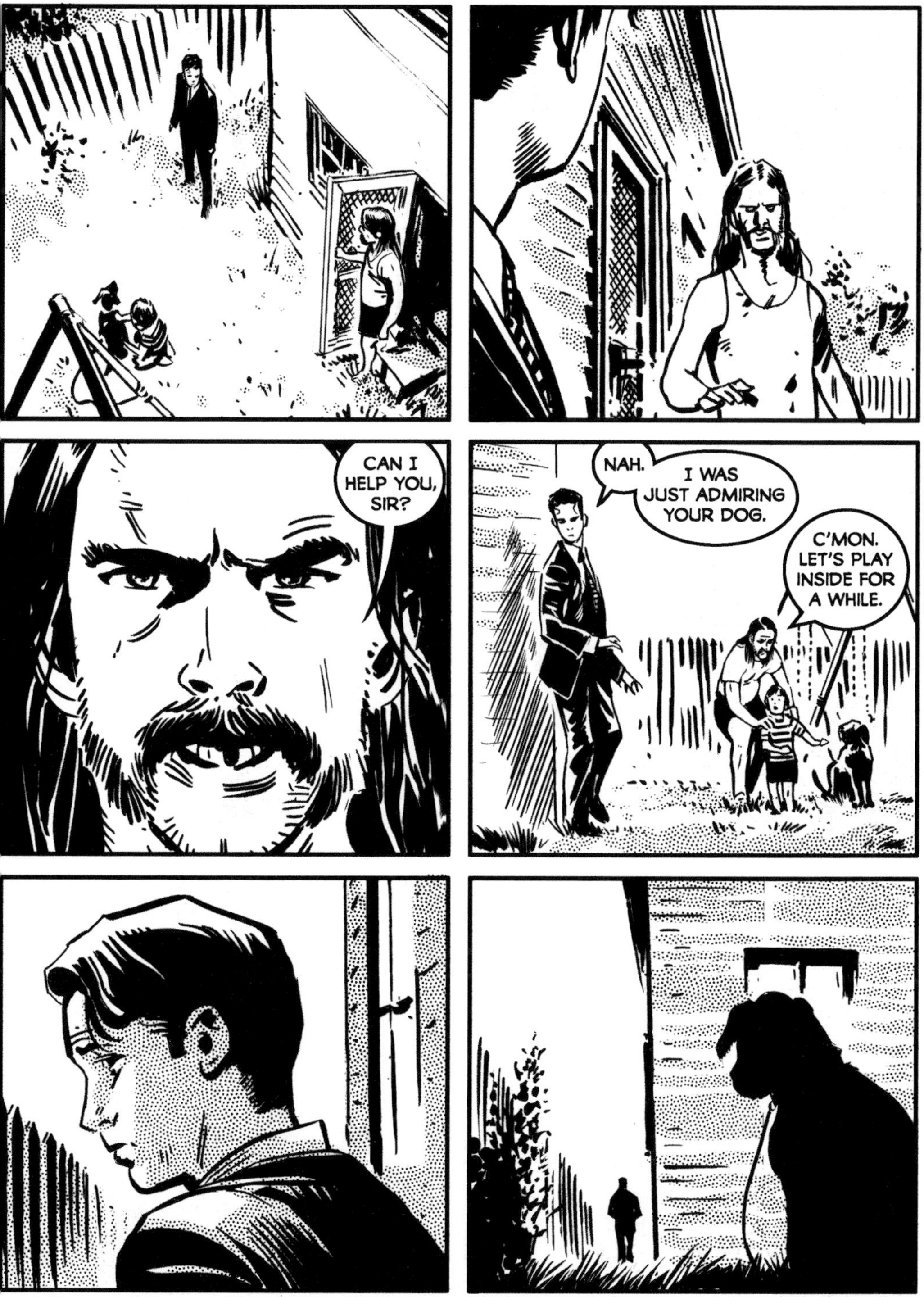
CAN I HELP YOU, SIR?
NAH.
I WAS JUST ADMIRING YOUR DOG.
C'MON. LET'S PLAY INSIDE FOR A WHILE.

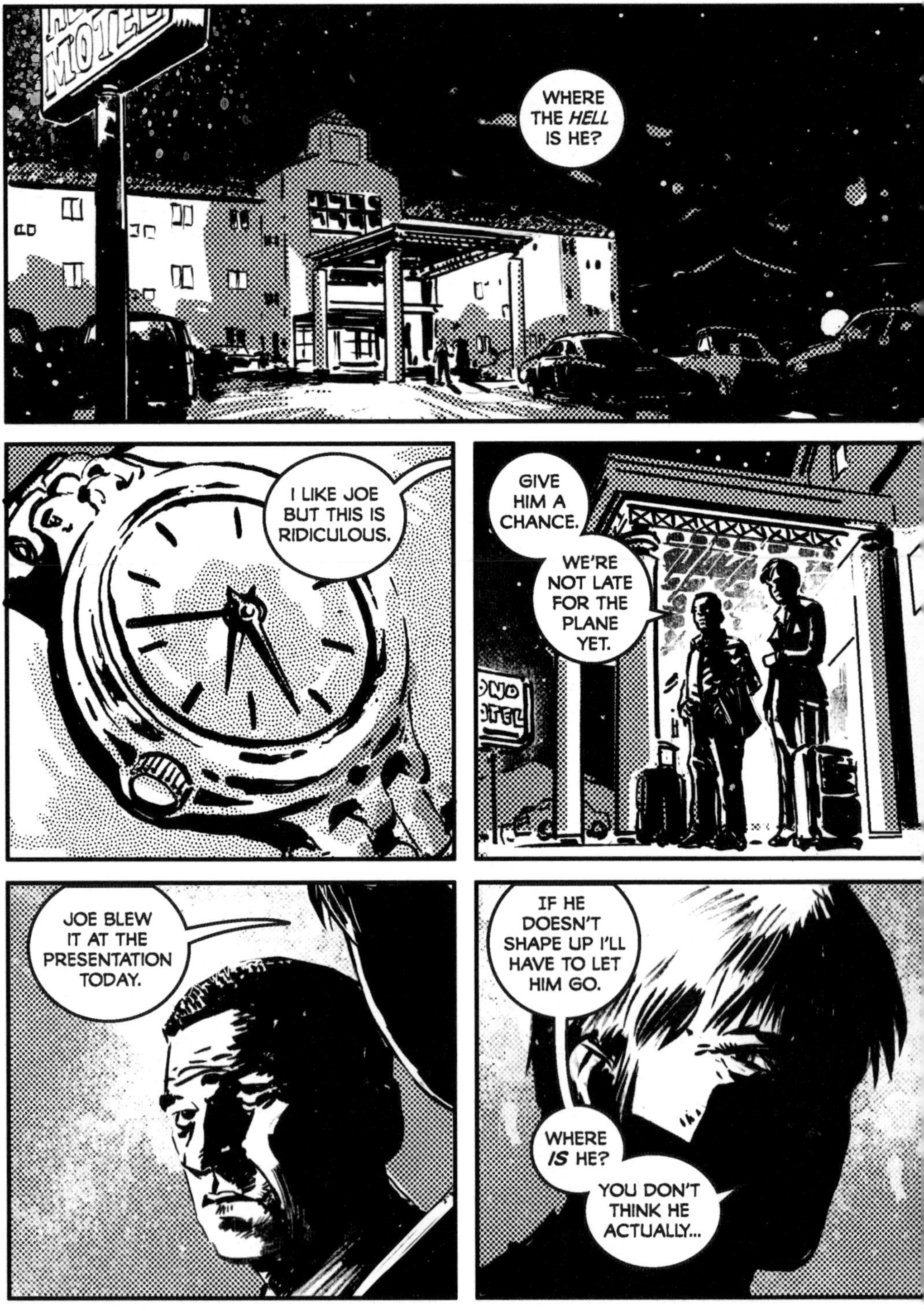
WHERE THE *HELL* IS HE?
I LIKE JOE BUT THIS IS RIDICULOUS.
GIVE HIM A CHANCE.
WE'RE NOT LATE FOR THE PLANE YET.
JOE BLEW IT AT THE PRESENTATION TODAY.
IF HE DOESN'T SHAPE UP I'LL HAVE TO LET HIM GO.
WHERE *IS* HE?
YOU DON'T THINK HE ACTUALLY...

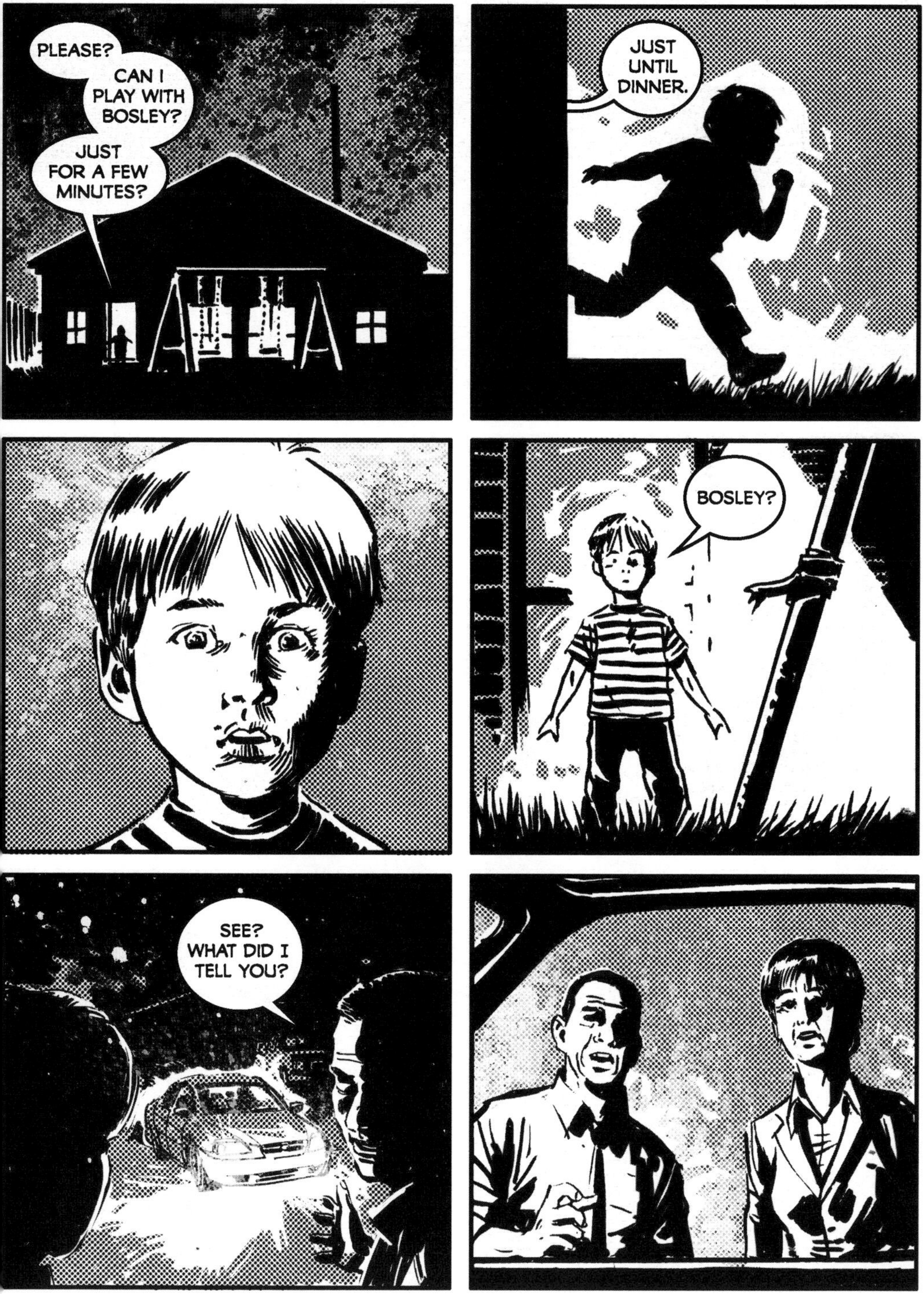
PLEASE?
CAN I PLAY WITH BOSLEY?
JUST FOR A FEW MINUTES?
JUST UNTIL DINNER.
BOSLEY?
SEE? WHAT DID I TELL YOU?

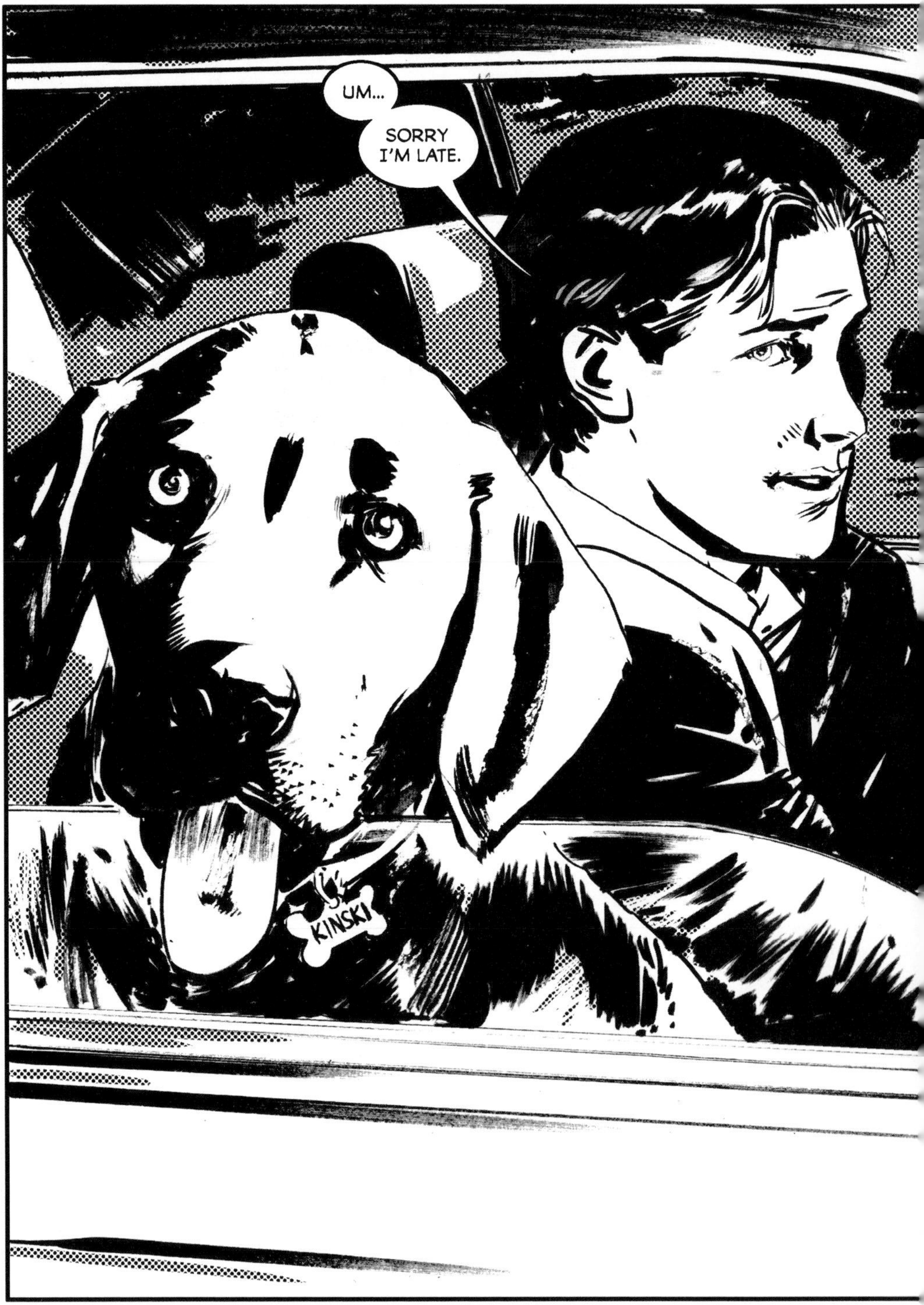
UM...
SORRY I'M LATE.
KINSKI

TWO

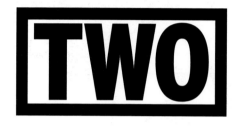

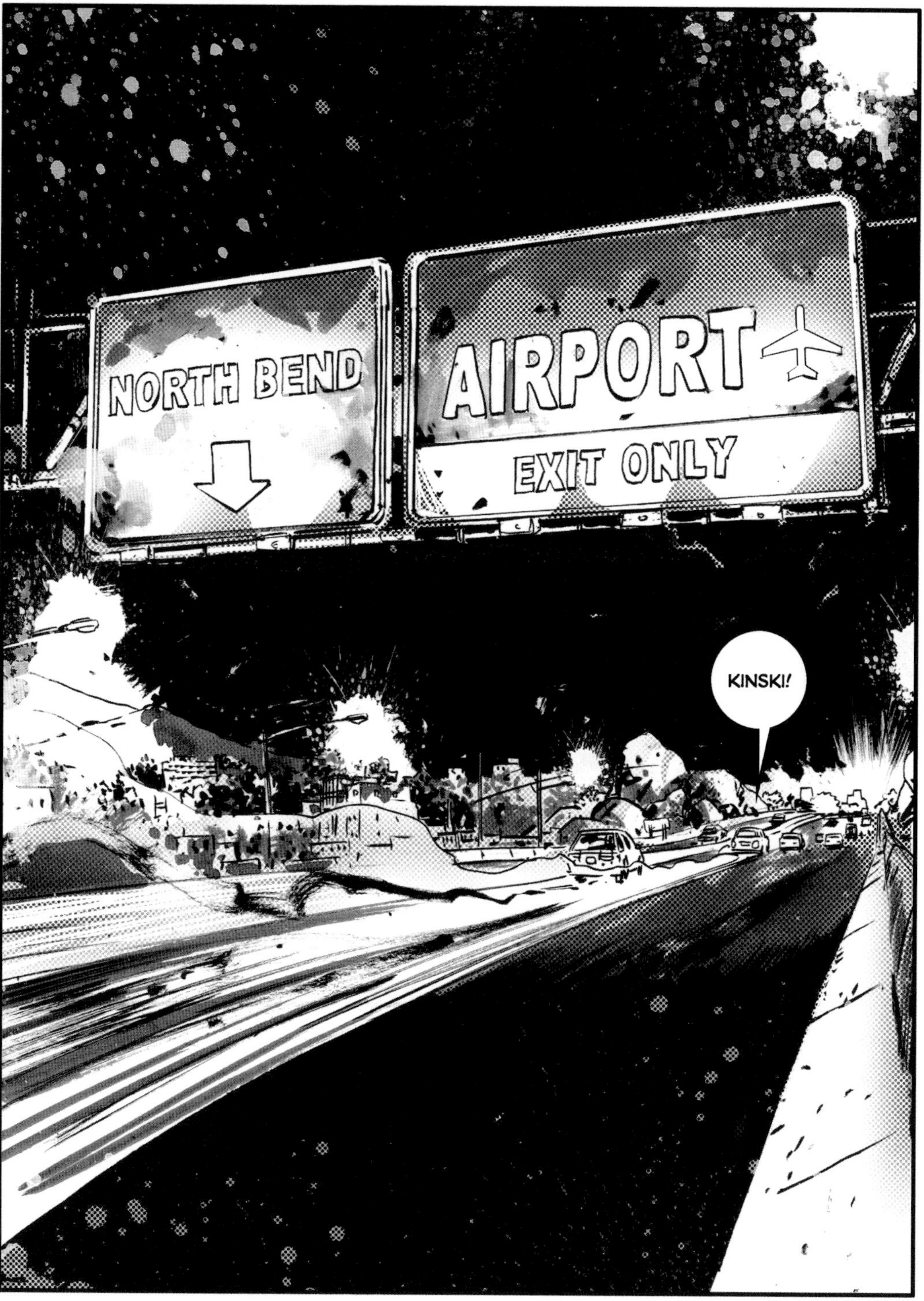
NORTH BEND
AIRPORT
EXIT ONLY
KINSKI!

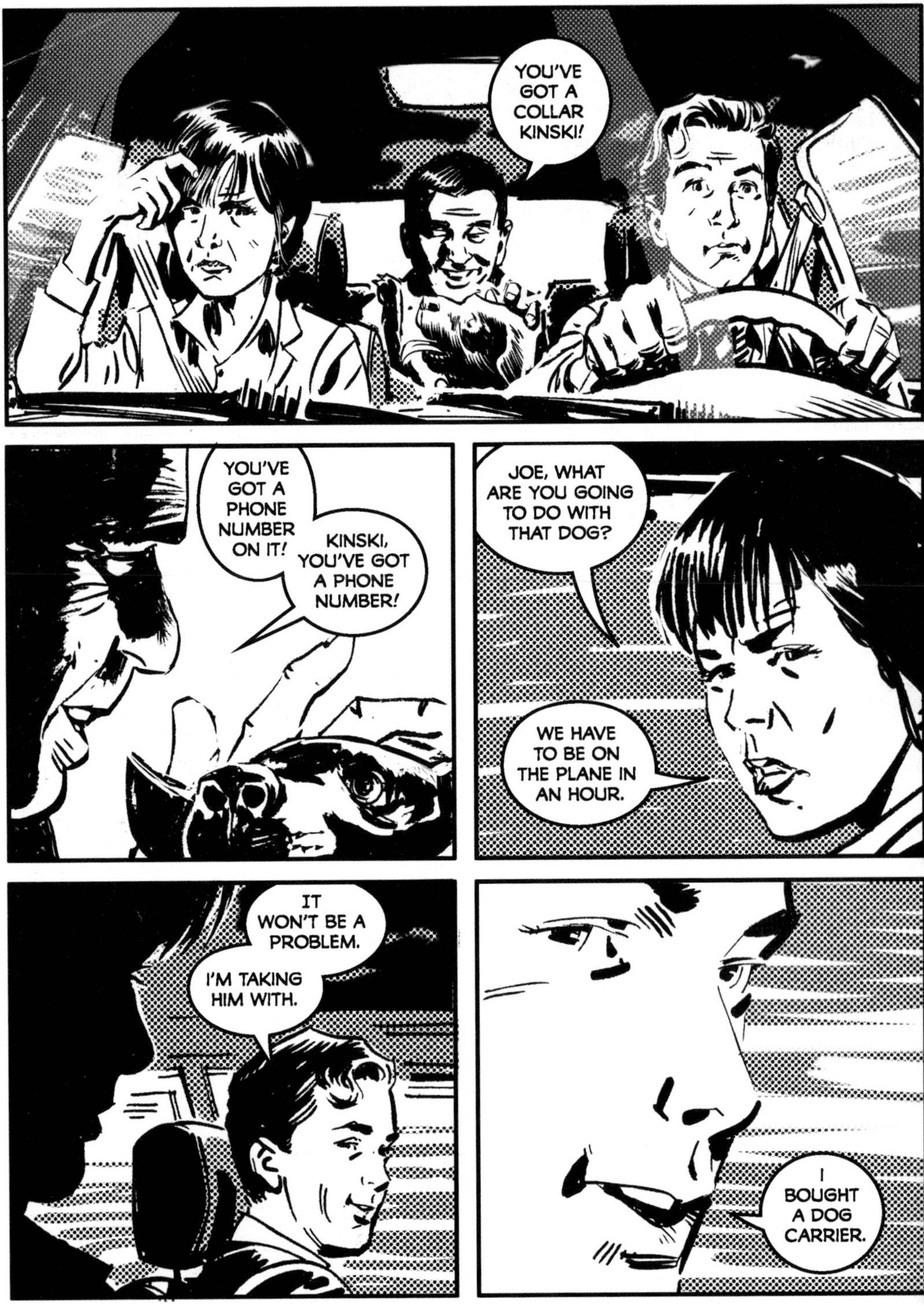
YOU'VE GOT A COLLAR KINSKI!
YOU'VE GOT A PHONE NUMBER ON IT!
KINSKI, YOU'VE GOT A PHONE NUMBER!
JOE, WHAT ARE YOU GOING TO DO WITH THAT DOG?
WE HAVE TO BE ON THE PLANE IN AN HOUR.
IT WON'T BE A PROBLEM.
I'M TAKING HIM WITH.
I BOUGHT A DOG CARRIER.

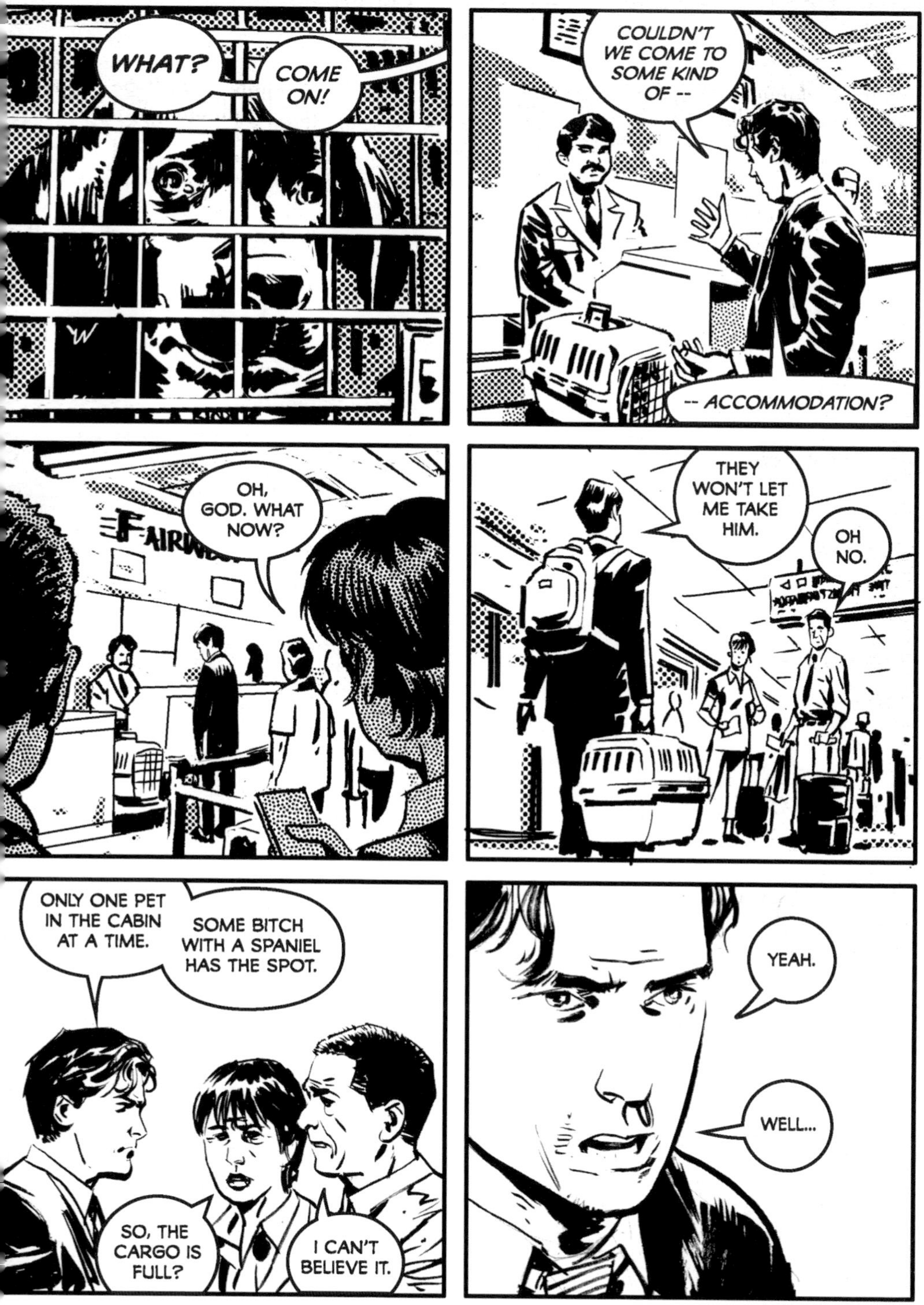
WHAT?
COME ON!
COULDN'T WE COME TO SOME KIND OF --
-- ACCOMMODATION?
OH, GOD. WHAT NOW?
THEY WON'T LET ME TAKE HIM.
OH NO.
ONLY ONE PET IN THE CABIN AT A TIME.
SOME BITCH WITH A SPANIEL HAS THE SPOT.
SO, THE CARGO IS FULL?
I CAN'T BELIEVE IT.
YEAH.
WELL...

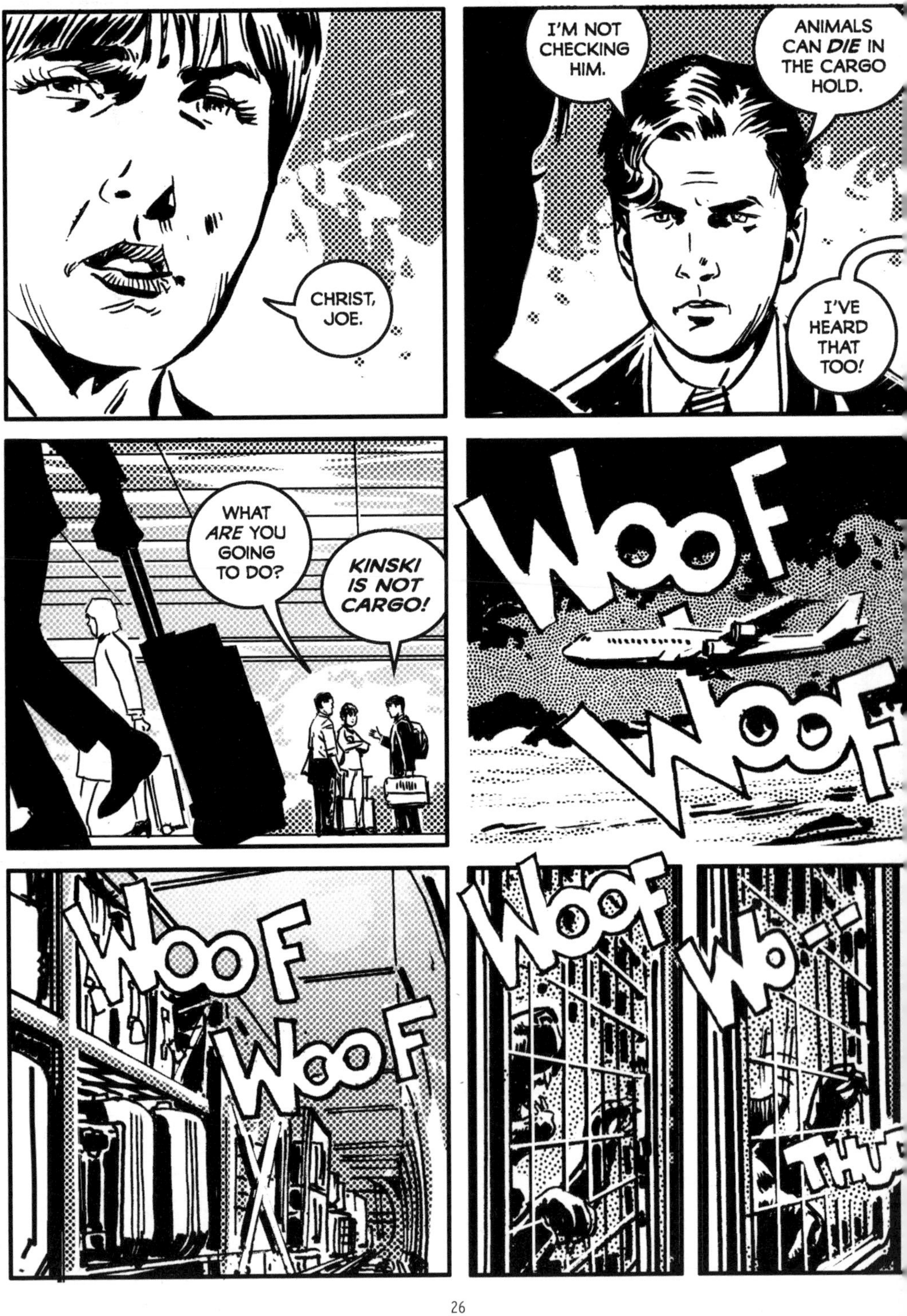
CHRIST, JOE.
I'M NOT CHECKING HIM.
ANIMALS CAN *DIE* IN THE CARGO HOLD.
I'VE HEARD THAT TOO!
WHAT *ARE* YOU GOING TO DO?
KINSKI IS NOT CARGO!
WOOF
WOOF
WOOF
WOOF
WOOF
WO--
THU

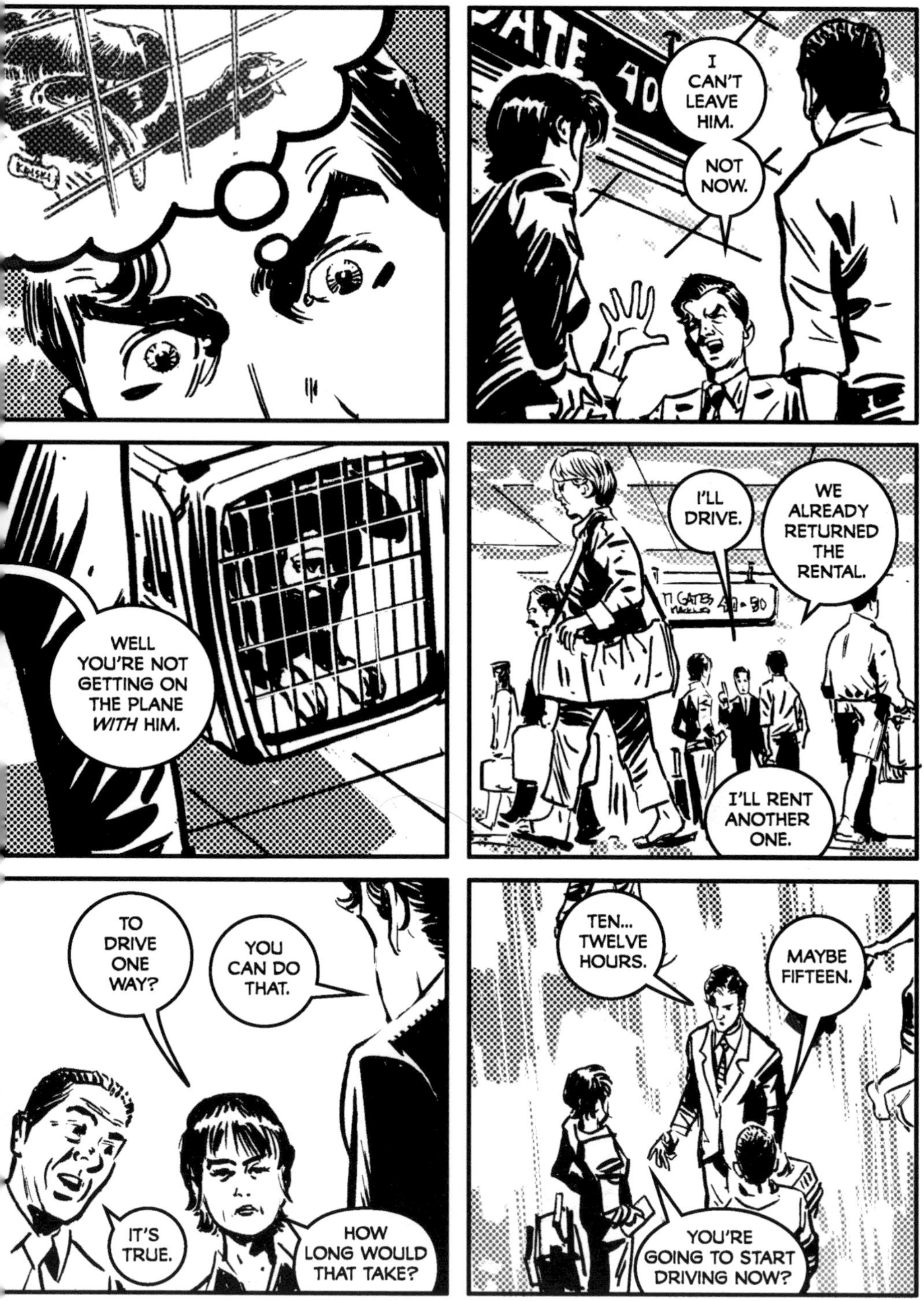
I CAN'T LEAVE HIM.
NOT NOW.
WELL YOU'RE NOT GETTING ON THE PLANE *WITH* HIM.
I'LL DRIVE.
WE ALREADY RETURNED THE RENTAL.
I'LL RENT ANOTHER ONE.
TO DRIVE ONE WAY?
YOU CAN DO THAT.
IT'S TRUE.
HOW LONG WOULD THAT TAKE?
TEN... TWELVE HOURS.
MAYBE FIFTEEN.
YOU'RE GOING TO START DRIVING NOW?

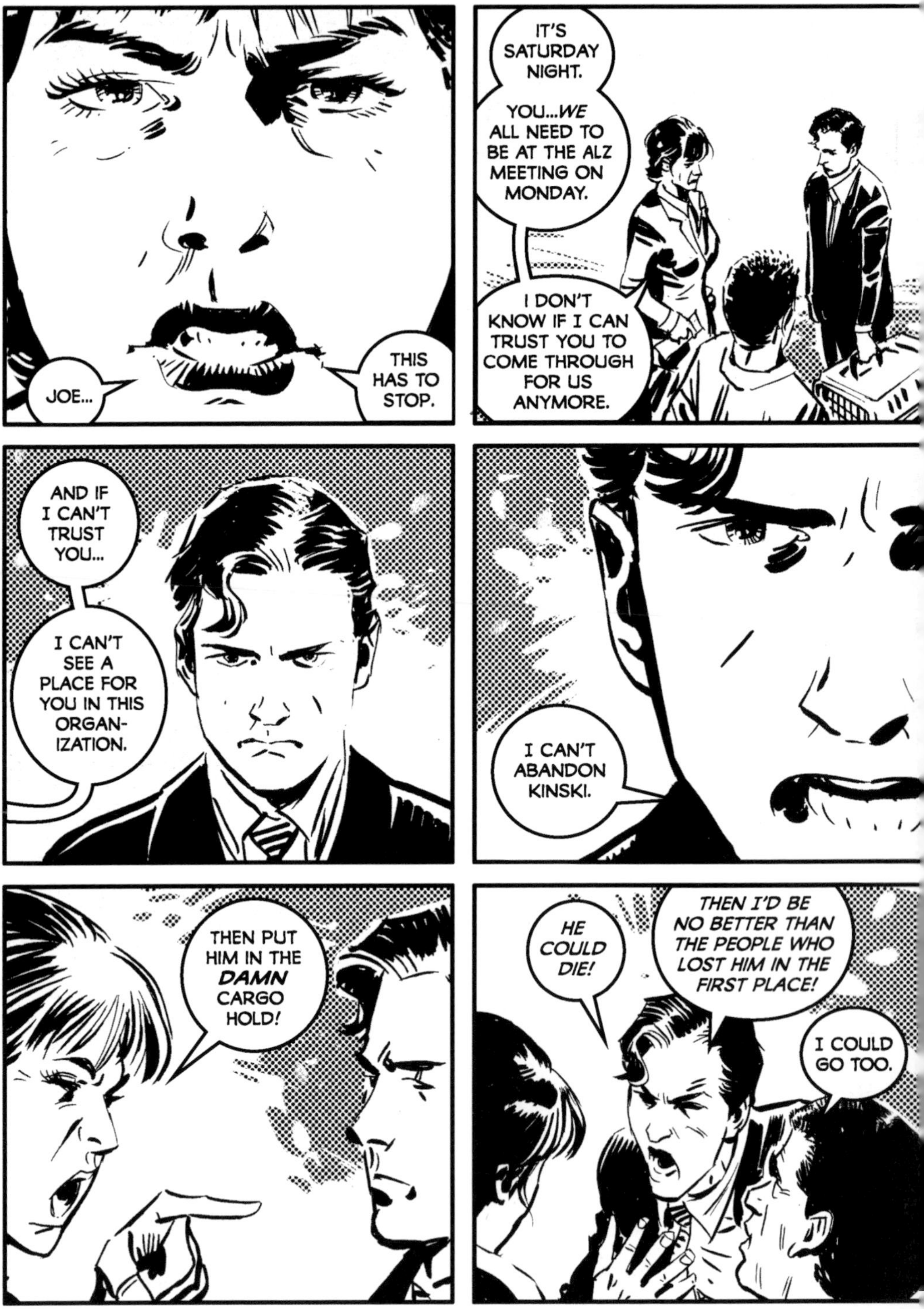
JOE...
THIS HAS TO STOP.
IT'S SATURDAY NIGHT.
YOU...*WE* ALL NEED TO BE AT THE ALZ MEETING ON MONDAY.
I DON'T KNOW IF I CAN TRUST YOU TO COME THROUGH FOR US ANYMORE.
AND IF I CAN'T TRUST YOU...
I CAN'T SEE A PLACE FOR YOU IN THIS ORGAN-IZATION.
I CAN'T ABANDON KINSKI.
THEN PUT HIM IN THE ***DAMN*** CARGO HOLD!
HE COULD DIE!
THEN I'D BE NO BETTER THAN THE PEOPLE WHO LOST HIM IN THE FIRST PLACE!
I COULD GO TOO.

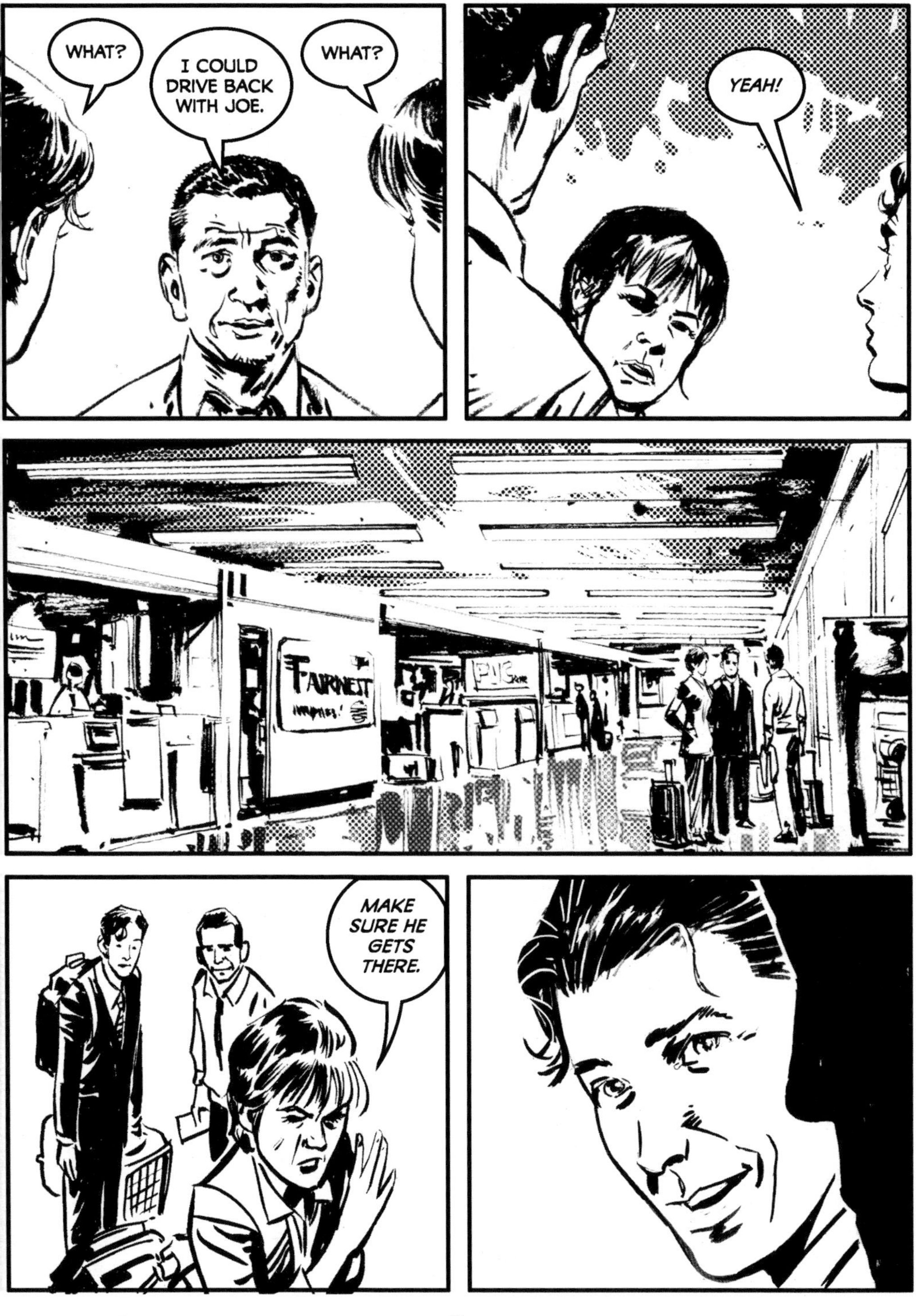
WHAT?
I COULD DRIVE BACK WITH JOE.
WHAT?
YEAH!
FAIRNEST
MAKE SURE HE GETS THERE.

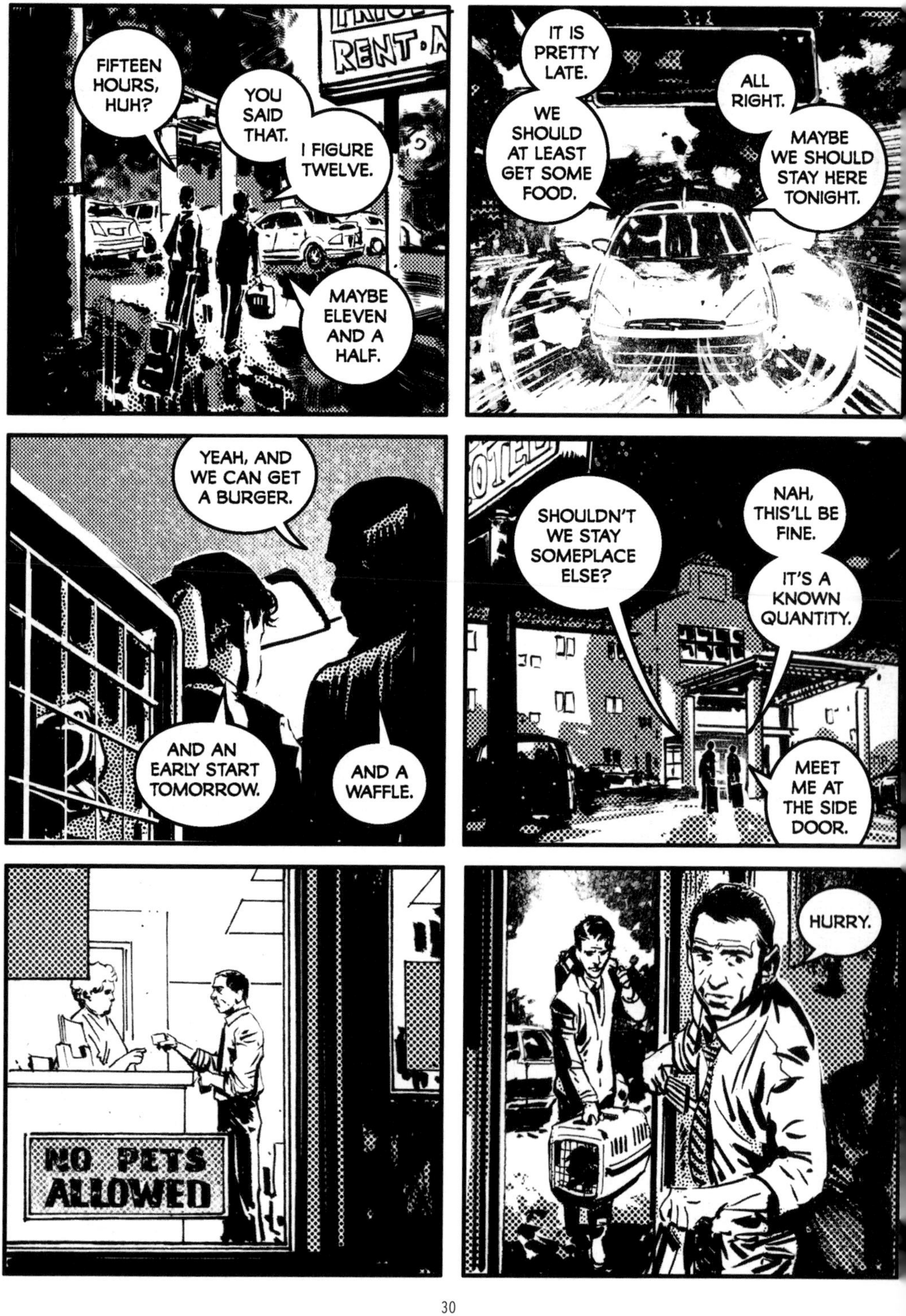
FIFTEEN HOURS, HUH?
YOU SAID THAT.
I FIGURE TWELVE.
MAYBE ELEVEN AND A HALF.
IT IS PRETTY LATE.
WE SHOULD AT LEAST GET SOME FOOD.
ALL RIGHT.
MAYBE WE SHOULD STAY HERE TONIGHT.
YEAH, AND WE CAN GET A BURGER.
AND AN EARLY START TOMORROW.
AND A WAFFLE.
SHOULDN'T WE STAY SOMEPLACE ELSE?
NAH, THIS'LL BE FINE.
IT'S A KNOWN QUANTITY.
MEET ME AT THE SIDE DOOR.
NO PETS ALLOWED
HURRY.

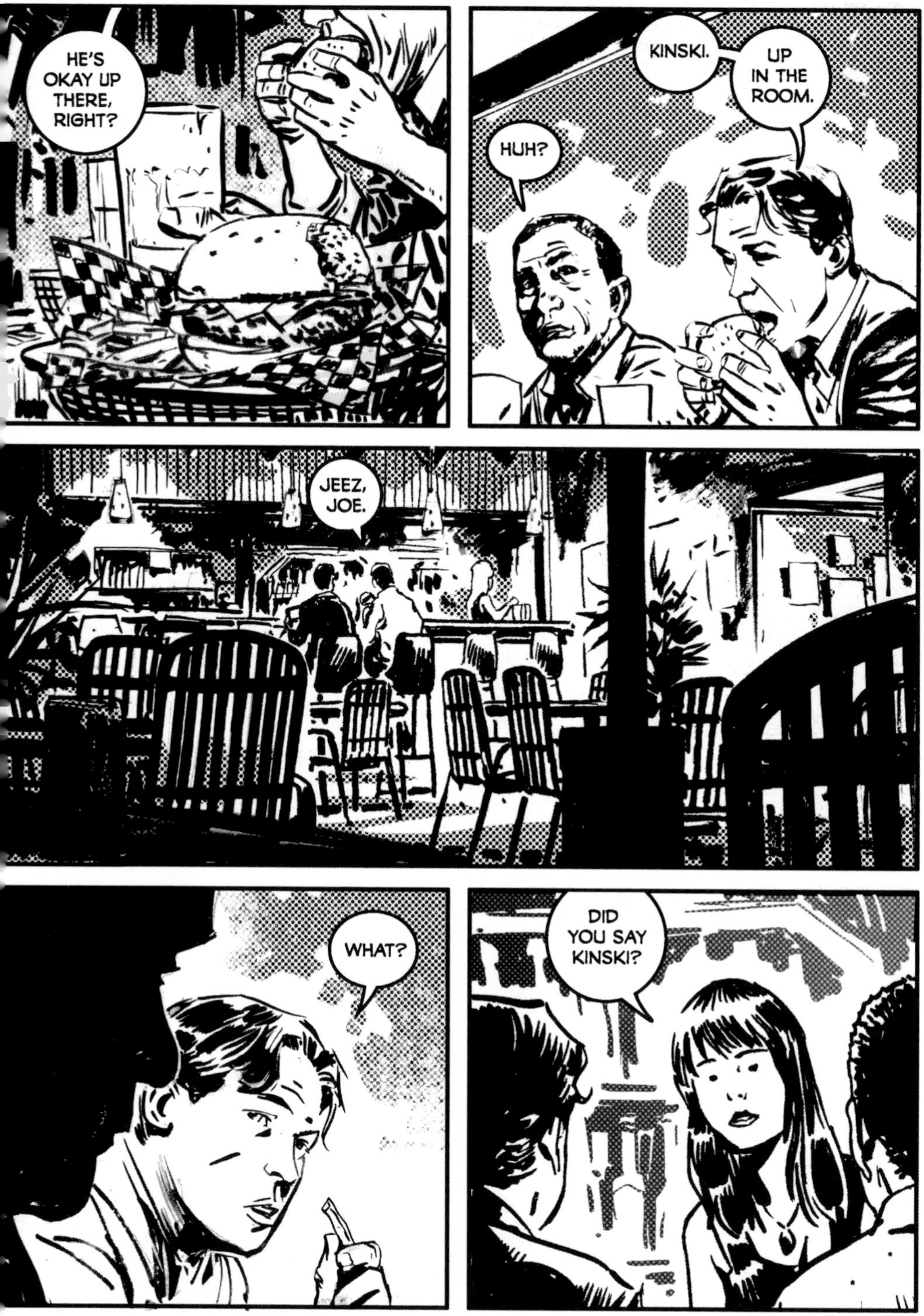
HE'S OKAY UP THERE, RIGHT?
KINSKI.
UP IN THE ROOM.
HUH?
JEEZ, JOE.
WHAT?
DID YOU SAY KINSKI?

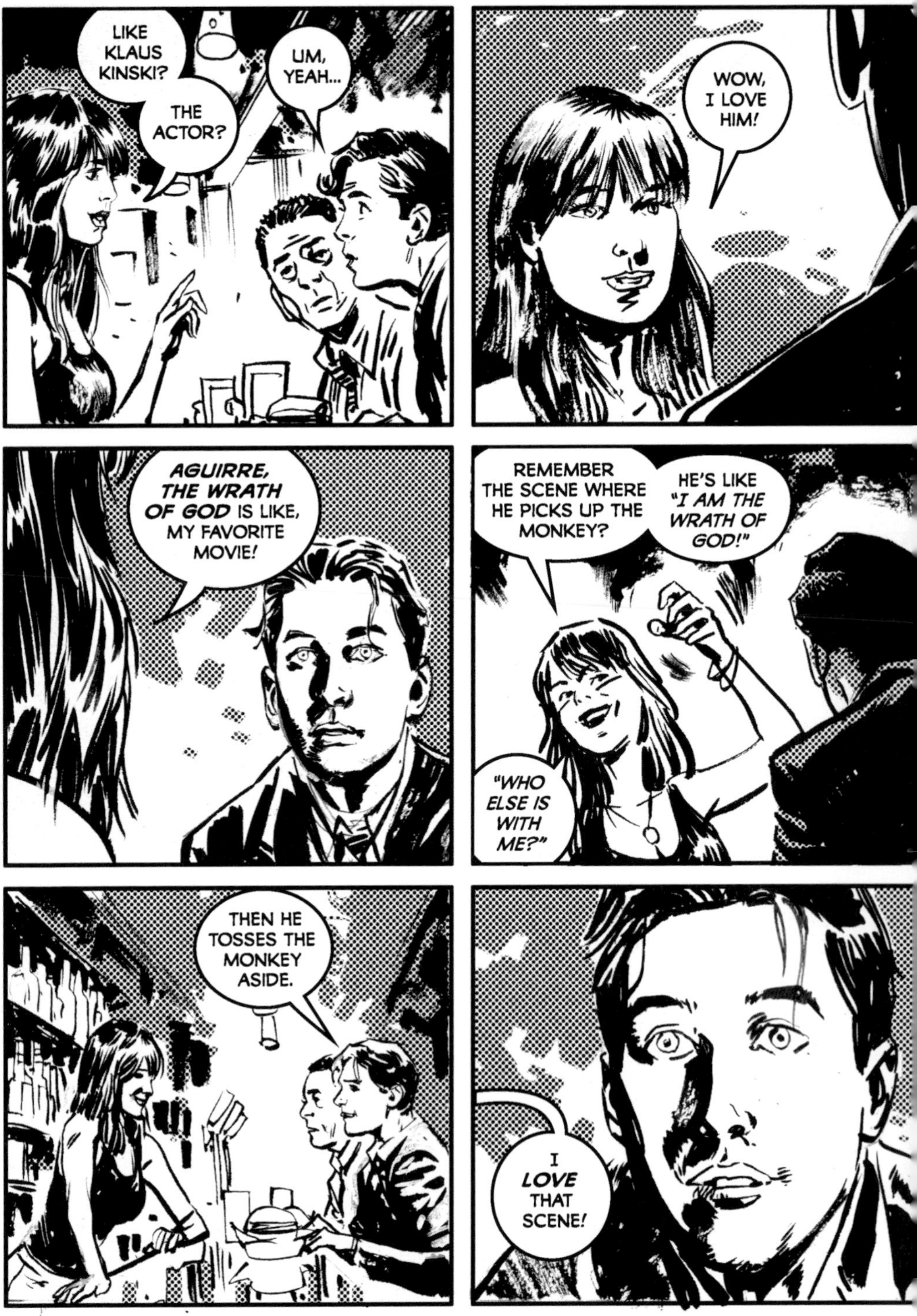
LIKE KLAUS KINSKI?
THE ACTOR?
UM, YEAH...
WOW, I LOVE HIM!
AGUIRRE, THE WRATH OF GOD IS LIKE, MY FAVORITE MOVIE!
REMEMBER THE SCENE WHERE HE PICKS UP THE MONKEY?
HE'S LIKE *"I AM THE WRATH OF GOD!"*
"WHO ELSE IS WITH ME?"
THEN HE TOSSES THE MONKEY ASIDE.
I *LOVE* THAT SCENE!

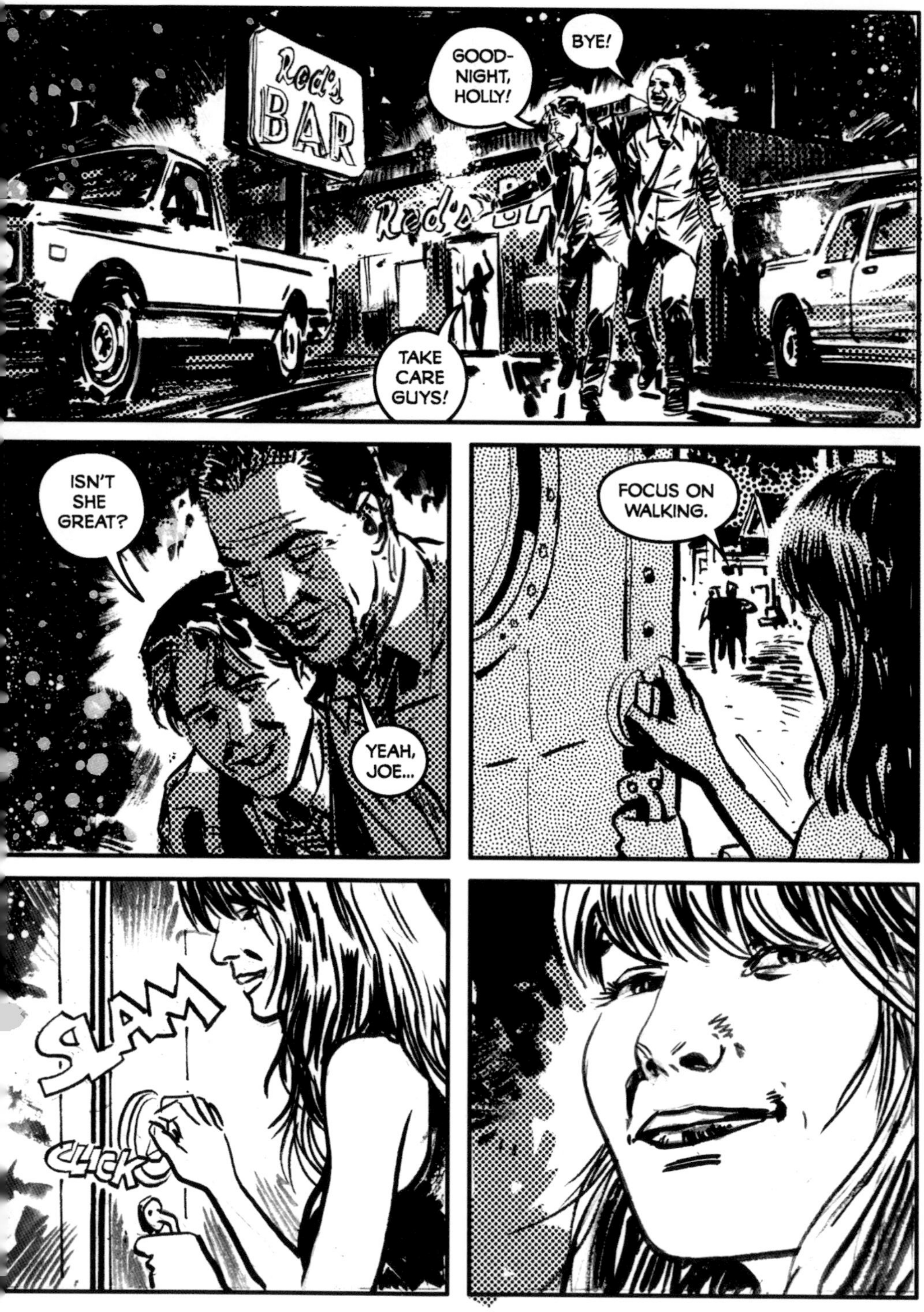
Red's BAR
GOOD-NIGHT, HOLLY!
BYE!
TAKE CARE GUYS!
ISN'T SHE GREAT?
YEAH, JOE...
FOCUS ON WALKING.
SLAM
CLICK

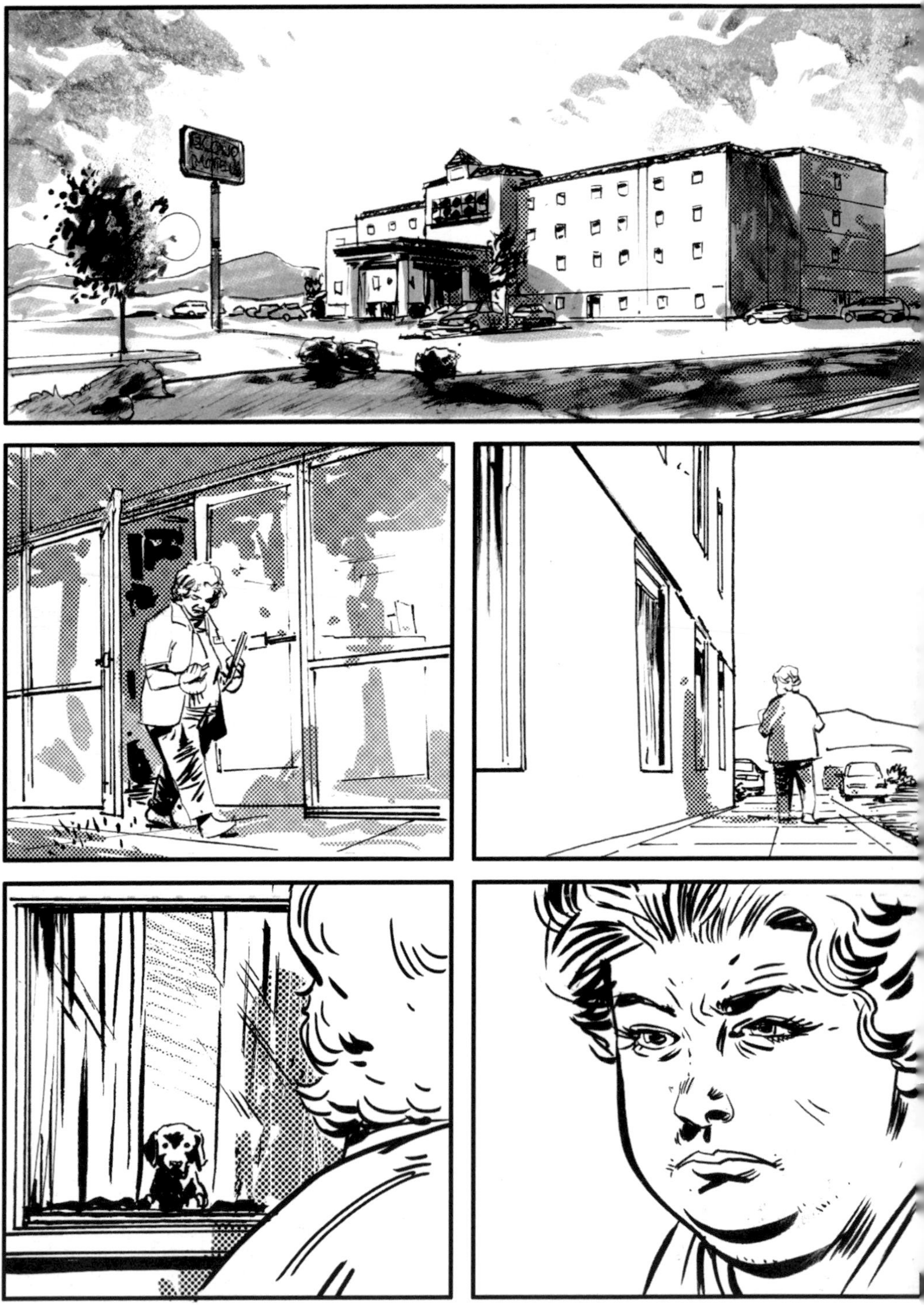

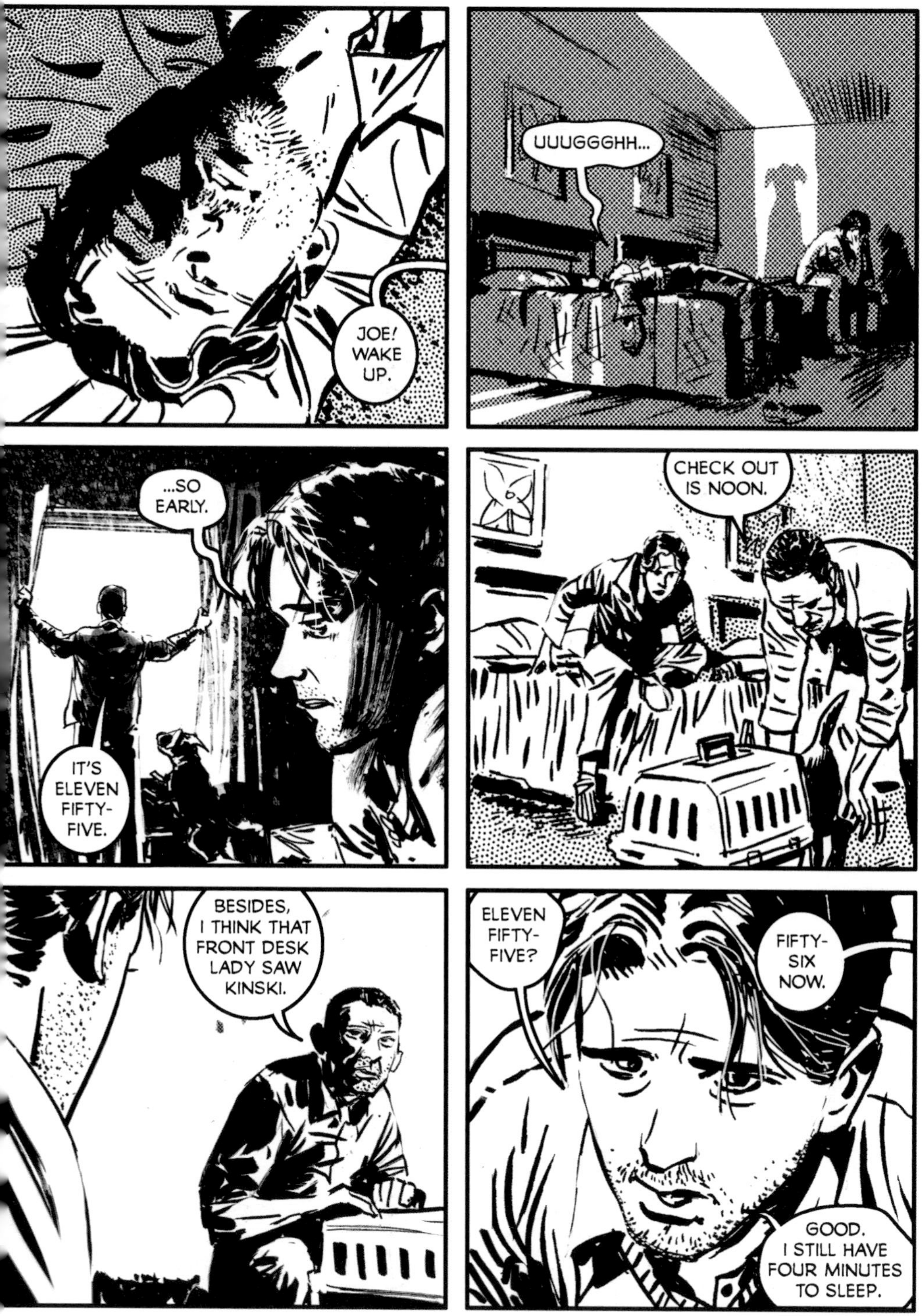

JOE! WAKE UP.
UUUGGGHH...
...SO EARLY.
IT'S ELEVEN FIFTY-FIVE.
CHECK OUT IS NOON.
BESIDES, I THINK THAT FRONT DESK LADY SAW KINSKI.
ELEVEN FIFTY-FIVE?
FIFTY-SIX NOW.
GOOD. I STILL HAVE FOUR MINUTES TO SLEEP.

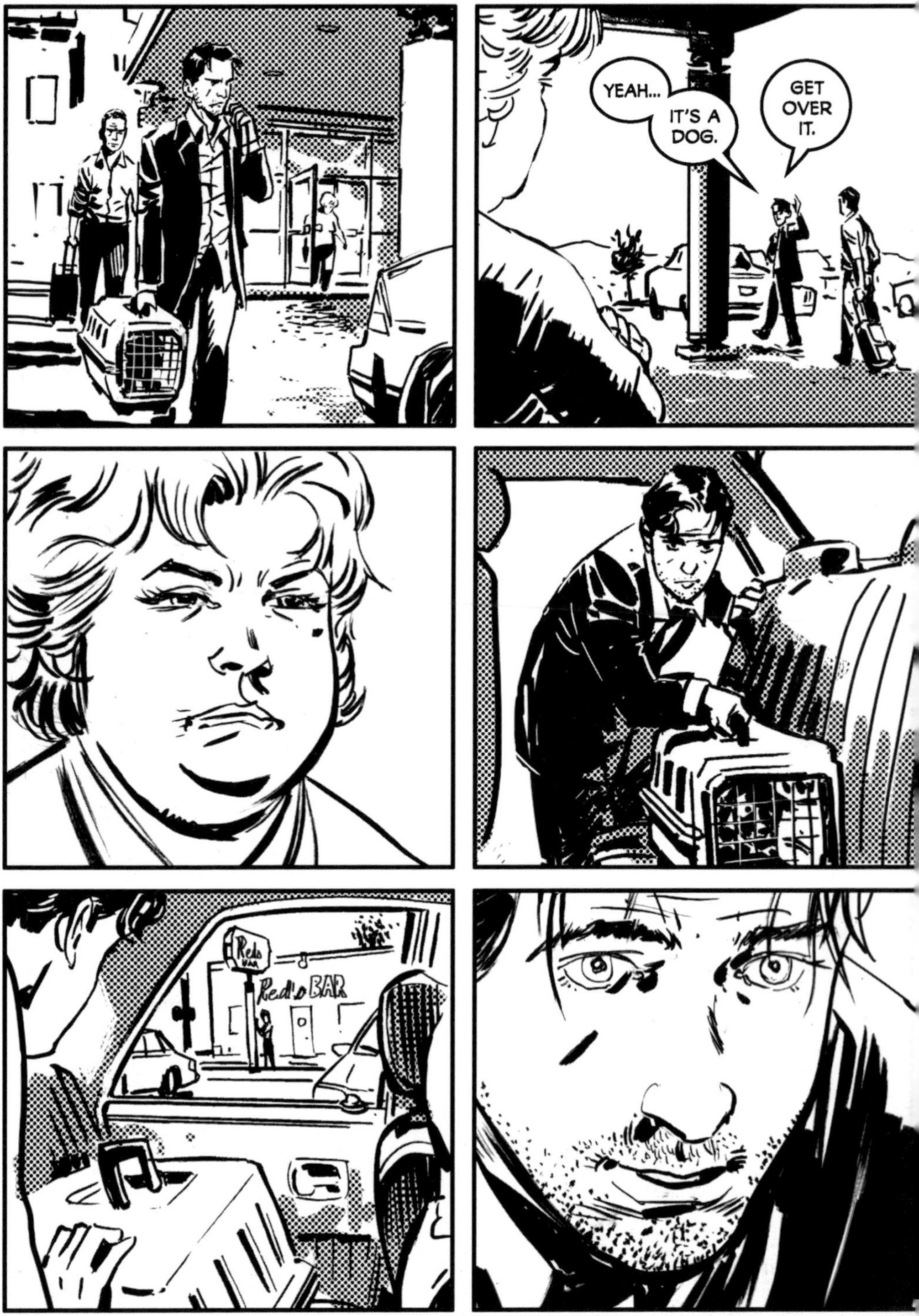
YEAH...
IT'S A DOG.
GET OVER IT.
Red's BAR

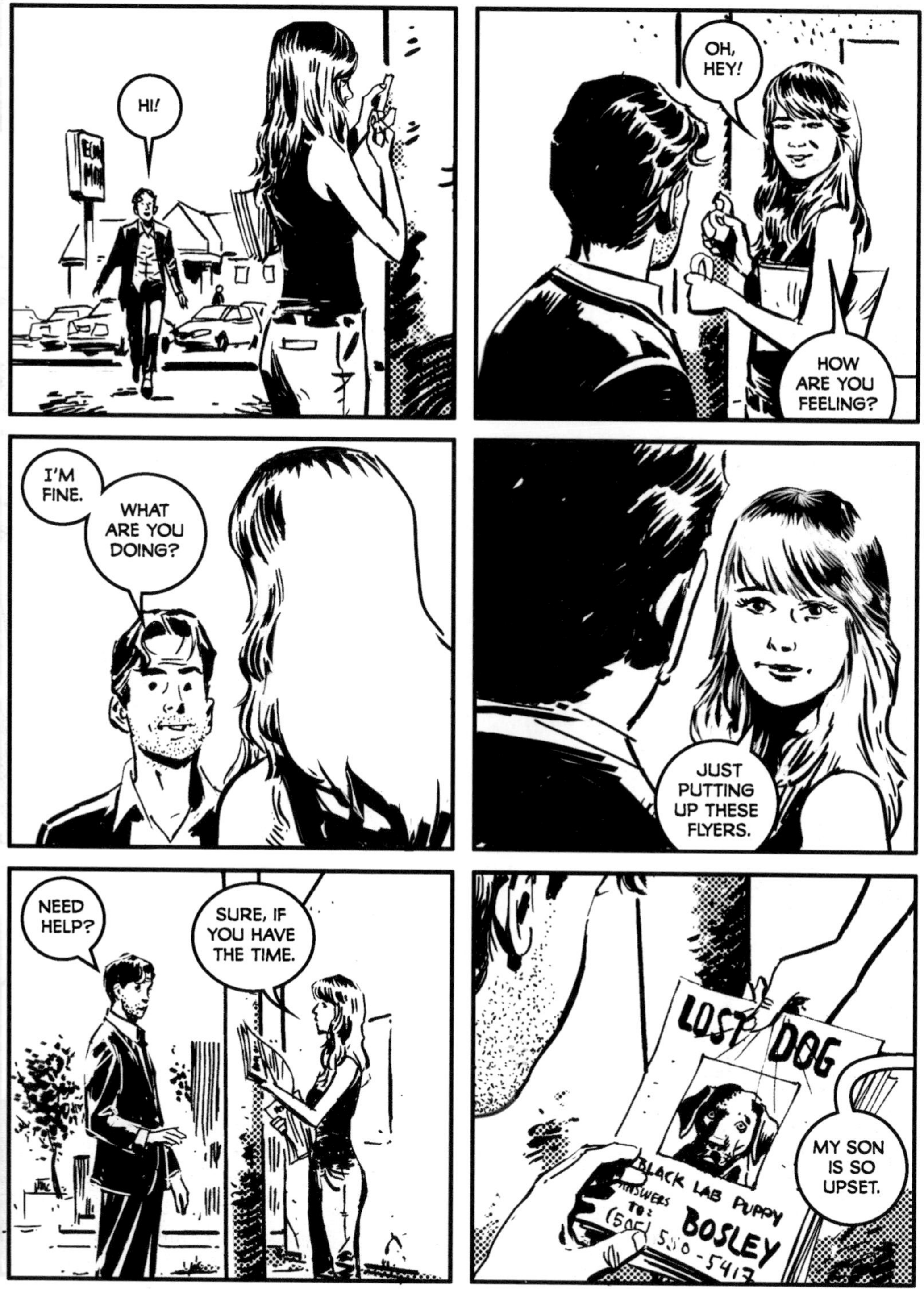
HI!
OH, HEY!
HOW ARE YOU FEELING?
I'M FINE.
WHAT ARE YOU DOING?
JUST PUTTING UP THESE FLYERS.
NEED HELP?
SURE, IF YOU HAVE THE TIME.
LOST DOG
BLACK LAB PUPPY
ANSWERS TO: BOSLEY
MY SON IS SO UPSET.

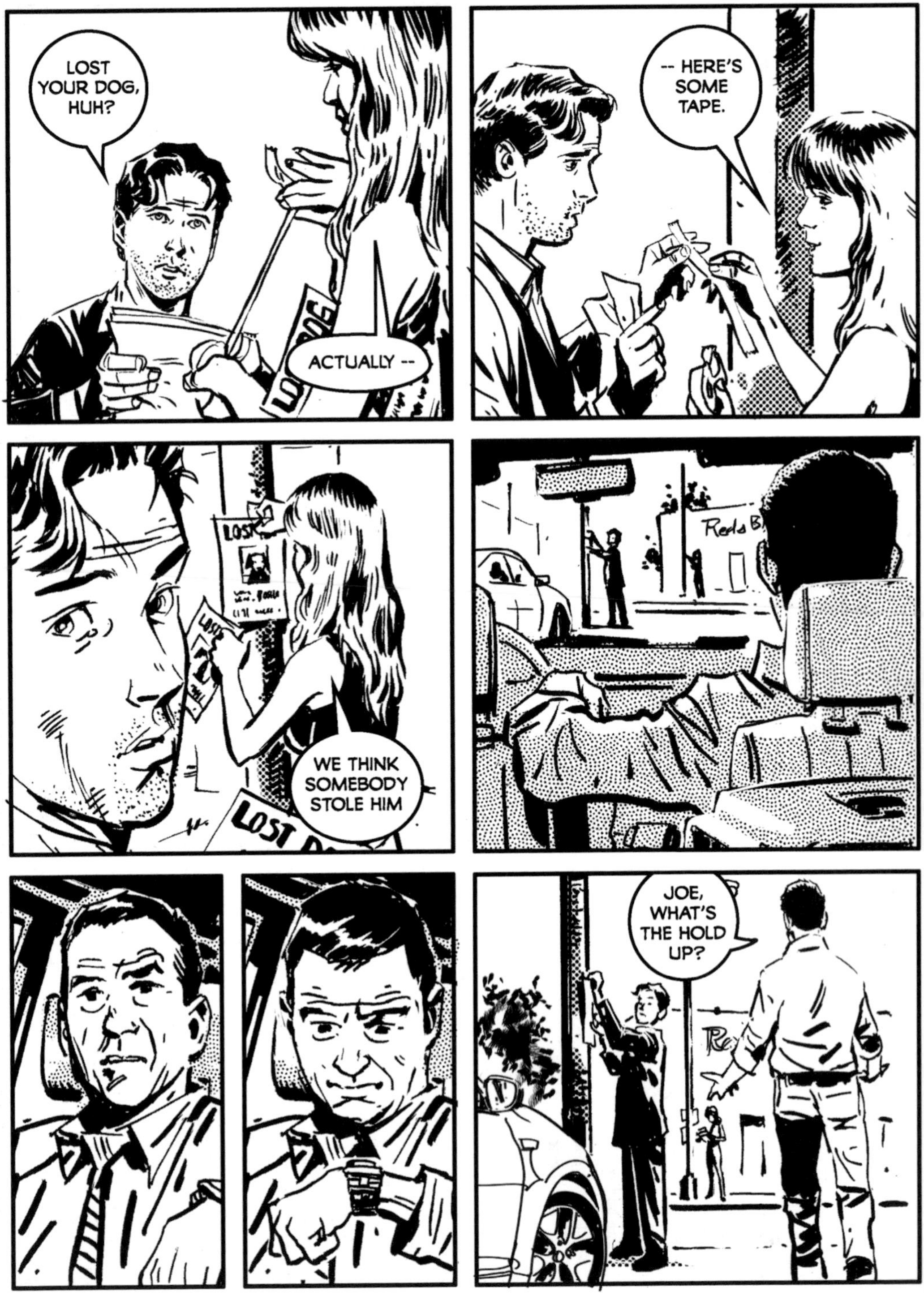
LOST YOUR DOG, HUH?
ACTUALLY --
-- HERE'S SOME TAPE.
LOST
WE THINK SOMEBODY STOLE HIM
LOST
JOE, WHAT'S THE HOLD UP?

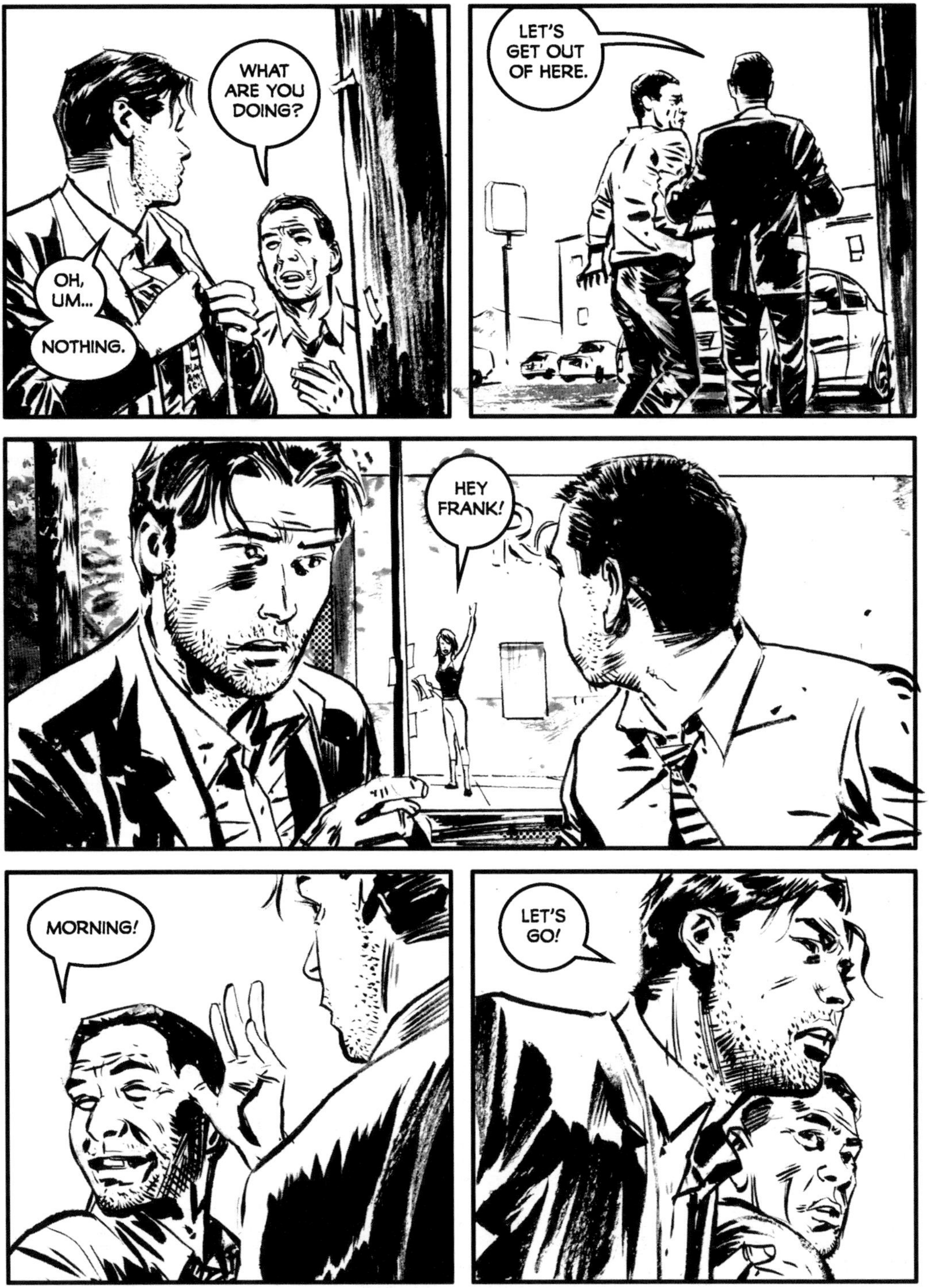
WHAT ARE YOU DOING?
OH, UM...
NOTHING.
LET'S GET OUT OF HERE.
HEY FRANK!
MORNING!
LET'S GO!

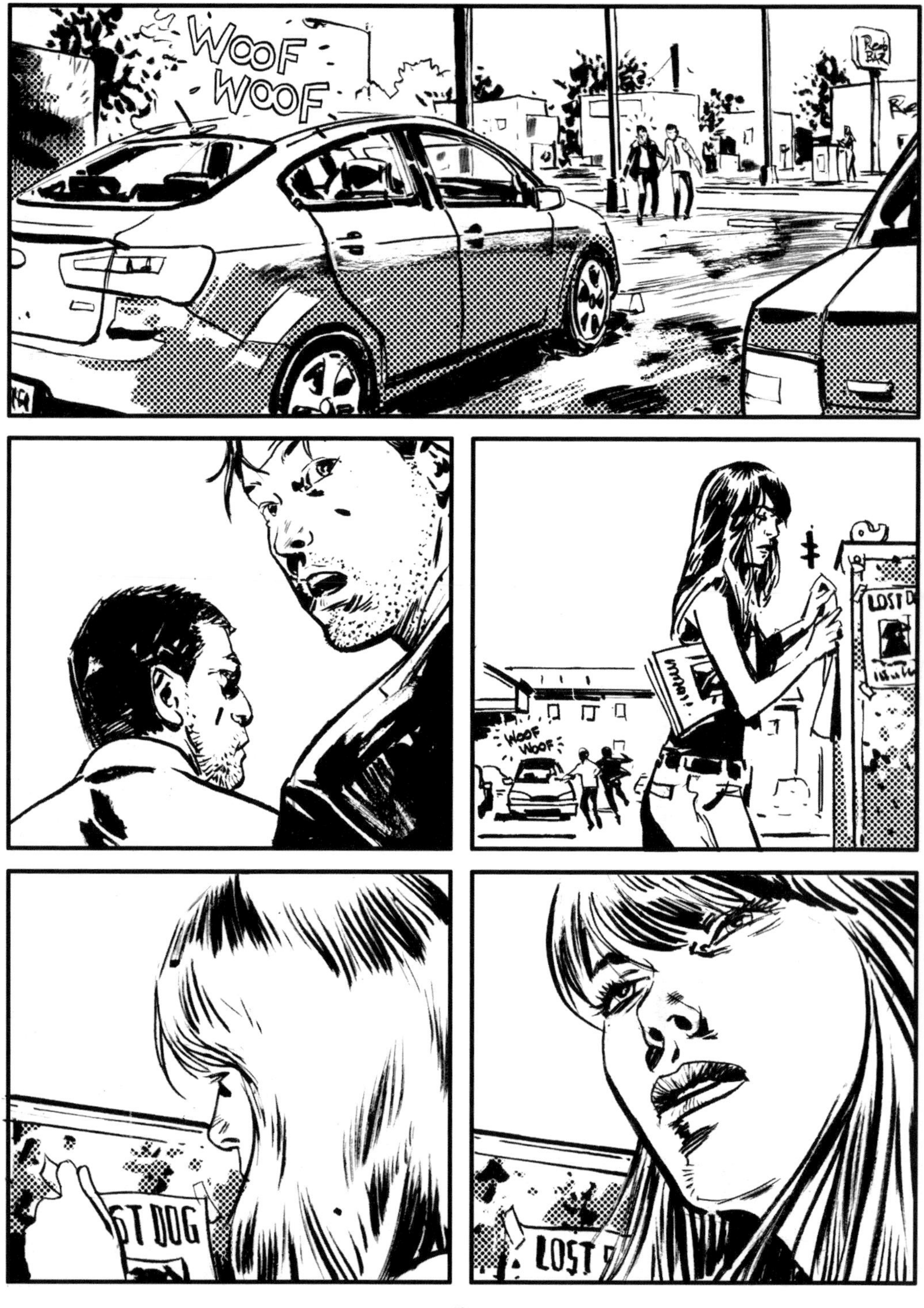
WOOF
WOOF
WOOF
WOOF
LOST D
ST DOG
LOST

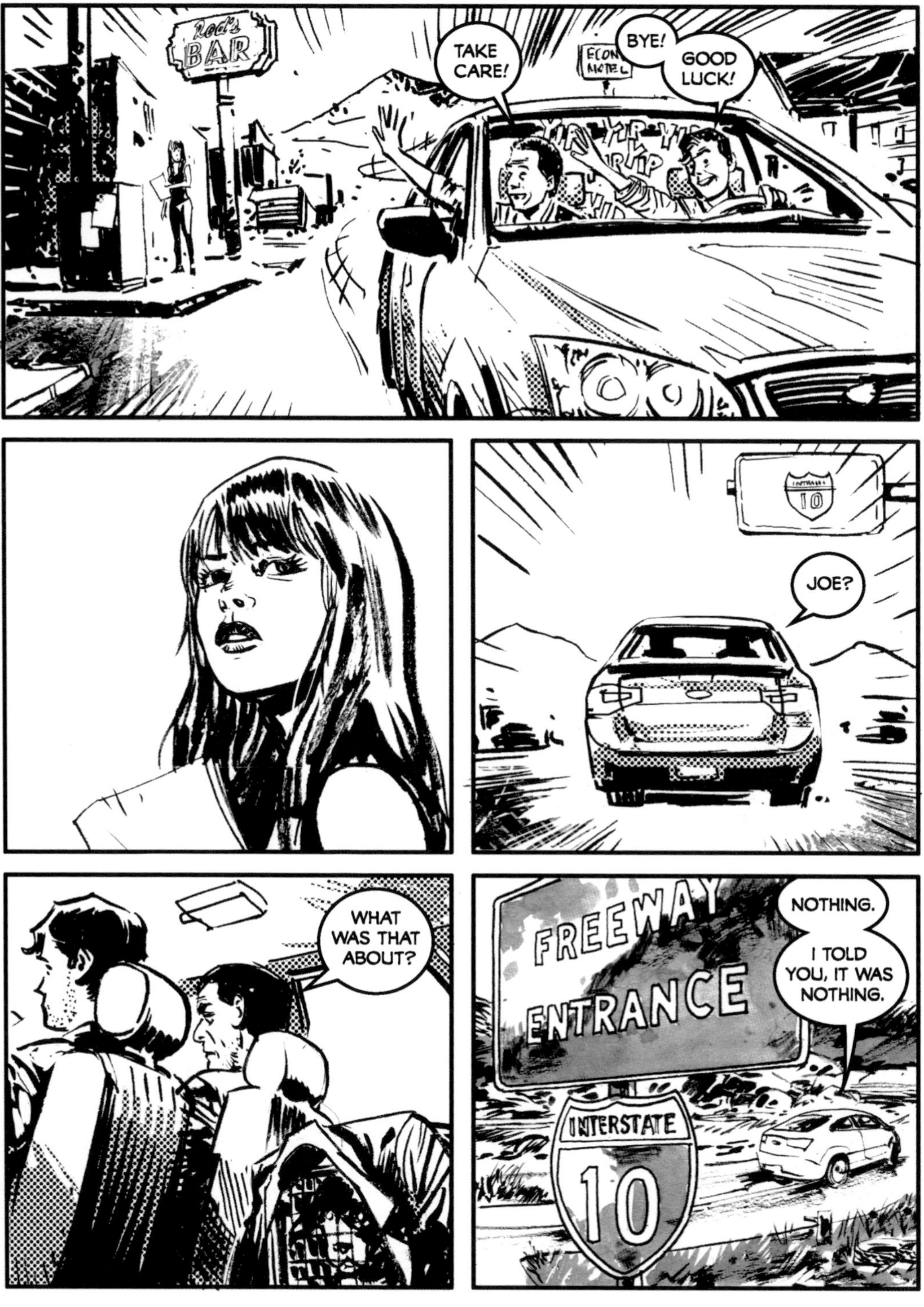
Rod's BAR
ECON MOTEL
TAKE CARE!
BYE!
GOOD LUCK!
JOE?
WHAT WAS THAT ABOUT?
FREEWAY ENTRANCE
INTERSTATE 10
NOTHING.
I TOLD YOU, IT WAS NOTHING.

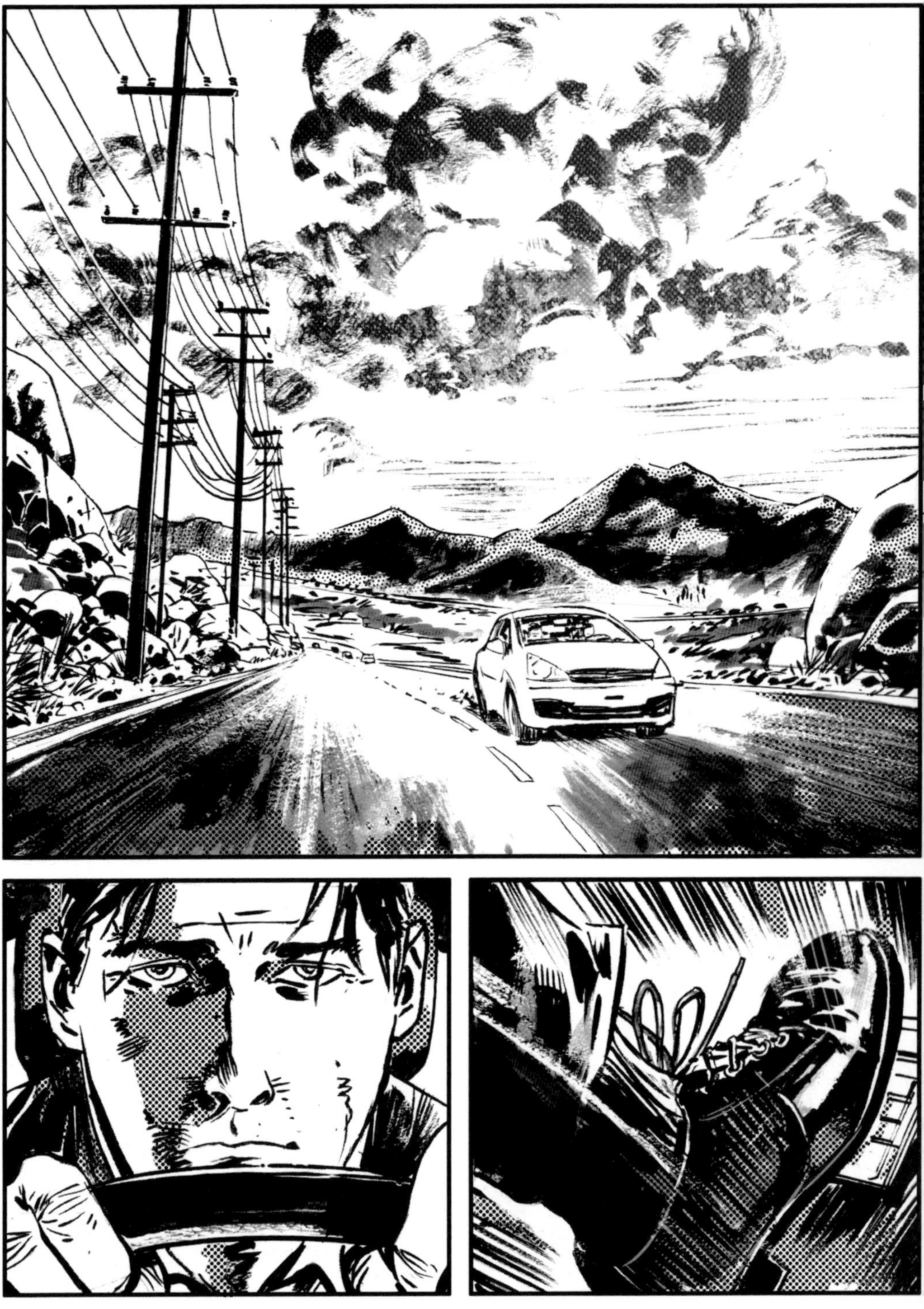

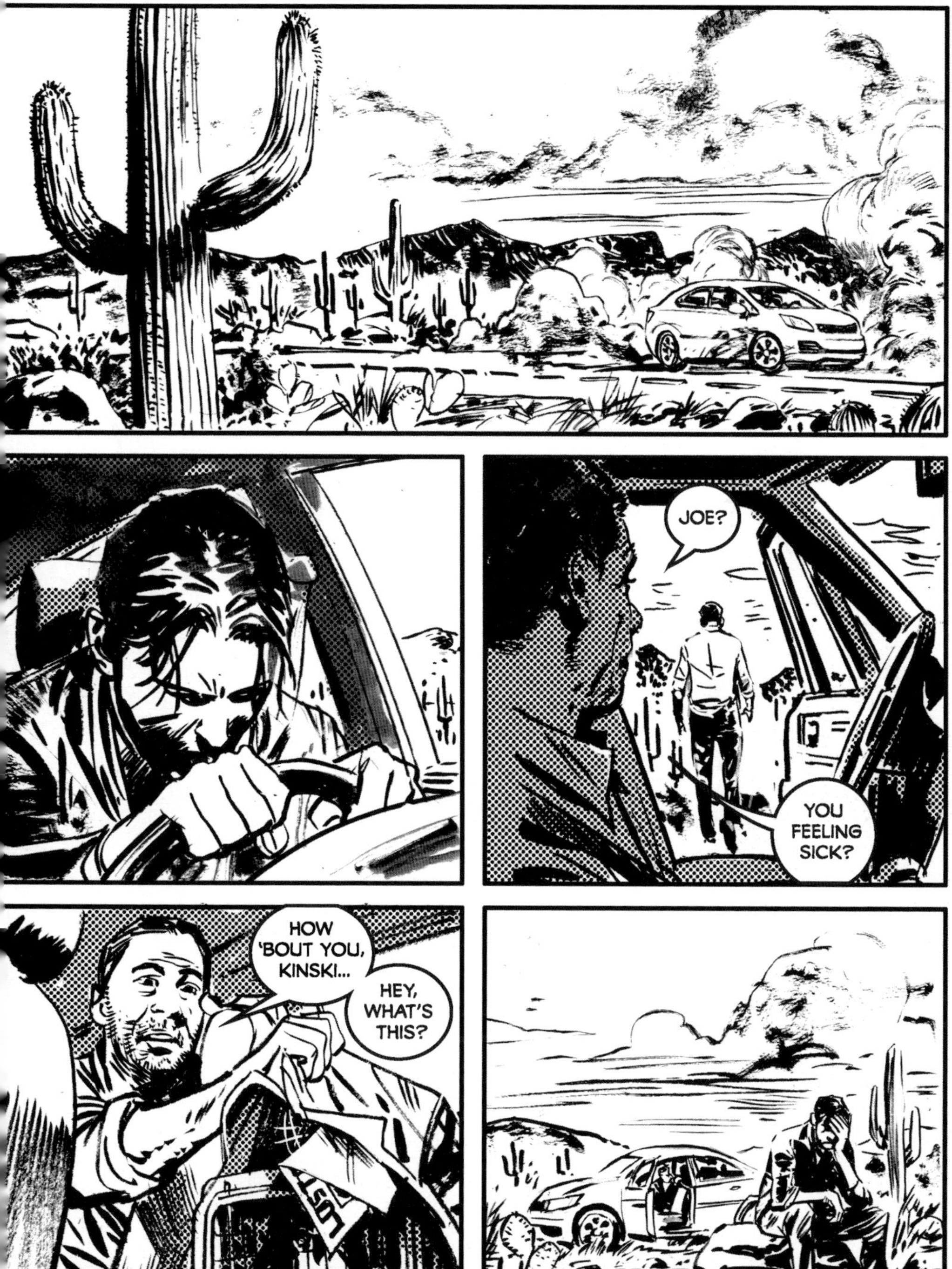
JOE?
YOU FEELING SICK?
HOW 'BOUT YOU, KINSKI...
HEY, WHAT'S THIS?

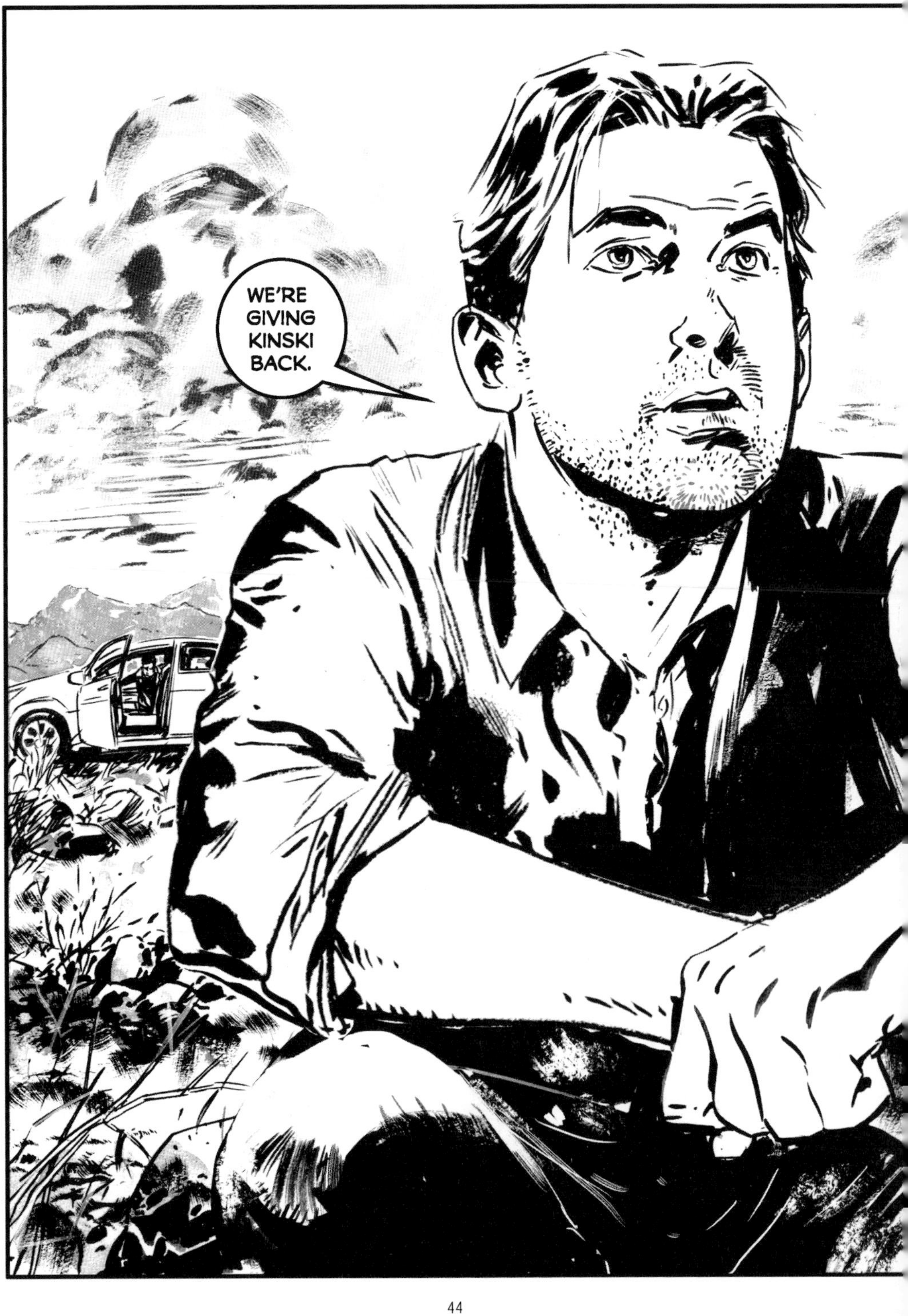
WE'RE GIVING KINSKI BACK.

THREE

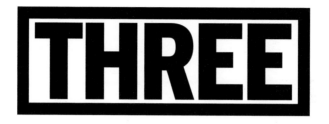

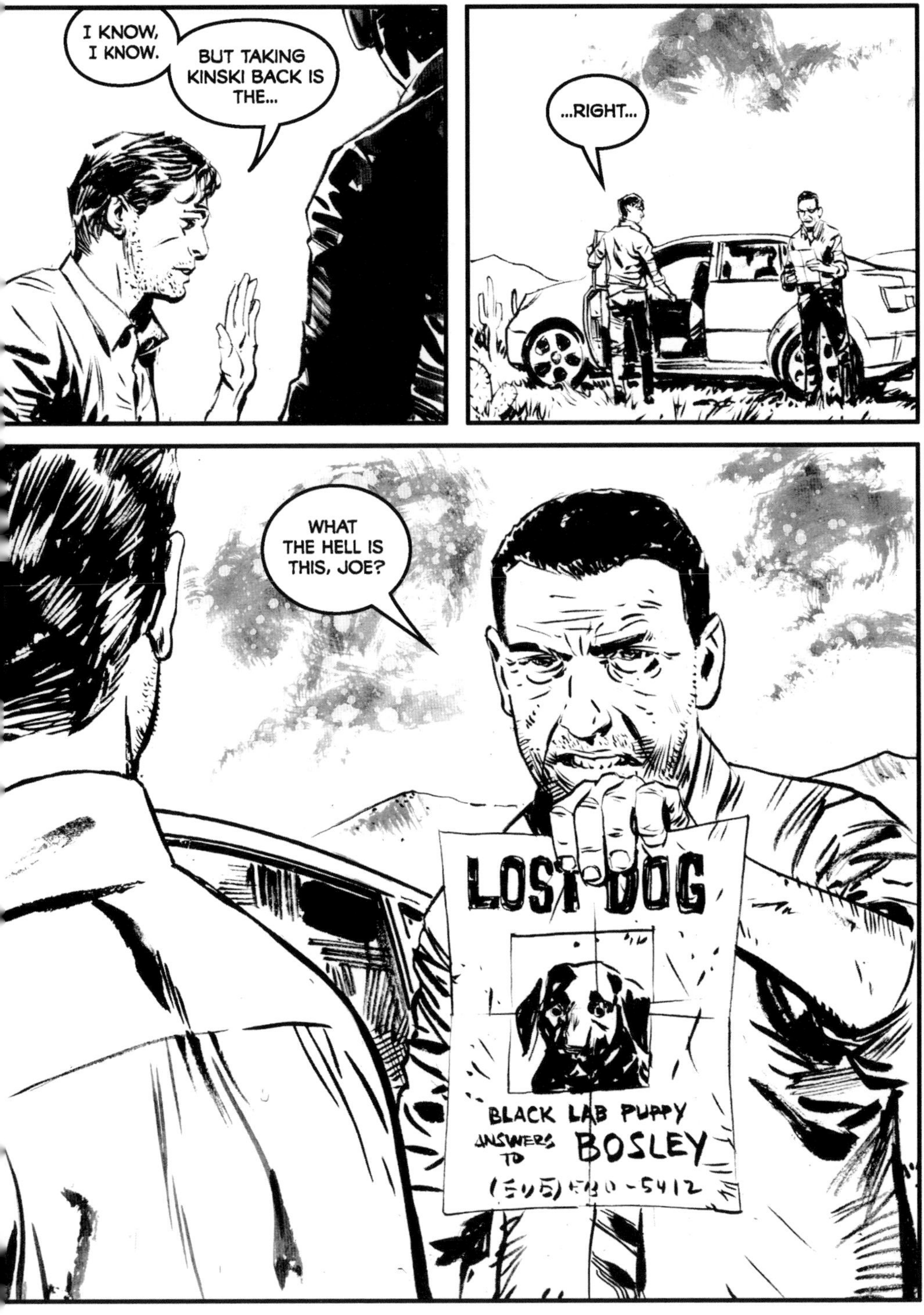
I KNOW, I KNOW.
BUT TAKING KINSKI BACK IS THE...
...RIGHT...
WHAT THE HELL IS THIS, JOE?
LOST DOG
BLACK LAB PUPPY
ANSWERS TO BOSLEY

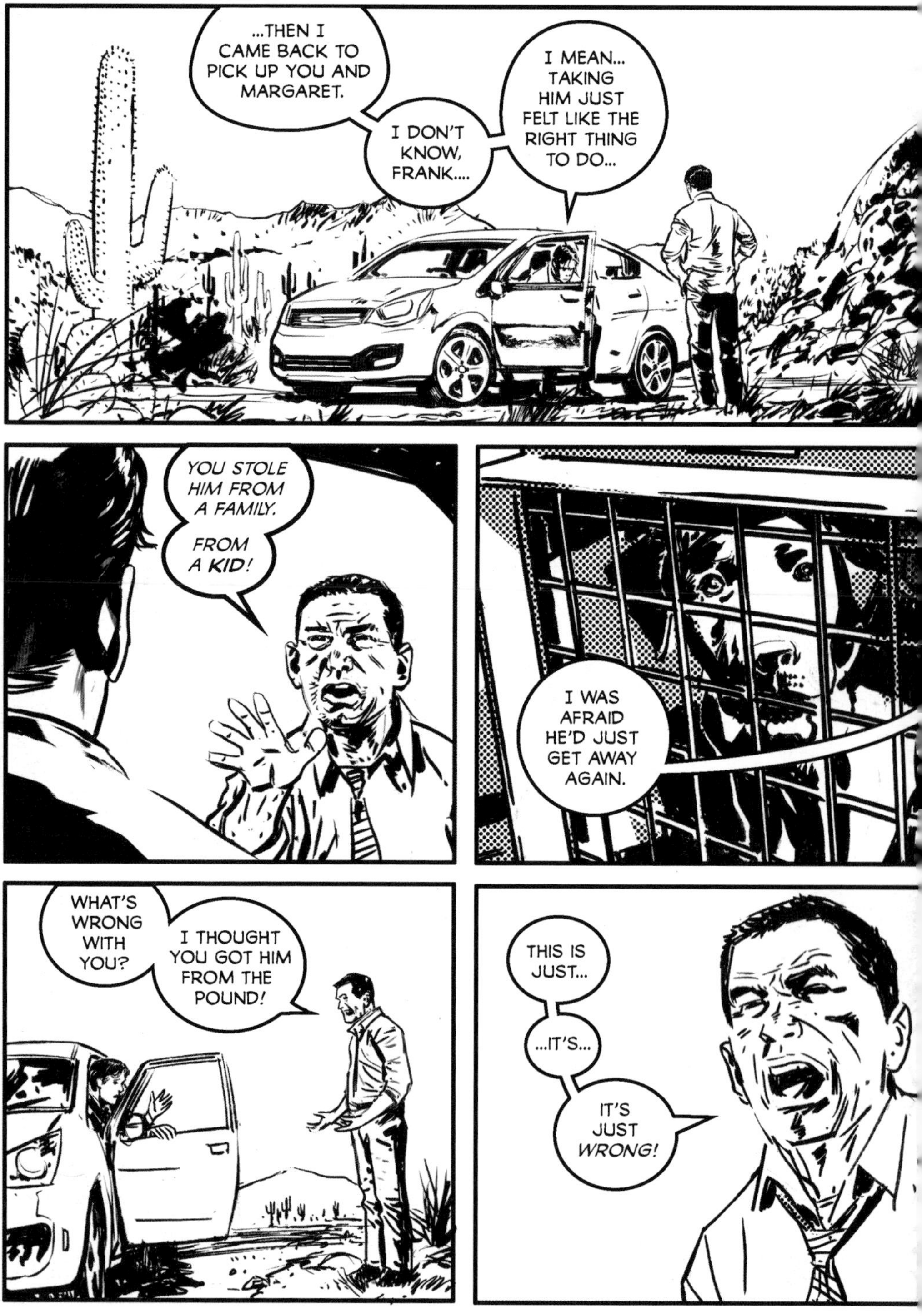
...THEN I CAME BACK TO PICK UP YOU AND MARGARET.
I DON'T KNOW, FRANK....
I MEAN... TAKING HIM JUST FELT LIKE THE RIGHT THING TO DO...
YOU STOLE HIM FROM A FAMILY.
*FROM A **KID**!*
I WAS AFRAID HE'D JUST GET AWAY AGAIN.
WHAT'S WRONG WITH YOU?
I THOUGHT YOU GOT HIM FROM THE POUND!
THIS IS JUST...
...IT'S...
IT'S JUST *WRONG!*

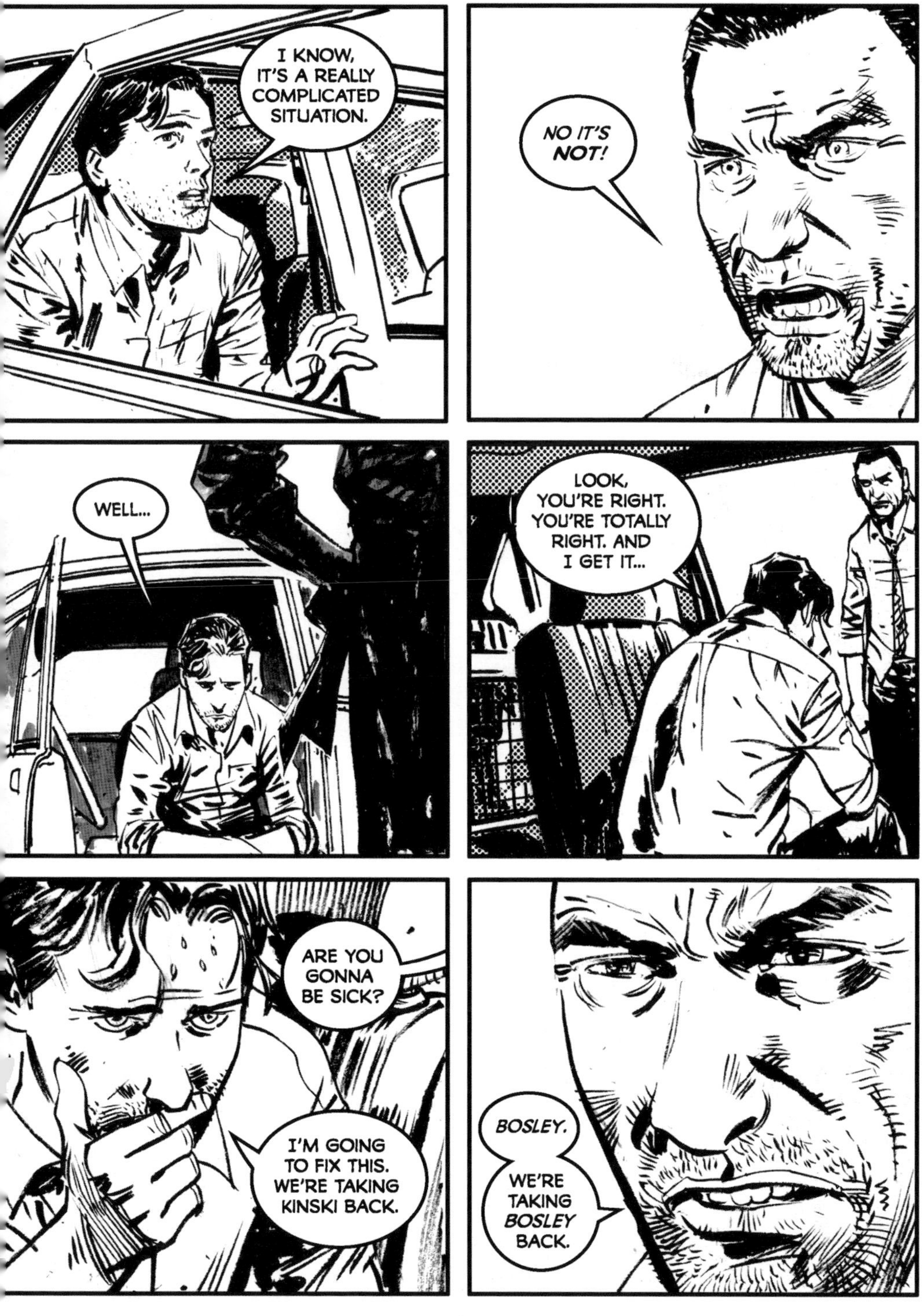
I KNOW, IT'S A REALLY COMPLICATED SITUATION.
NO IT'S ***NOT!***
WELL...
LOOK, YOU'RE RIGHT. YOU'RE TOTALLY RIGHT. AND I GET IT...
ARE YOU GONNA BE SICK?
I'M GOING TO FIX THIS. WE'RE TAKING KINSKI BACK.
BOSLEY.
WE'RE TAKING *BOSLEY* BACK.

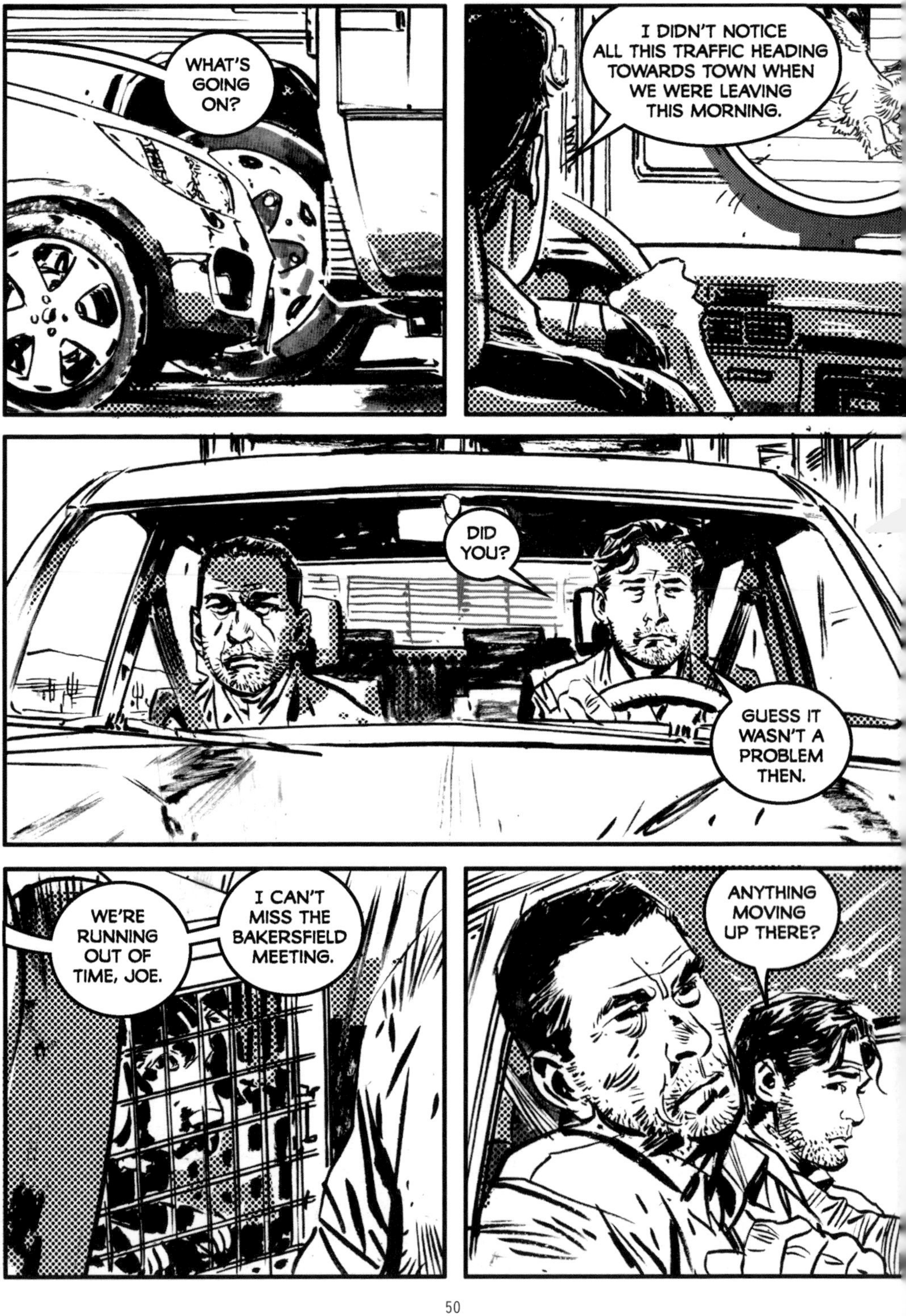
WHAT'S GOING ON?
I DIDN'T NOTICE ALL THIS TRAFFIC HEADING TOWARDS TOWN WHEN WE WERE LEAVING THIS MORNING.
DID YOU?
GUESS IT WASN'T A PROBLEM THEN.
WE'RE RUNNING OUT OF TIME, JOE.
I CAN'T MISS THE BAKERSFIELD MEETING.
ANYTHING MOVING UP THERE?

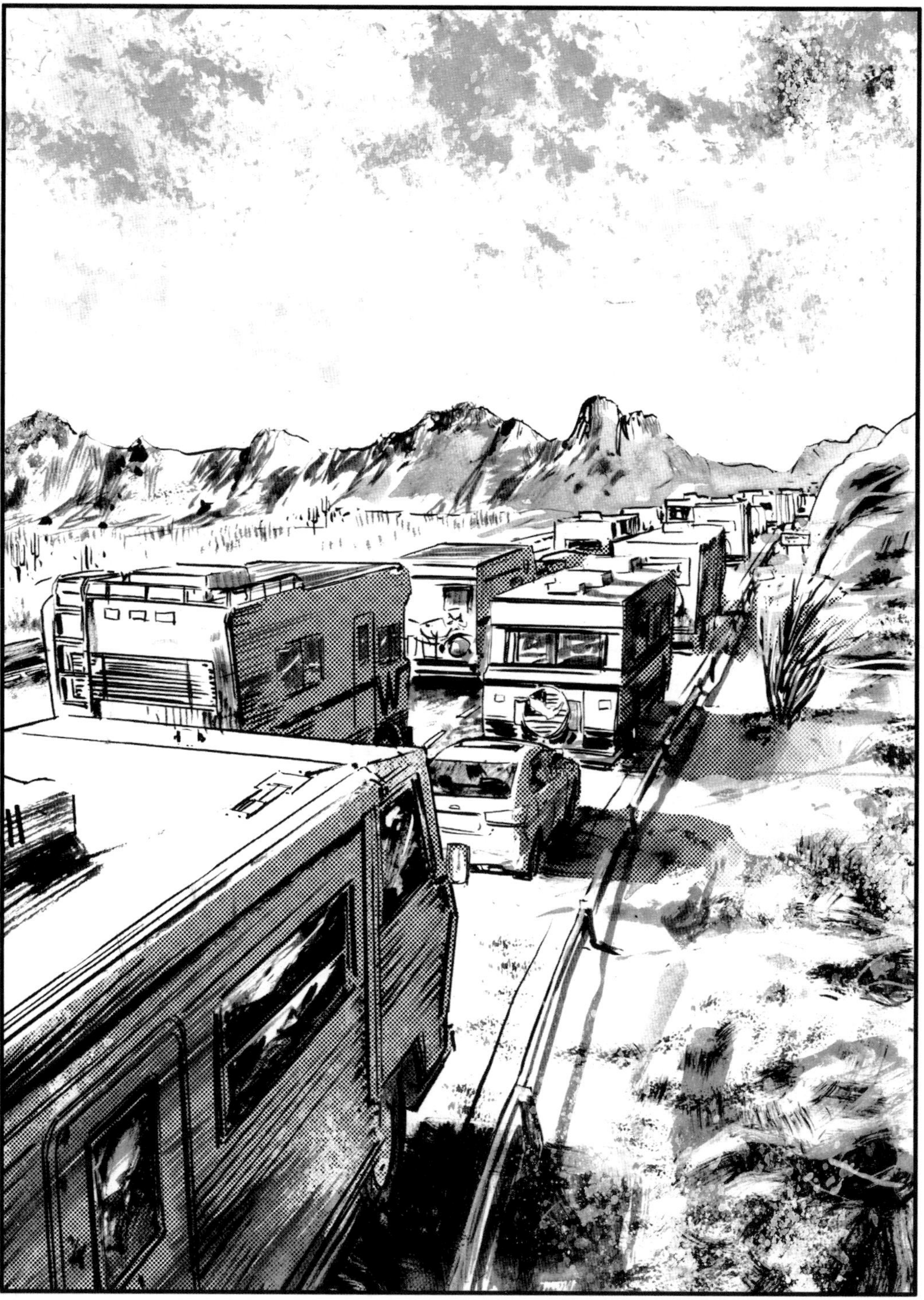

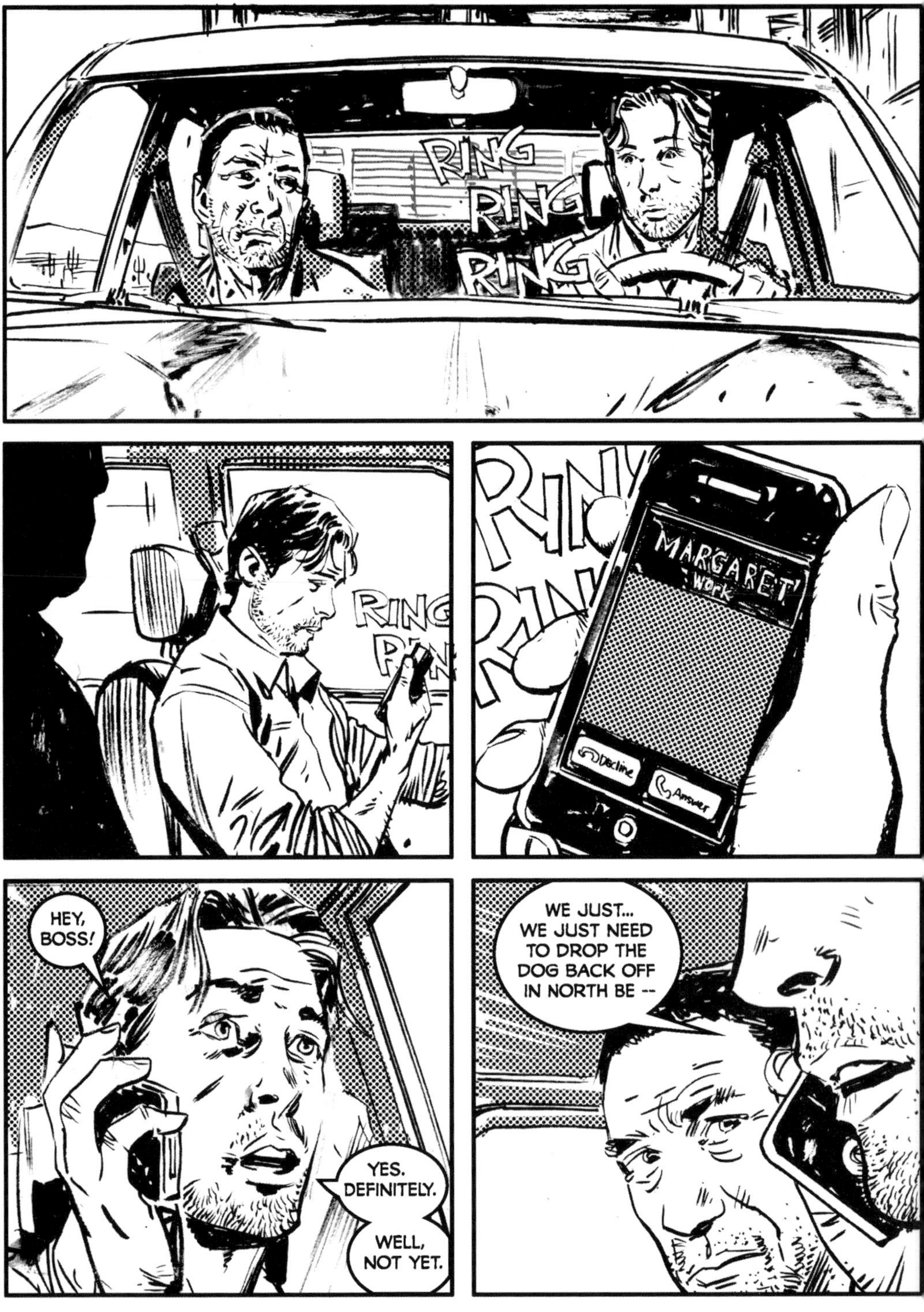
RING
RING
RING
RING
MARGARET
work
Decline
Answer
HEY, BOSS!
YES. DEFINITELY.
WELL, NOT YET.
WE JUST... WE JUST NEED TO DROP THE DOG BACK OFF IN NORTH BE --

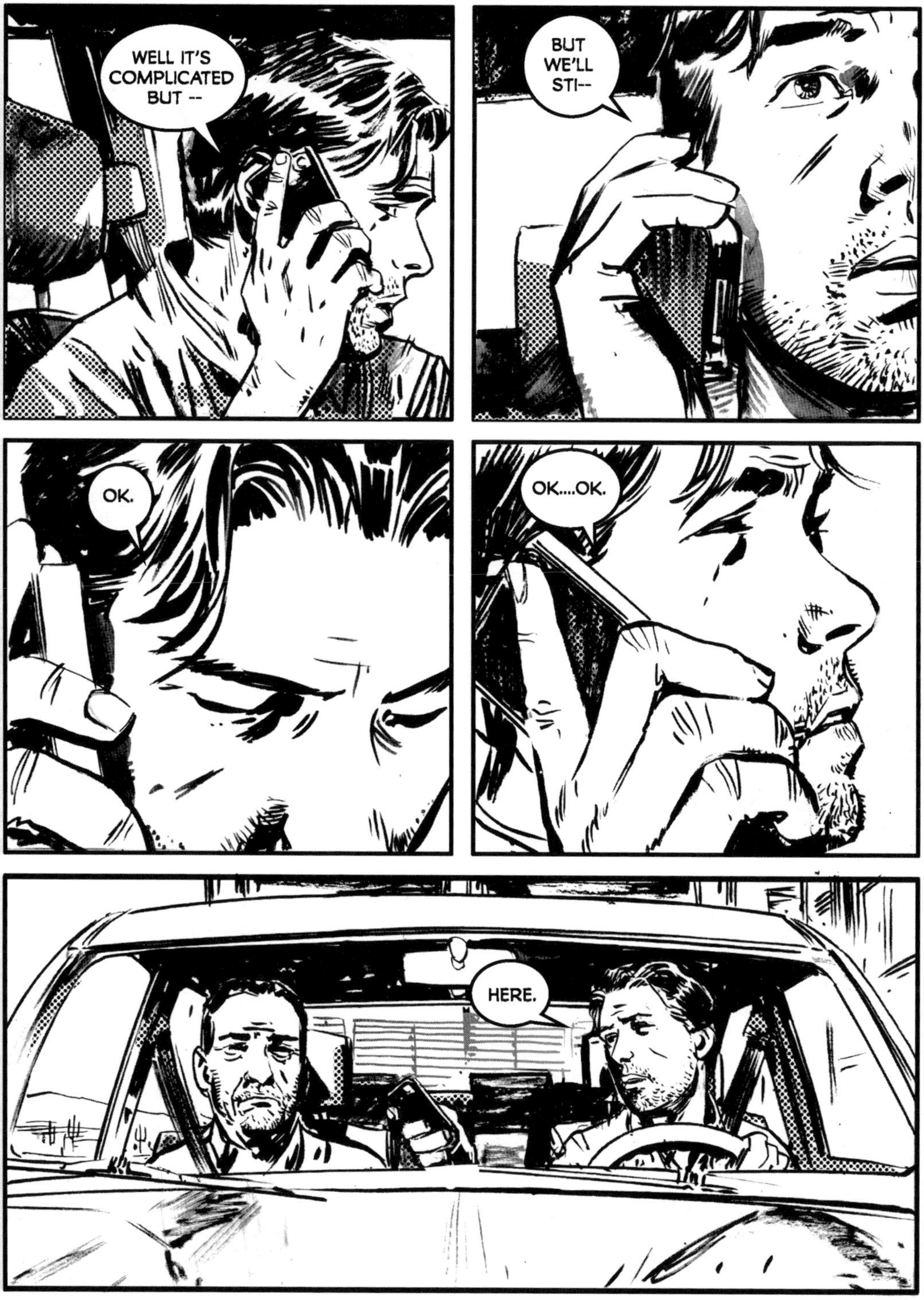
WELL IT'S COMPLICATED BUT --
BUT WE'LL STI--
OK.
OK....OK.
HERE.

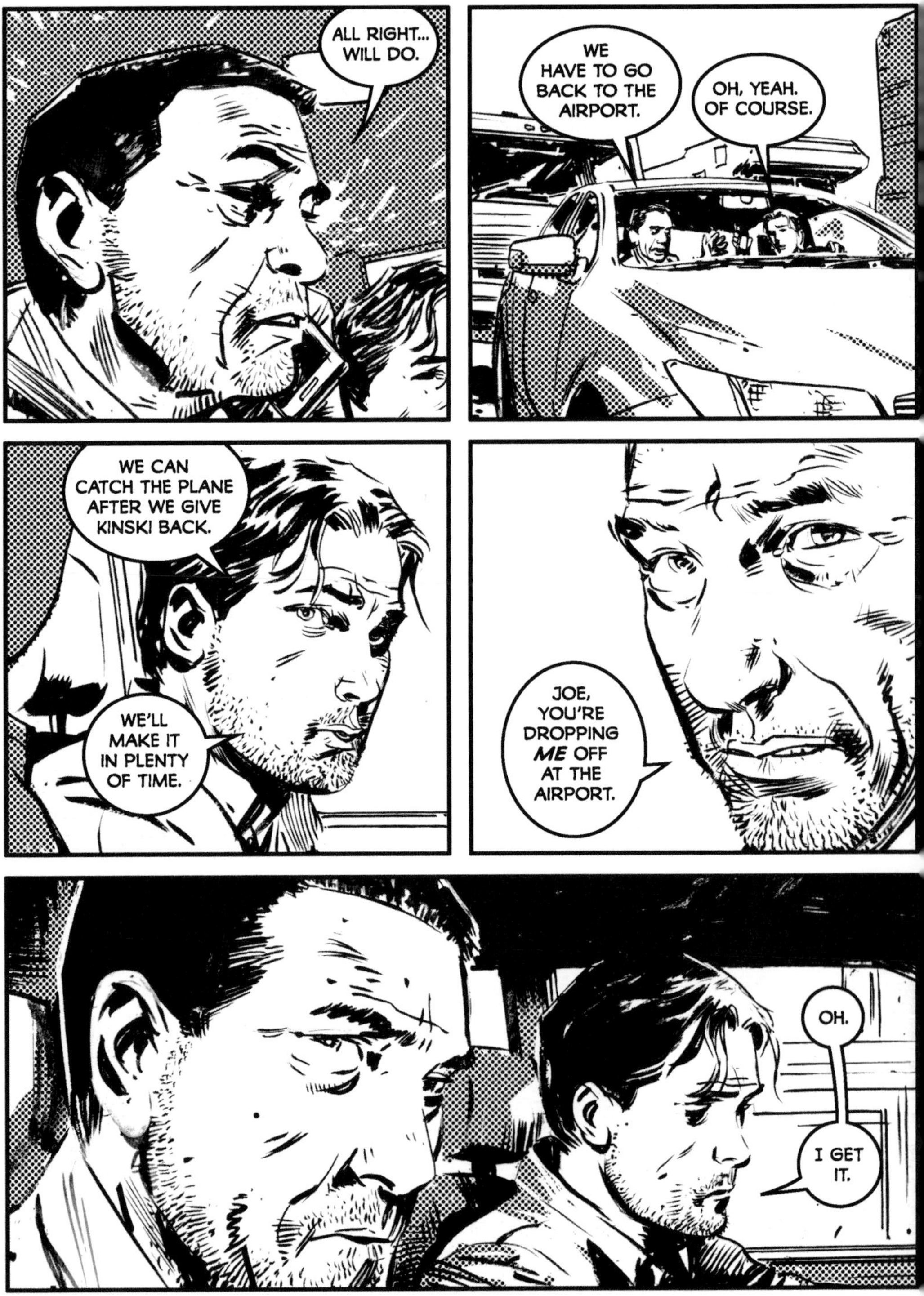
ALL RIGHT... WILL DO.
WE HAVE TO GO BACK TO THE AIRPORT.
OH, YEAH. OF COURSE.
WE CAN CATCH THE PLANE AFTER WE GIVE KINSKI BACK.
WE'LL MAKE IT IN PLENTY OF TIME.
JOE, YOU'RE DROPPING *ME* OFF AT THE AIRPORT.
OH.
I GET IT.

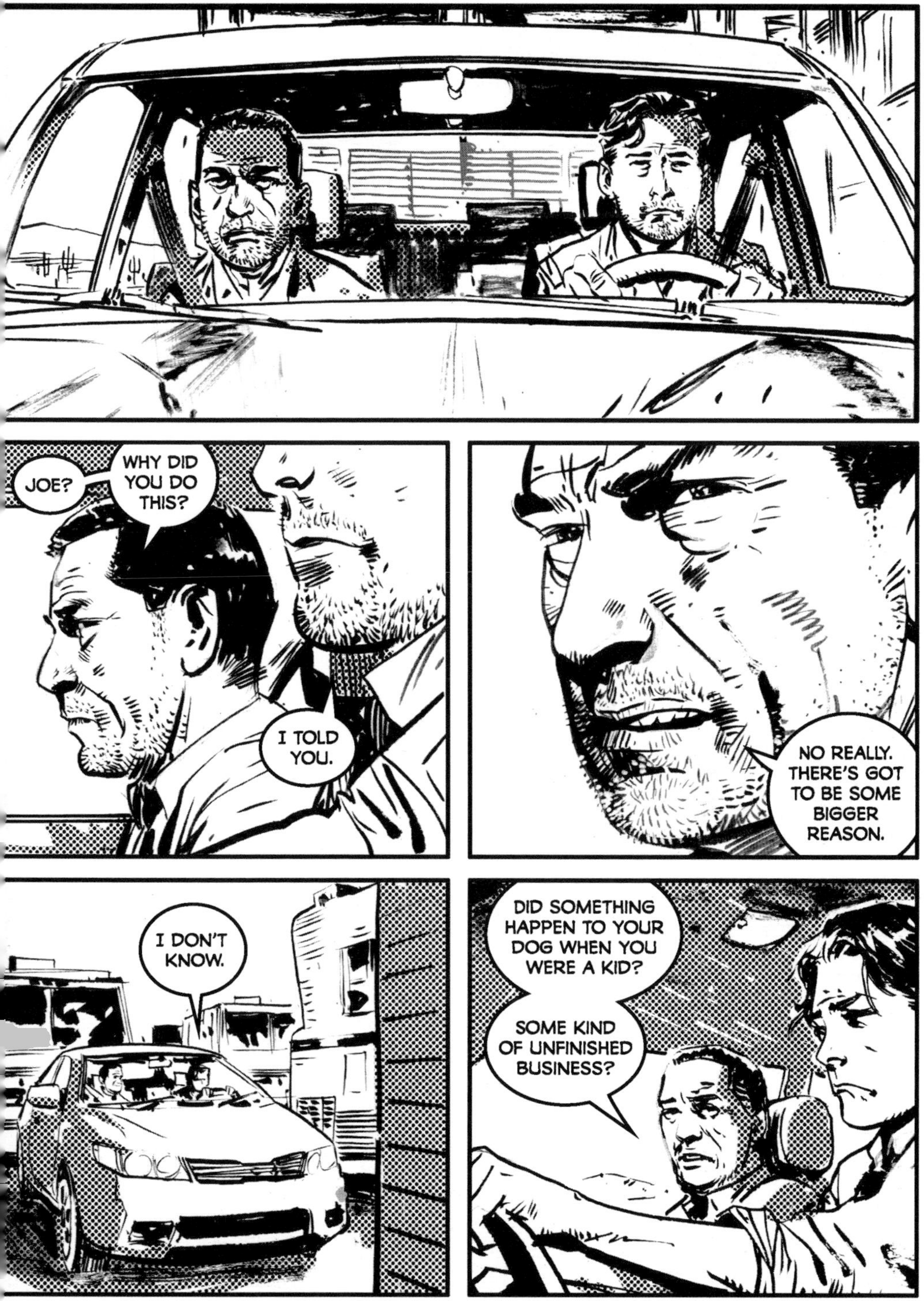
JOE?
WHY DID YOU DO THIS?
I TOLD YOU.
NO REALLY. THERE'S GOT TO BE SOME BIGGER REASON.
I DON'T KNOW.
DID SOMETHING HAPPEN TO YOUR DOG WHEN YOU WERE A KID?
SOME KIND OF UNFINISHED BUSINESS?

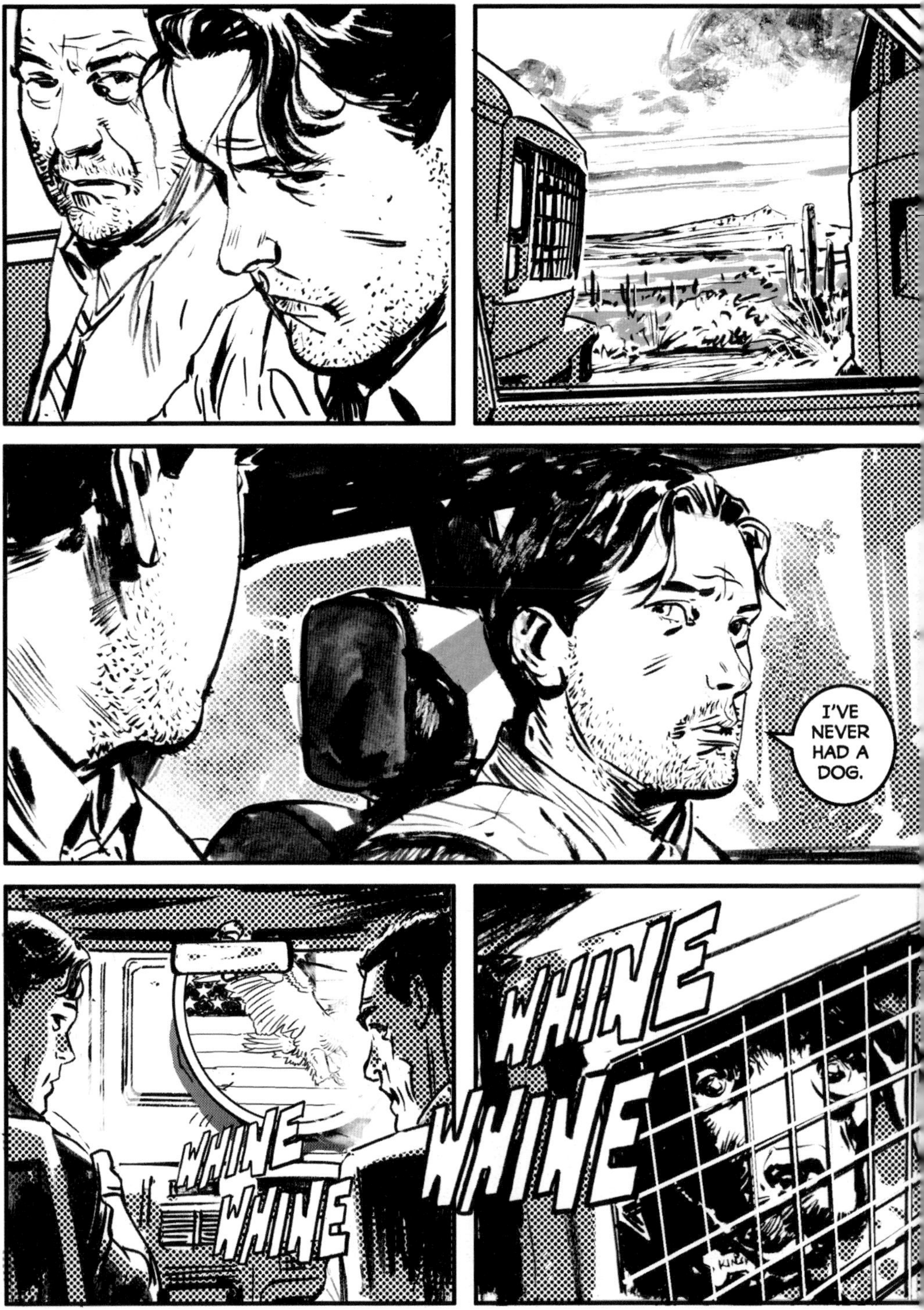
I'VE NEVER HAD A DOG.
WHINE
WHINE
WHINE
WHINE

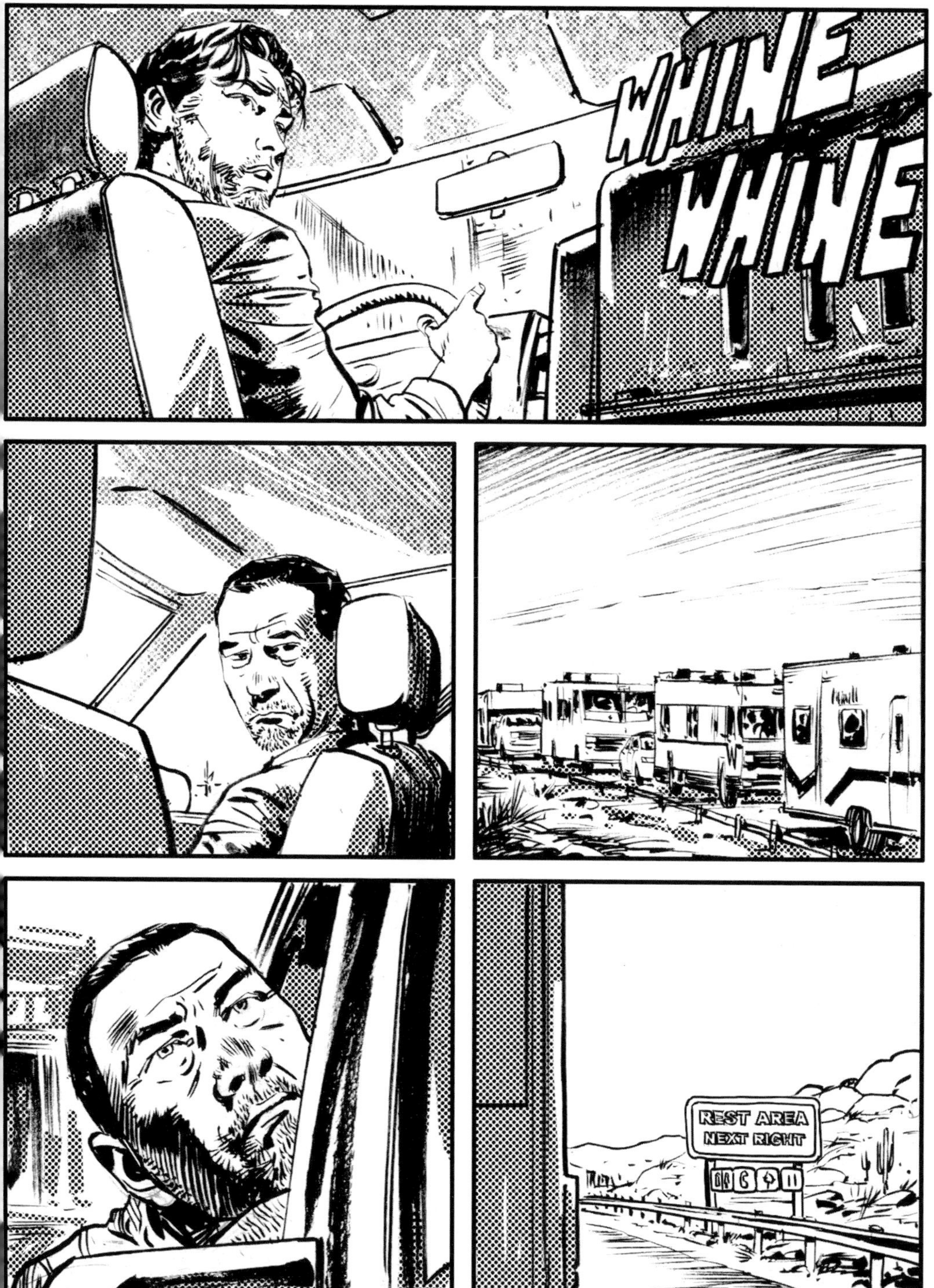
WHINE
WHINE
WHINE
REST AREA
NEXT RIGHT

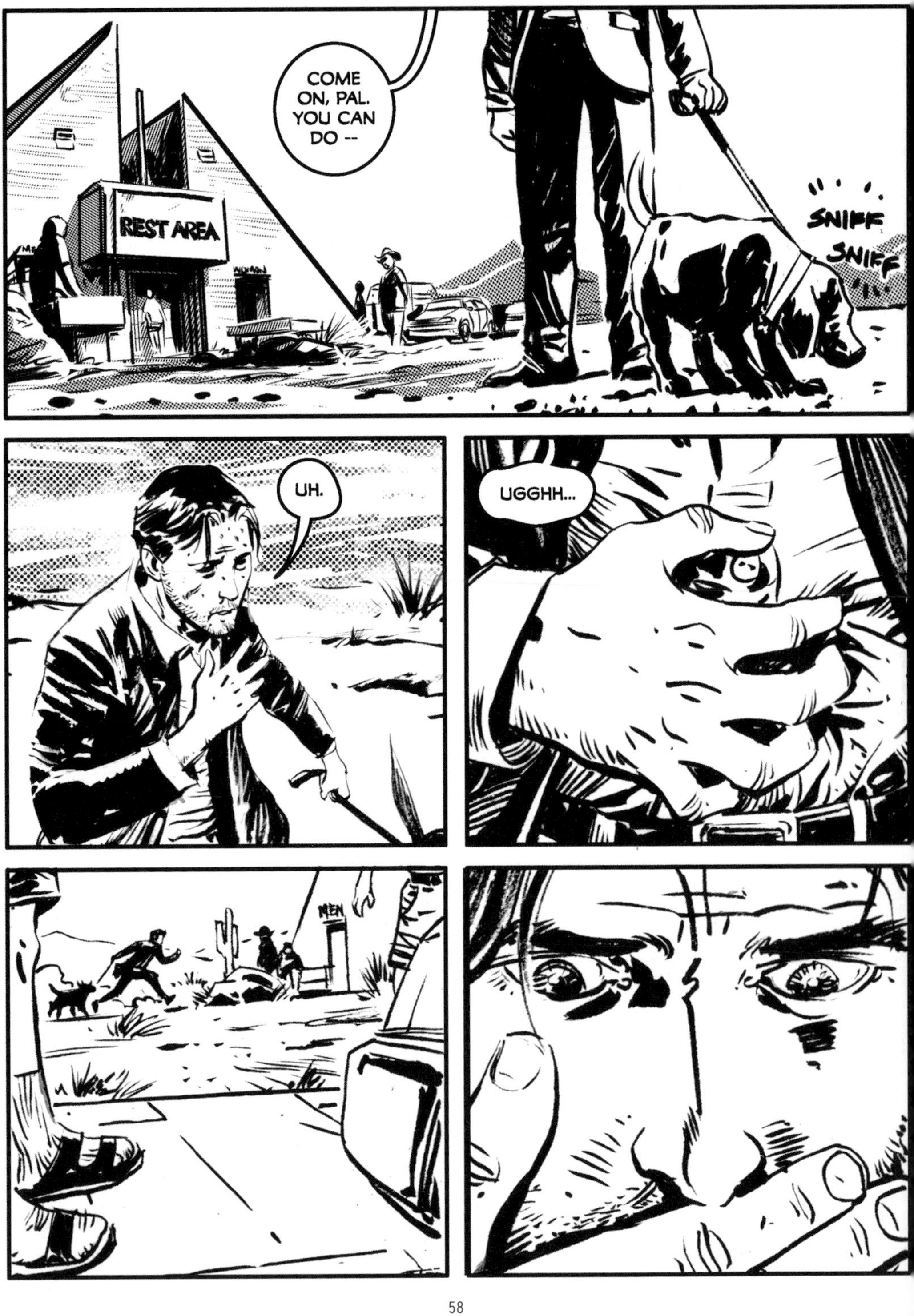
COME ON, PAL. YOU CAN DO --
REST AREA
SNIFF
SNIFF
UH.
UGGHH...
MEN

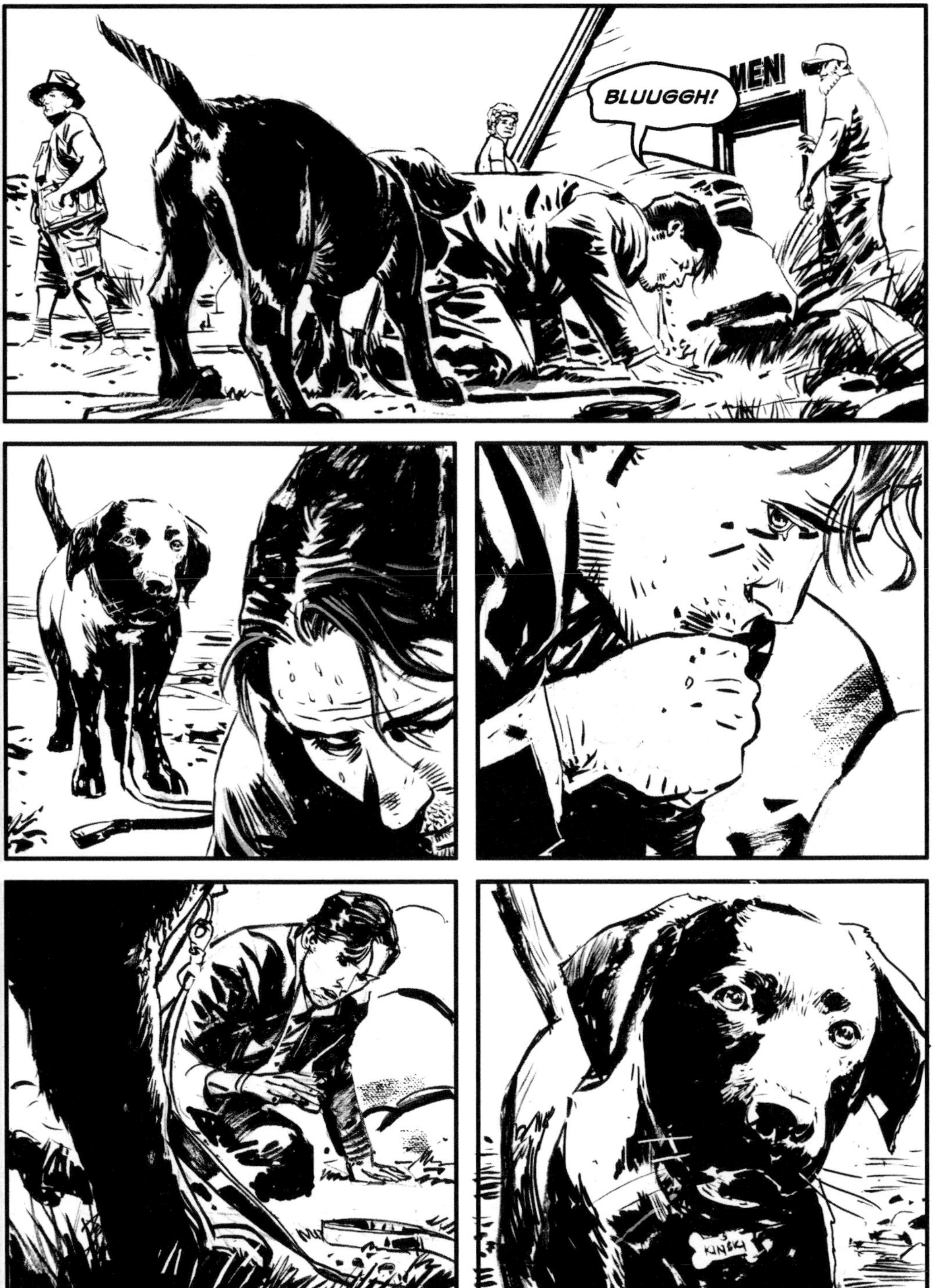
MEN
BLUUGGH!

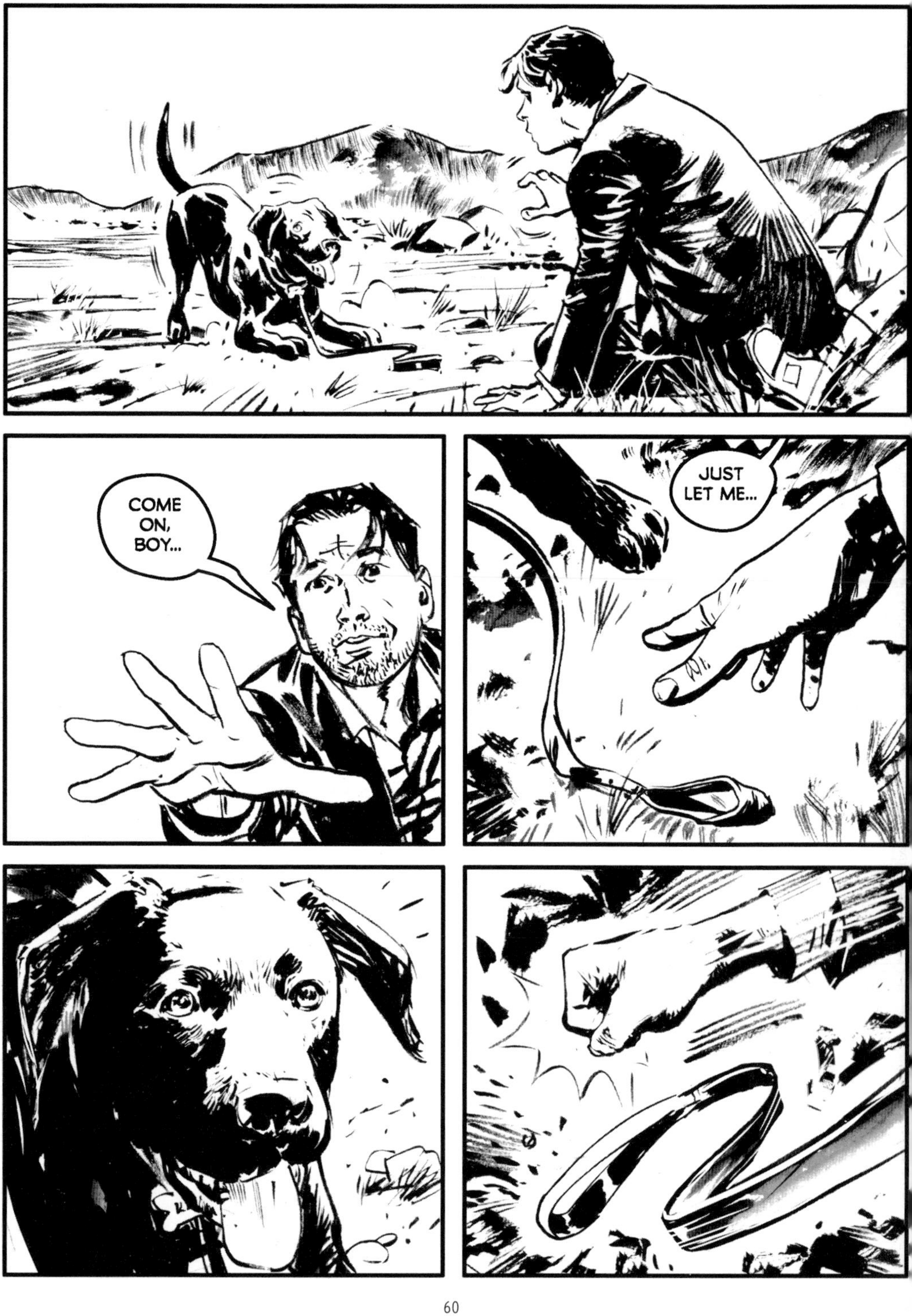
COME ON, BOY...
JUST LET ME...

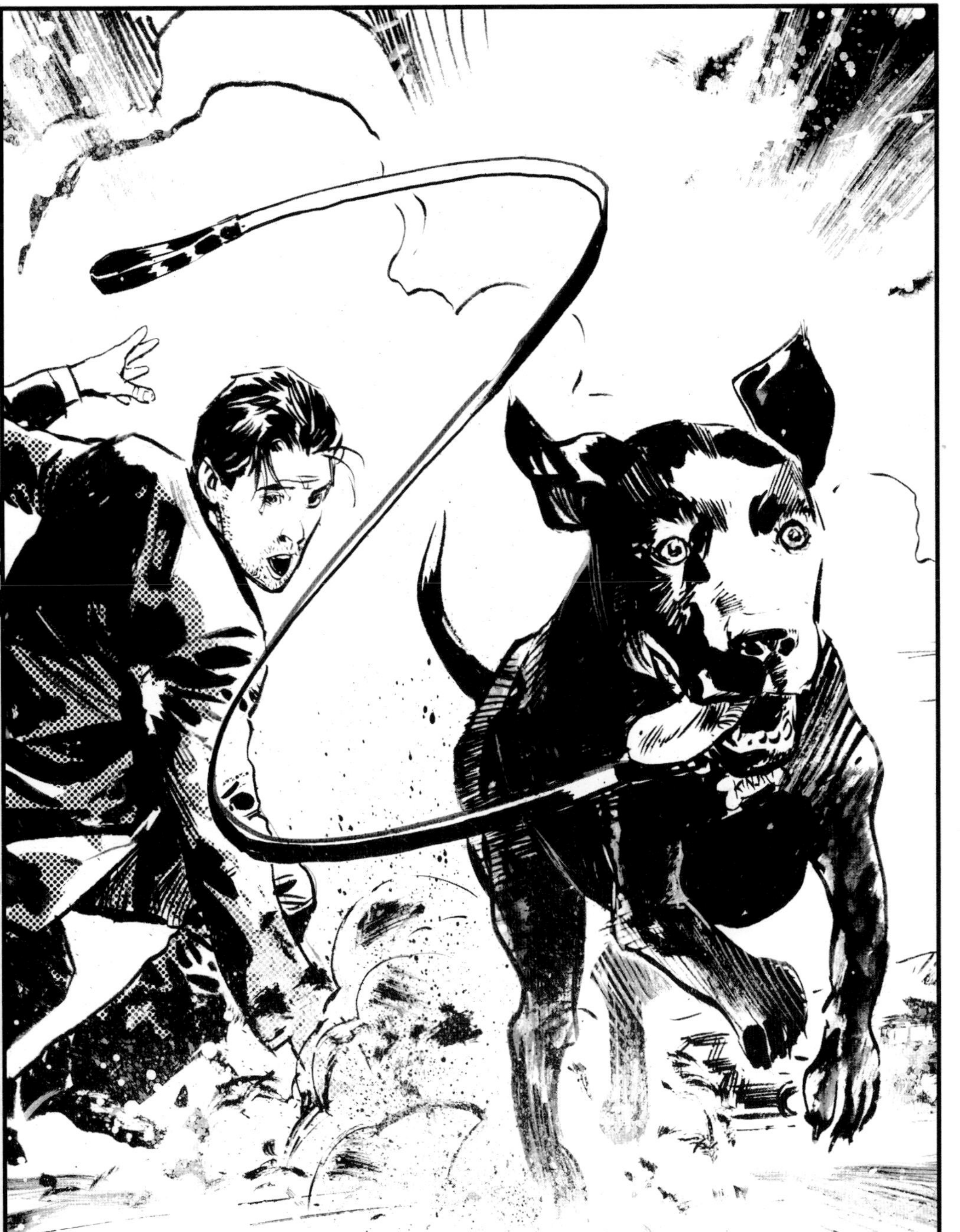

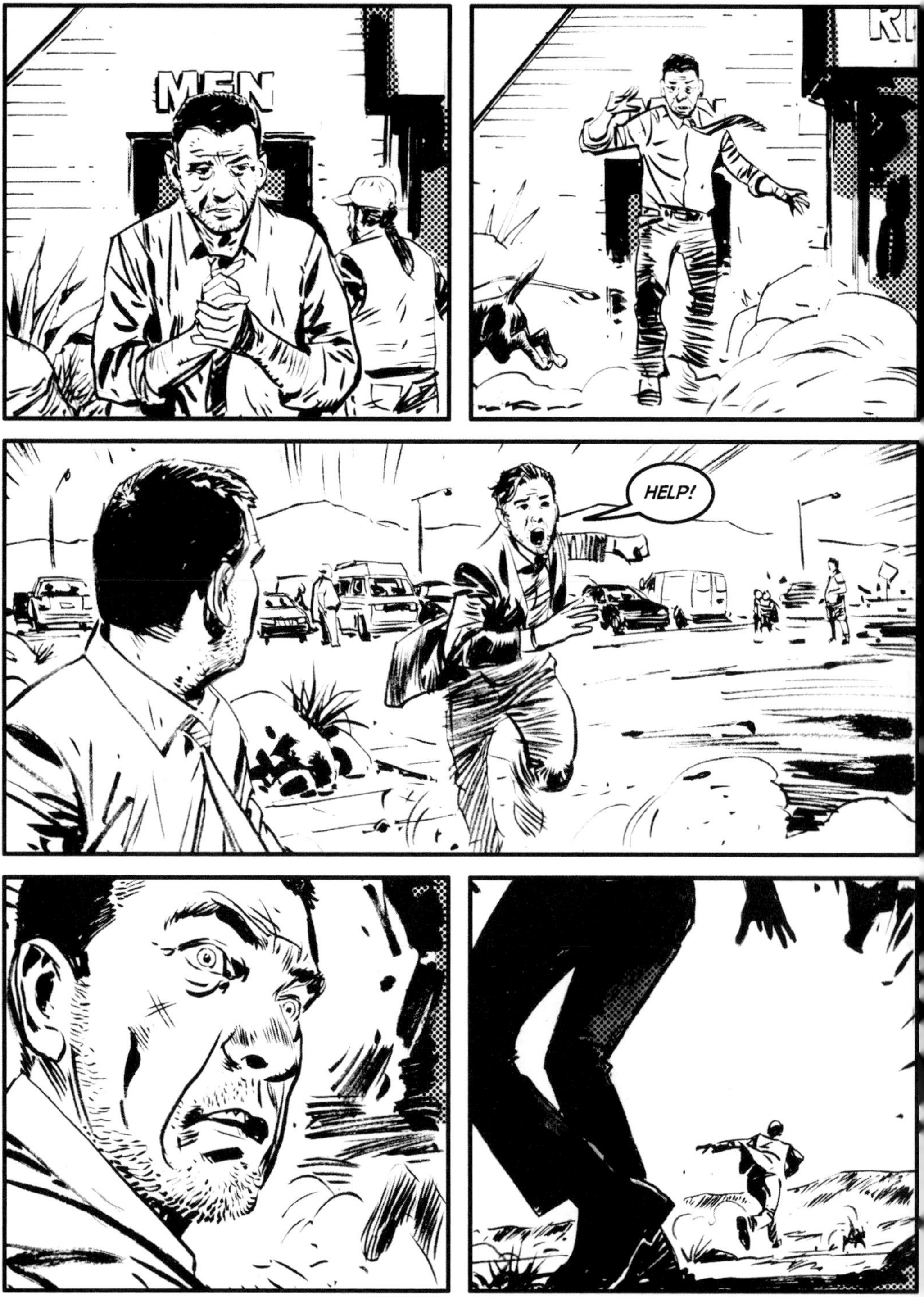
MEN
HELP!

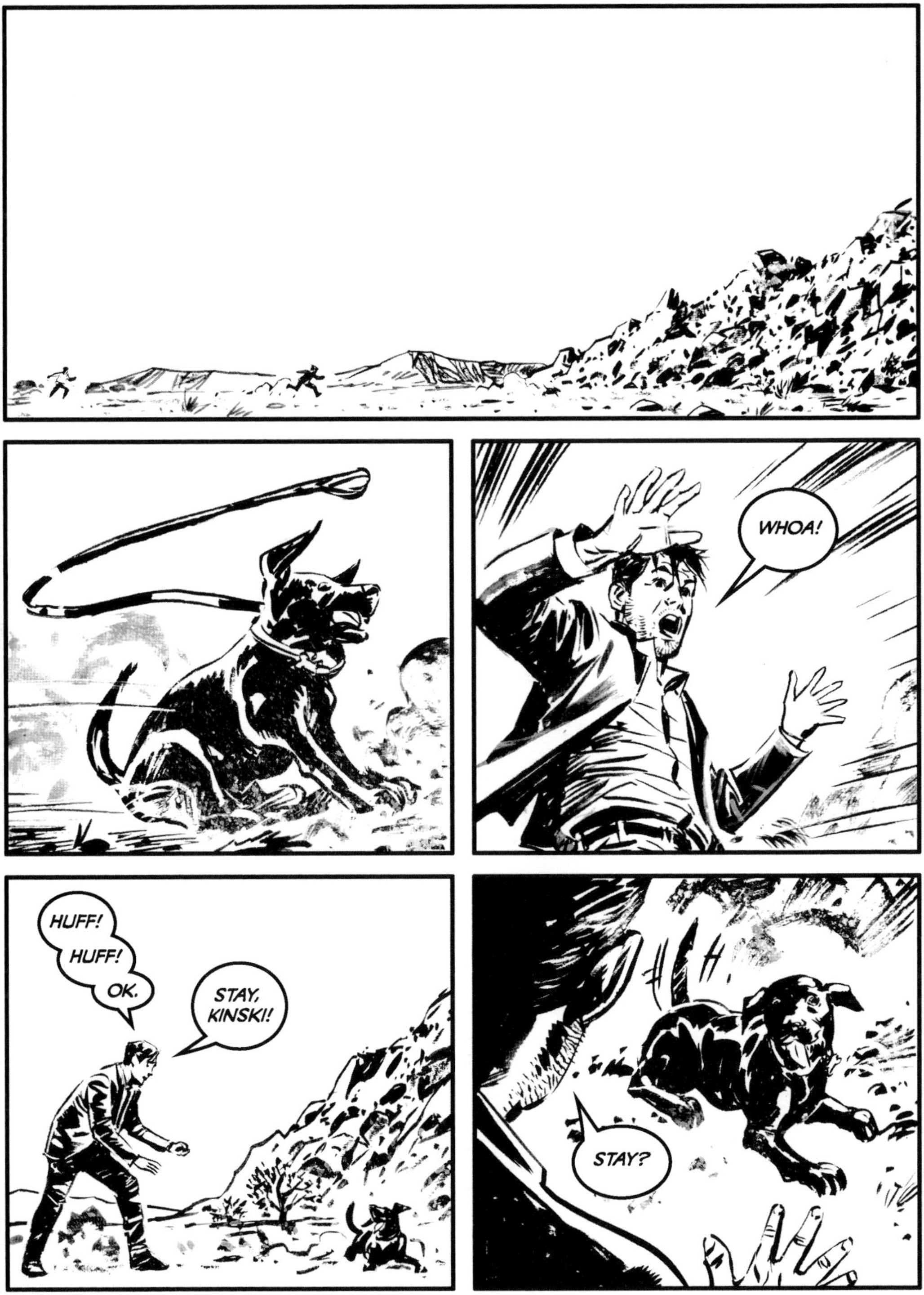
WHOA!
HUFF! HUFF! OK.
STAY, KINSKI!
STAY?

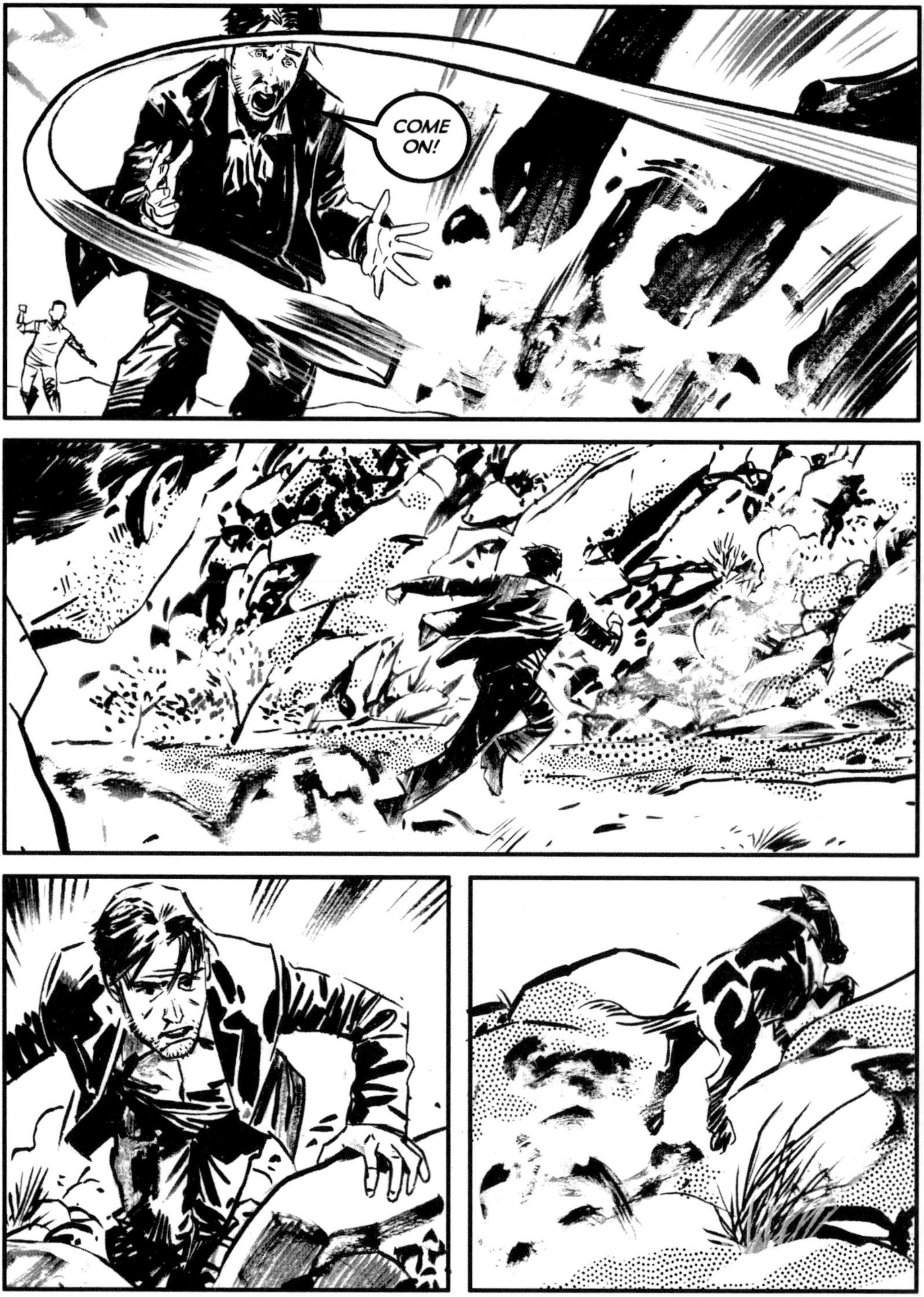
COME ON!

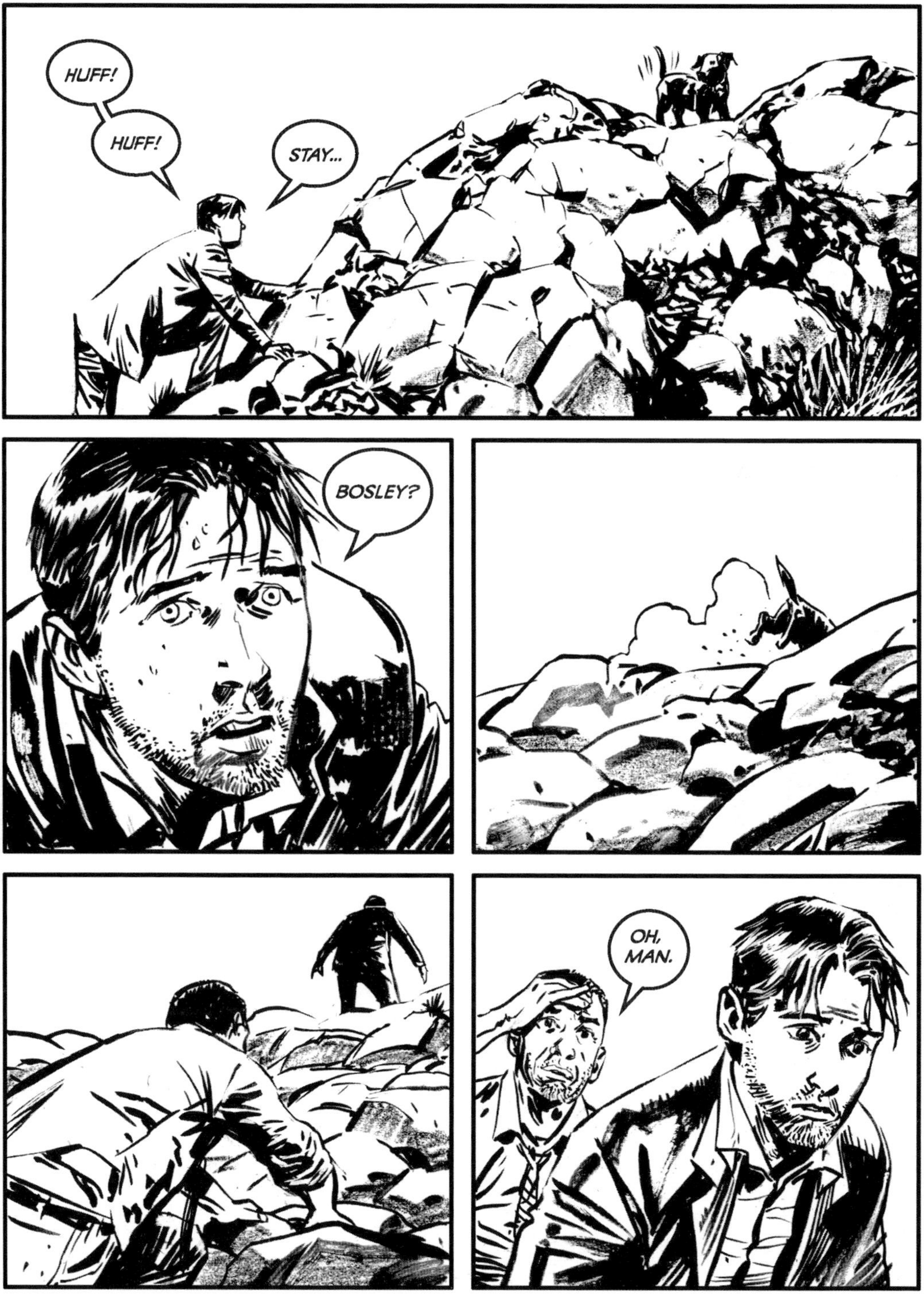
HUFF!
HUFF!
STAY...
BOSLEY?
OH, MAN.

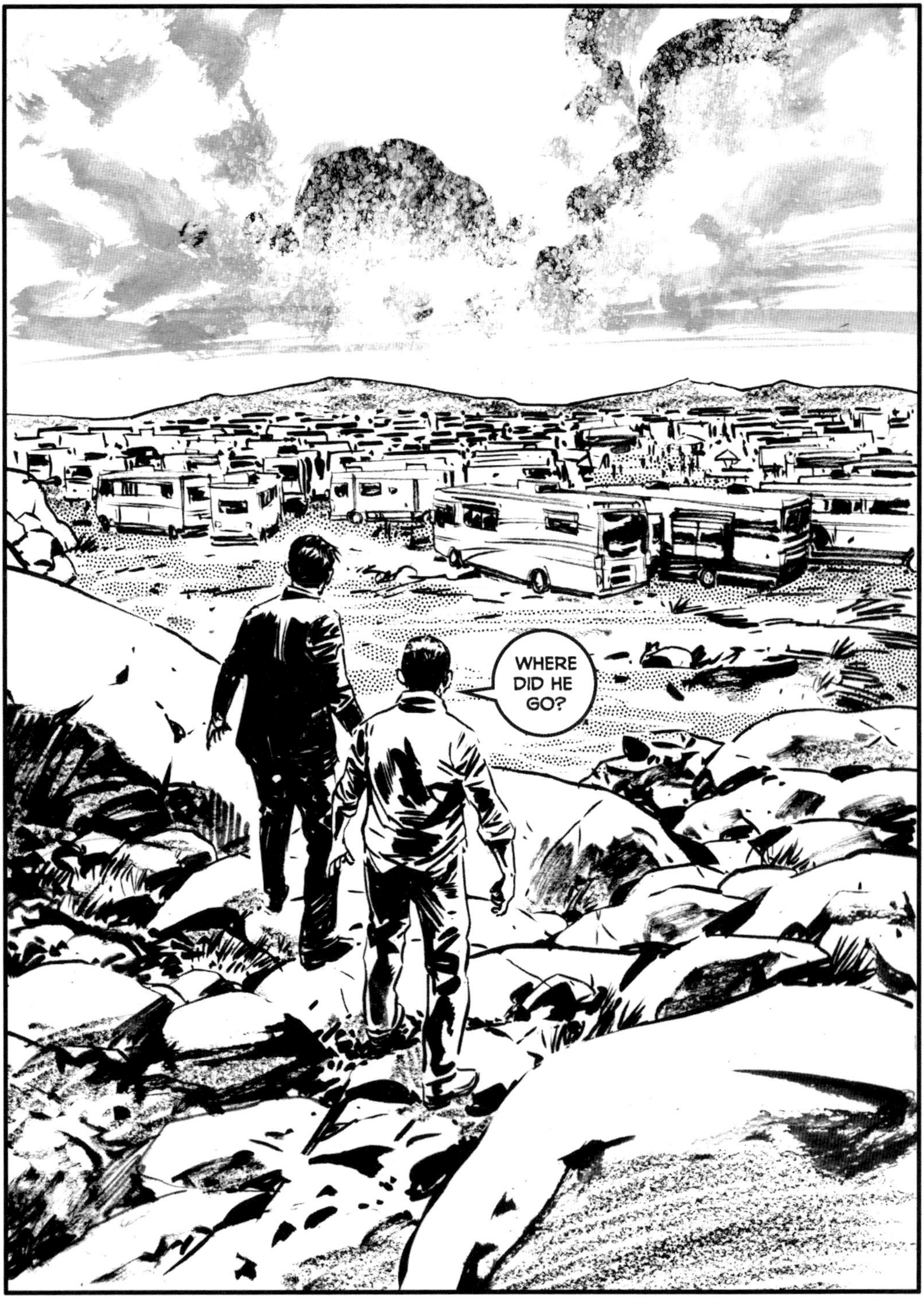
WHERE DID HE GO?

FOUR

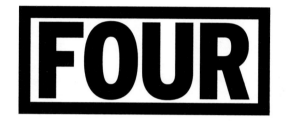

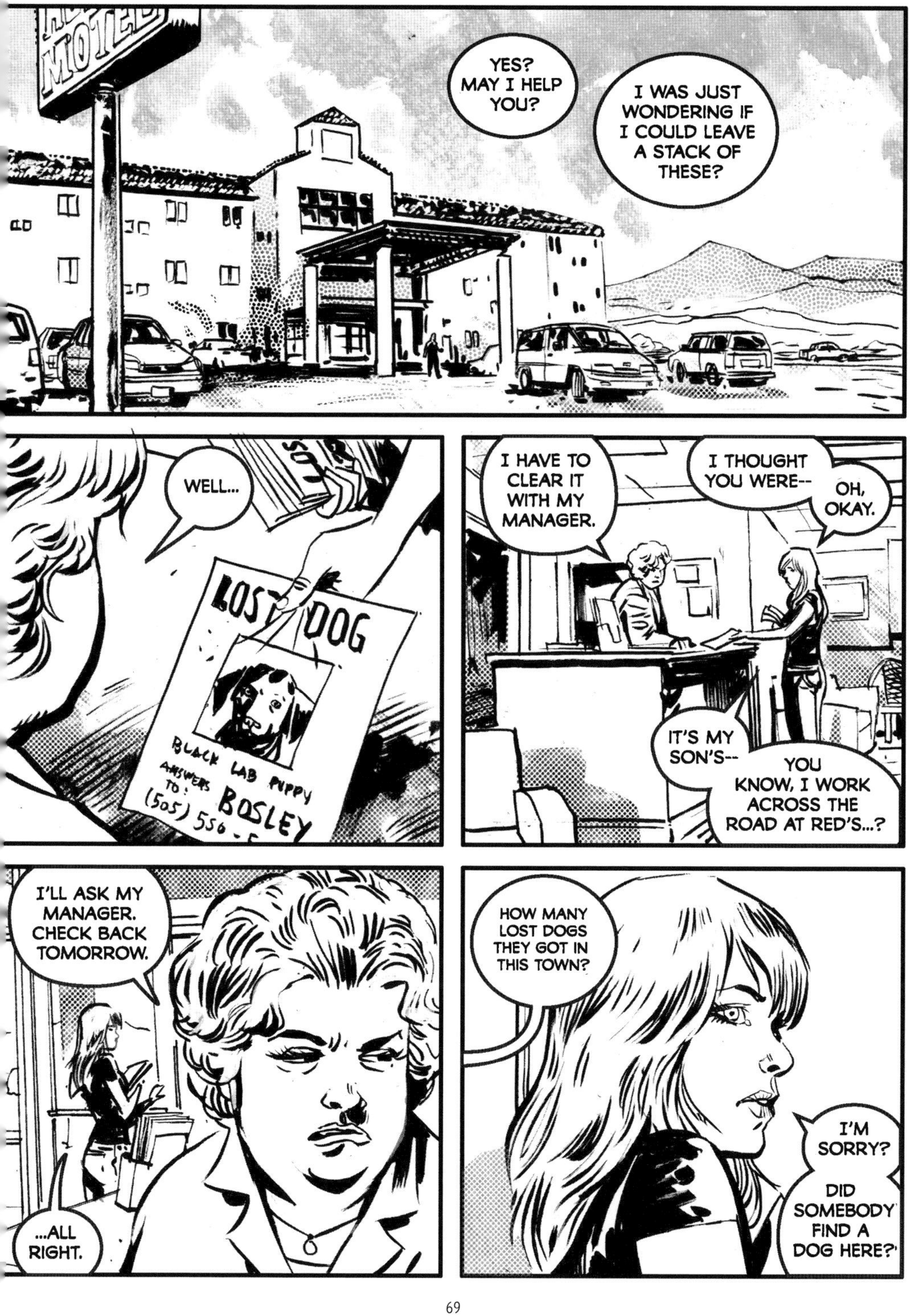

MOTEL
YES? MAY I HELP YOU?
I WAS JUST WONDERING IF I COULD LEAVE A STACK OF THESE?
WELL...
LOST DOG
BLACK LAB PUPPY
ANSWERS TO: BOSLEY
(505) 556-
I HAVE TO CLEAR IT WITH MY MANAGER.
I THOUGHT YOU WERE--
OH, OKAY.
IT'S MY SON'S--
YOU KNOW, I WORK ACROSS THE ROAD AT RED'S...?
I'LL ASK MY MANAGER. CHECK BACK TOMORROW.
...ALL RIGHT.
HOW MANY LOST DOGS THEY GOT IN THIS TOWN?
I'M SORRY?
DID SOMEBODY FIND A DOG HERE?

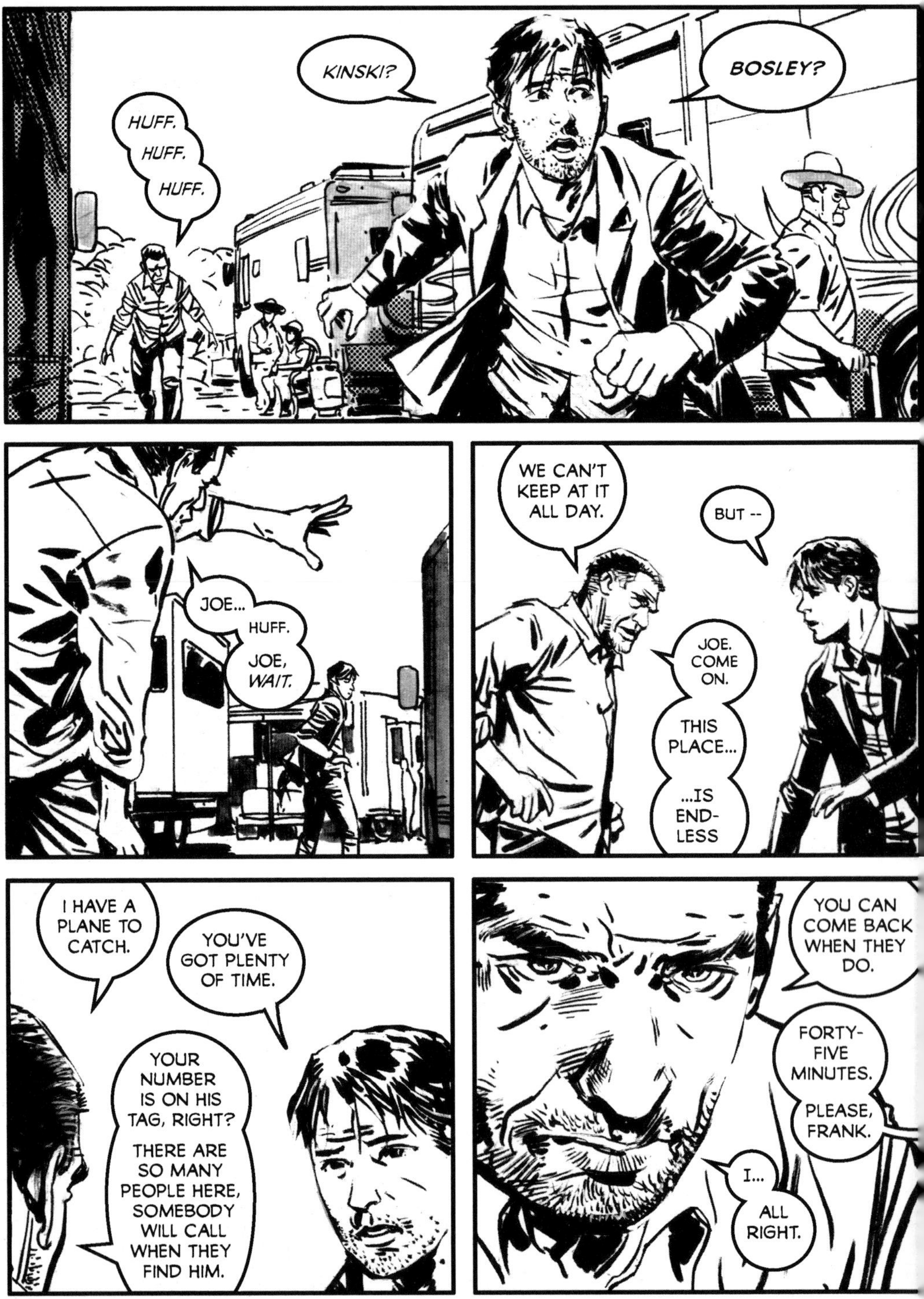
HUFF. HUFF. HUFF.
KINSKI?
BOSLEY?
JOE...
HUFF.
JOE, WAIT.
WE CAN'T KEEP AT IT ALL DAY.
BUT --
JOE. COME ON.
THIS PLACE...
...IS END-LESS
I HAVE A PLANE TO CATCH.
YOU'VE GOT PLENTY OF TIME.
YOUR NUMBER IS ON HIS TAG, RIGHT?
THERE ARE SO MANY PEOPLE HERE, SOMEBODY WILL CALL WHEN THEY FIND HIM.
YOU CAN COME BACK WHEN THEY DO.
FORTY-FIVE MINUTES.
PLEASE, FRANK.
I...
ALL RIGHT.

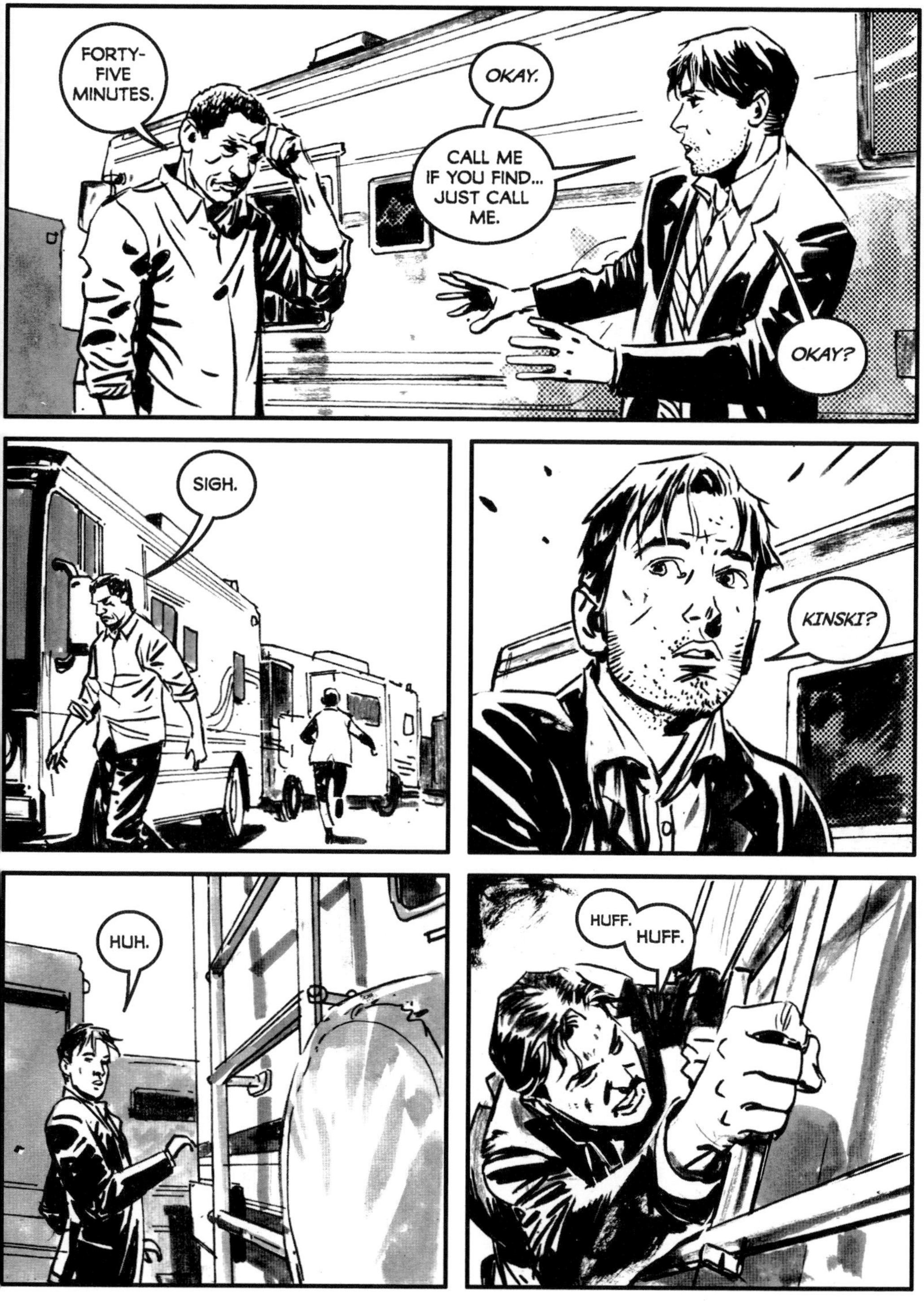
FORTY-FIVE MINUTES.
OKAY.
CALL ME IF YOU FIND... JUST CALL ME.
OKAY?
SIGH.
KINSKI?
HUH.
HUFF.
HUFF.

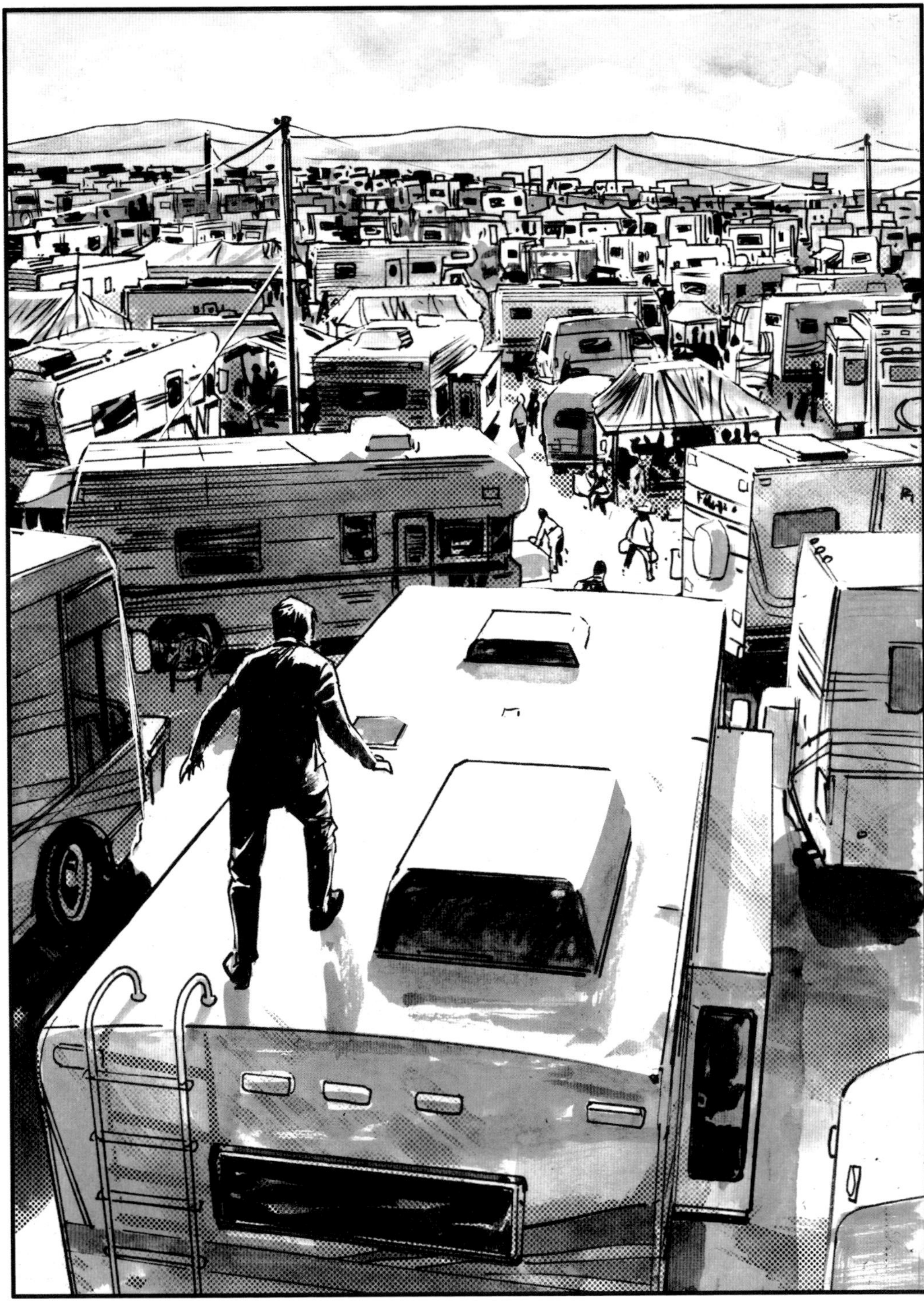

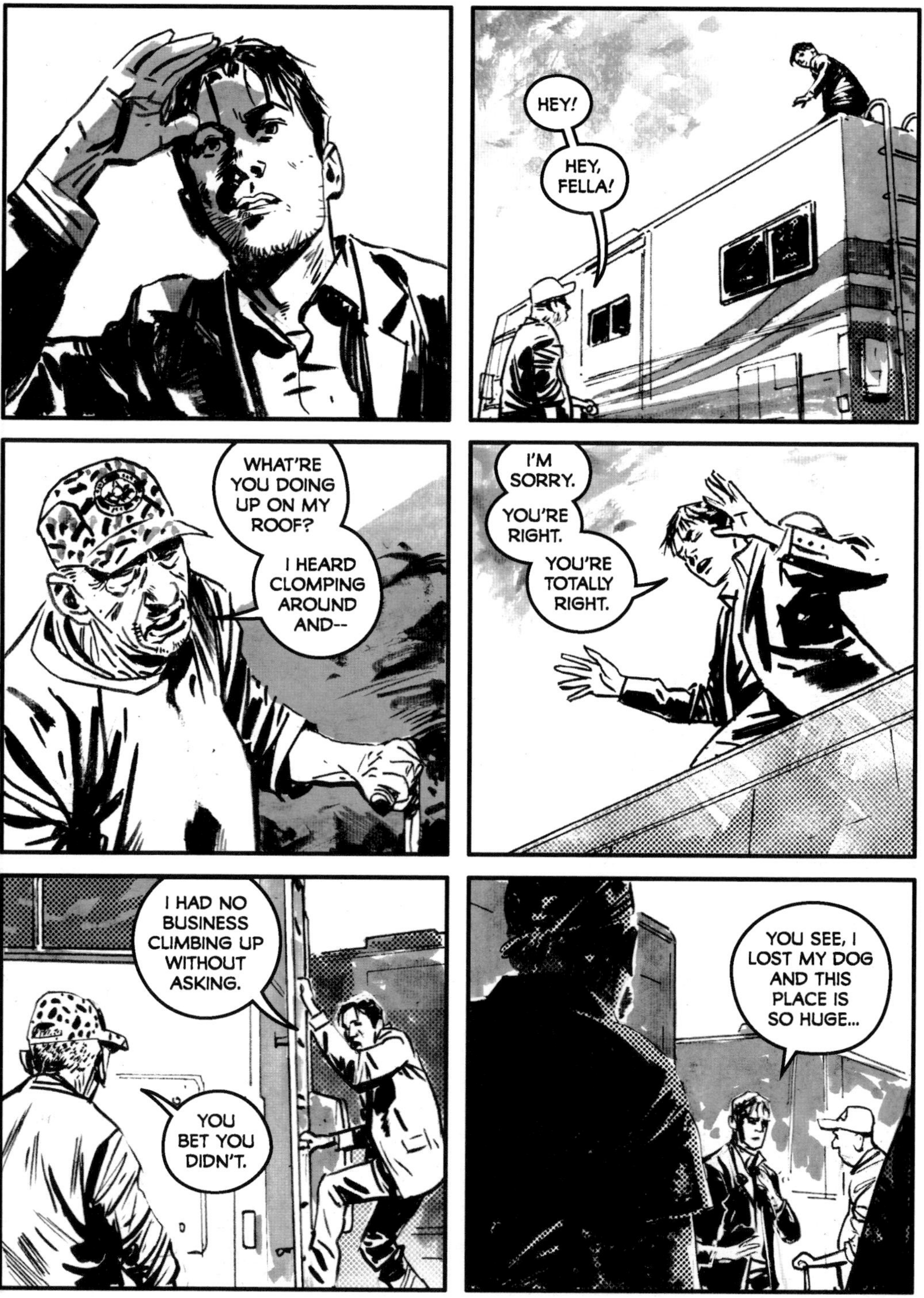
HEY!
HEY, FELLA!
WHAT'RE YOU DOING UP ON MY ROOF?
I HEARD CLOMPING AROUND AND--
I'M SORRY.
YOU'RE RIGHT.
YOU'RE TOTALLY RIGHT.
I HAD NO BUSINESS CLIMBING UP WITHOUT ASKING.
YOU BET YOU DIDN'T.
YOU SEE, I LOST MY DOG AND THIS PLACE IS SO HUGE...

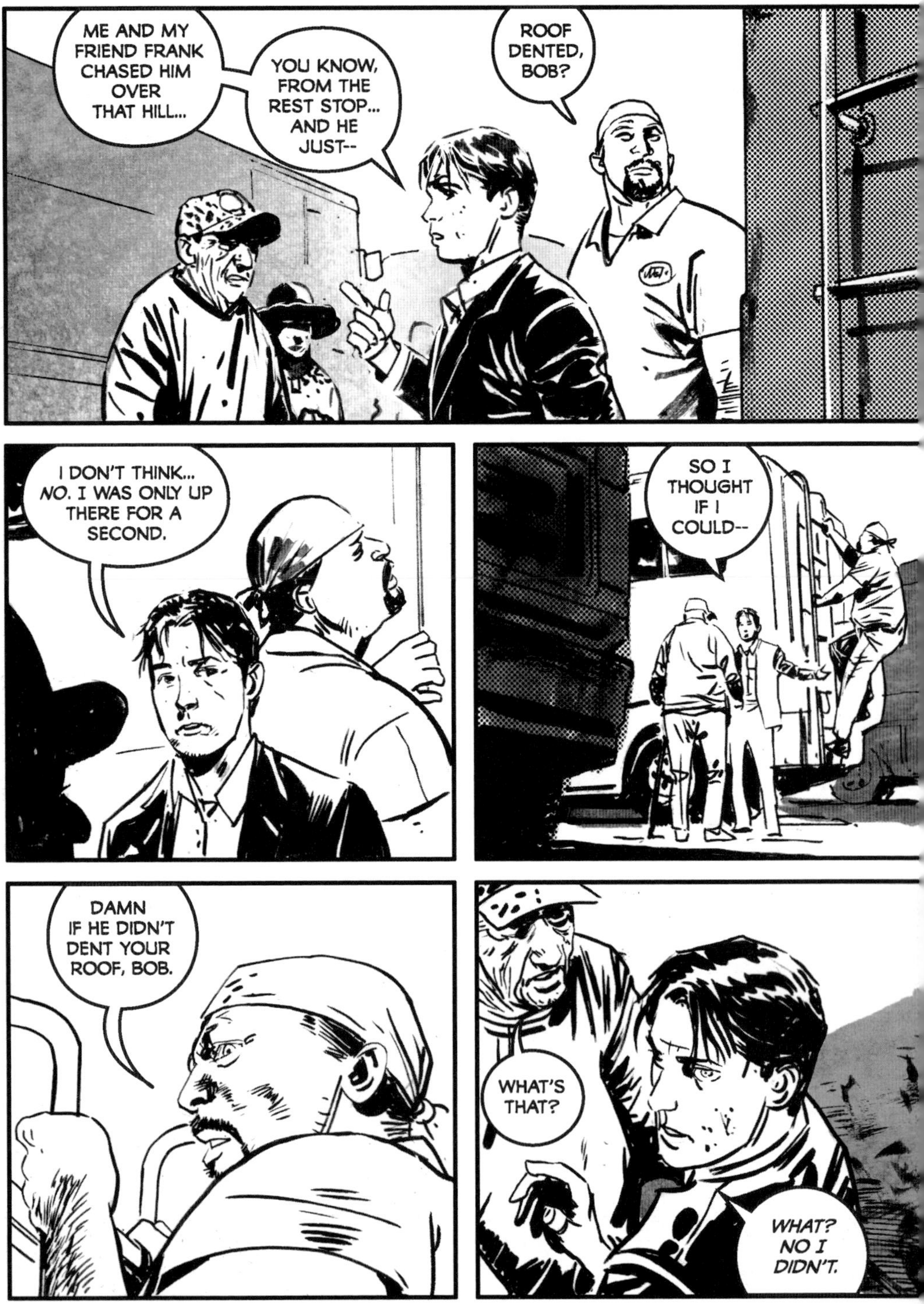
ME AND MY FRIEND FRANK CHASED HIM OVER THAT HILL...
YOU KNOW, FROM THE REST STOP... AND HE JUST--
ROOF DENTED, BOB?
I DON'T THINK... *NO*. I WAS ONLY UP THERE FOR A SECOND.
SO I THOUGHT IF I COULD--
DAMN IF HE DIDN'T DENT YOUR ROOF, BOB.
WHAT'S THAT?
WHAT? NO I DIDN'T.

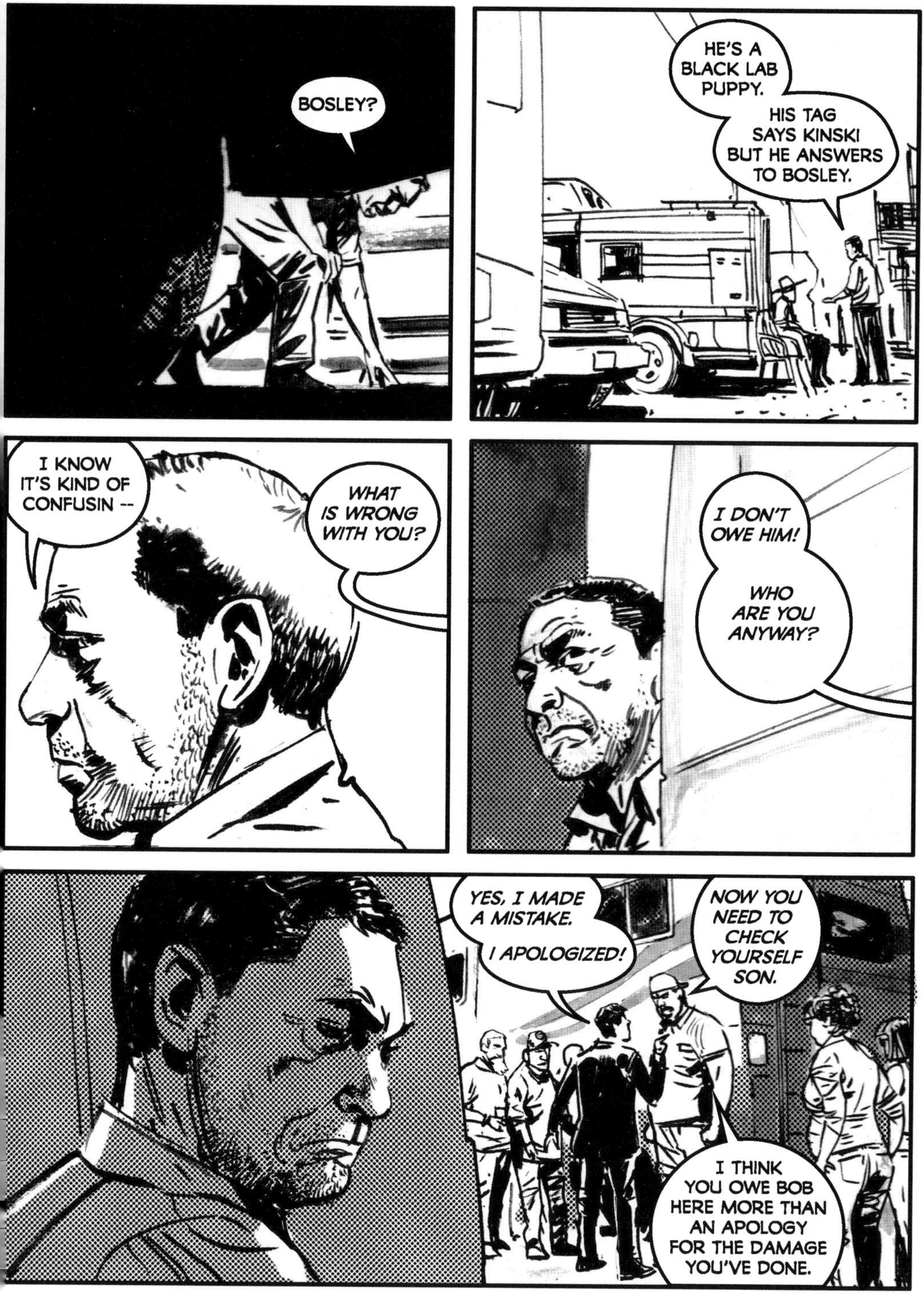
BOSLEY?
HE'S A BLACK LAB PUPPY.
HIS TAG SAYS KINSKI BUT HE ANSWERS TO BOSLEY.
I KNOW IT'S KIND OF CONFUSIN --
WHAT IS WRONG WITH YOU?
I DON'T OWE HIM!
WHO ARE YOU ANYWAY?
YES, I MADE A MISTAKE.
I APOLOGIZED!
NOW YOU NEED TO CHECK YOURSELF SON.
I THINK YOU OWE BOB HERE MORE THAN AN APOLOGY FOR THE DAMAGE YOU'VE DONE.

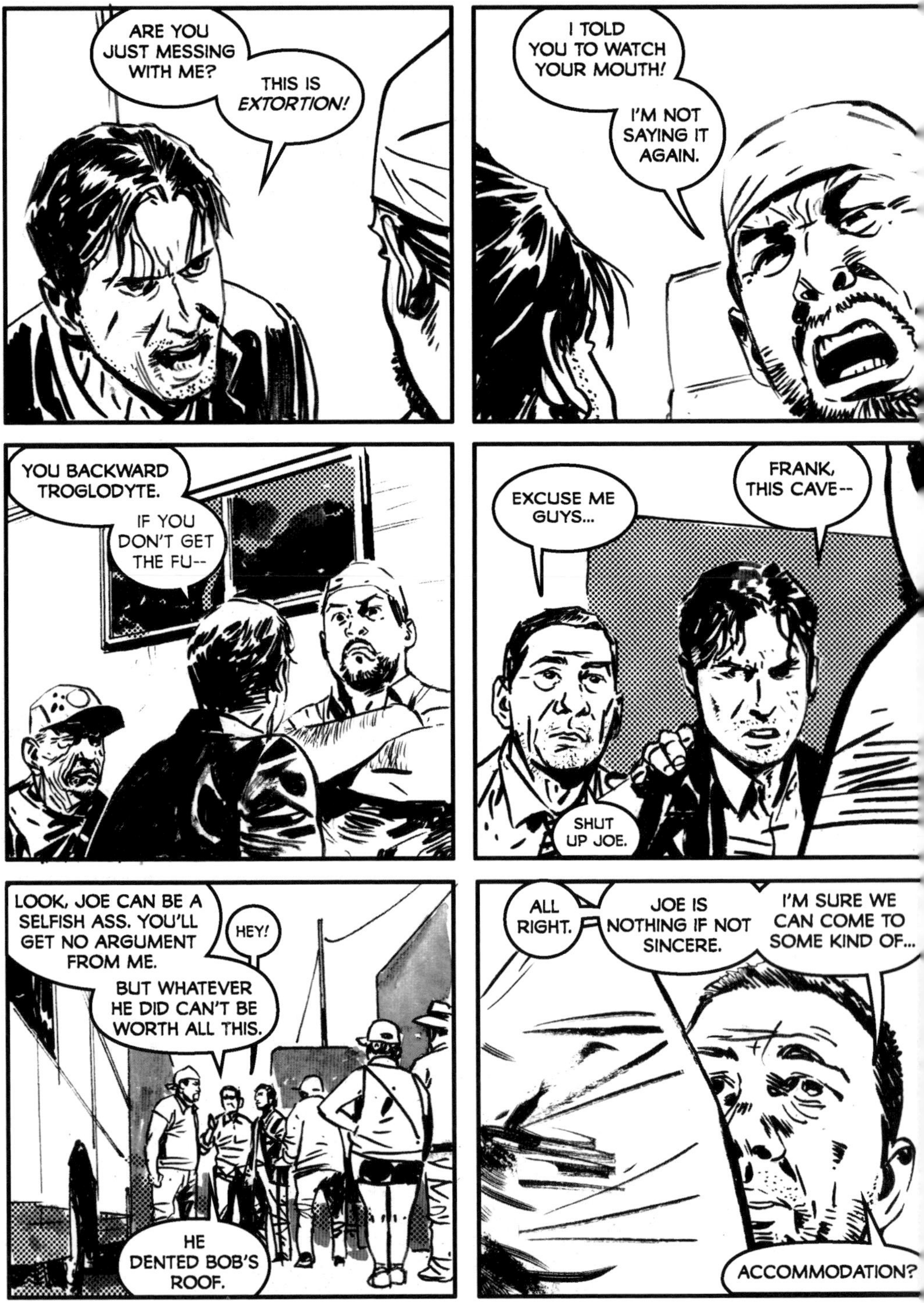
ARE YOU JUST MESSING WITH ME?
THIS IS *EXTORTION!*
I TOLD YOU TO WATCH YOUR MOUTH!
I'M NOT SAYING IT AGAIN.
YOU BACKWARD TROGLODYTE.
IF YOU DON'T GET THE FU--
EXCUSE ME GUYS...
FRANK, THIS CAVE--
SHUT UP JOE.
LOOK, JOE CAN BE A SELFISH ASS. YOU'LL GET NO ARGUMENT FROM ME.
HEY!
BUT WHATEVER HE DID CAN'T BE WORTH ALL THIS.
HE DENTED BOB'S ROOF.
ALL RIGHT.
JOE IS NOTHING IF NOT SINCERE.
I'M SURE WE CAN COME TO SOME KIND OF...
ACCOMMODATION?

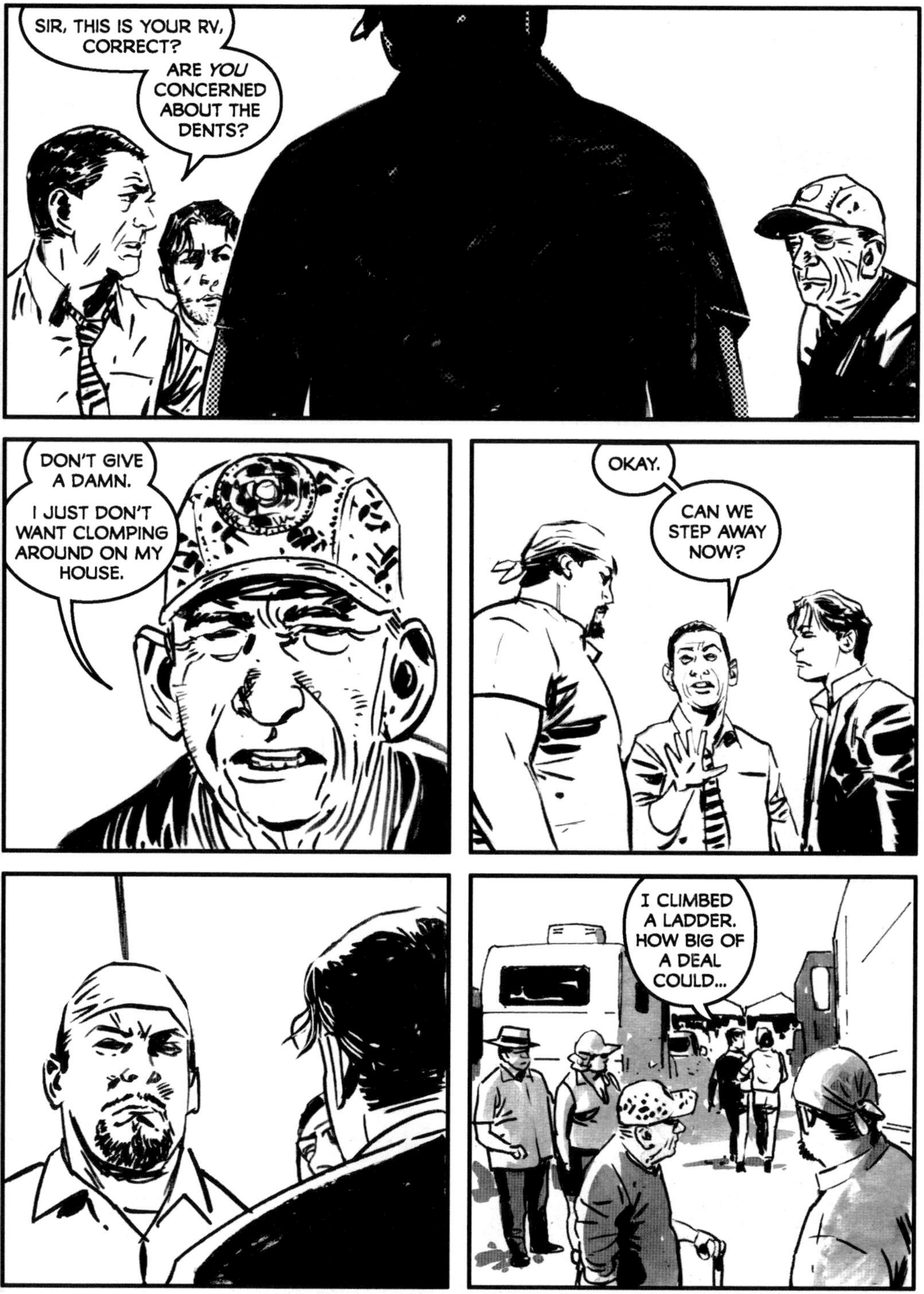
SIR, THIS IS YOUR RV, CORRECT?
ARE *YOU* CONCERNED ABOUT THE DENTS?
DON'T GIVE A DAMN.
I JUST DON'T WANT CLOMPING AROUND ON MY HOUSE.
OKAY.
CAN WE STEP AWAY NOW?
I CLIMBED A LADDER. HOW BIG OF A DEAL COULD...

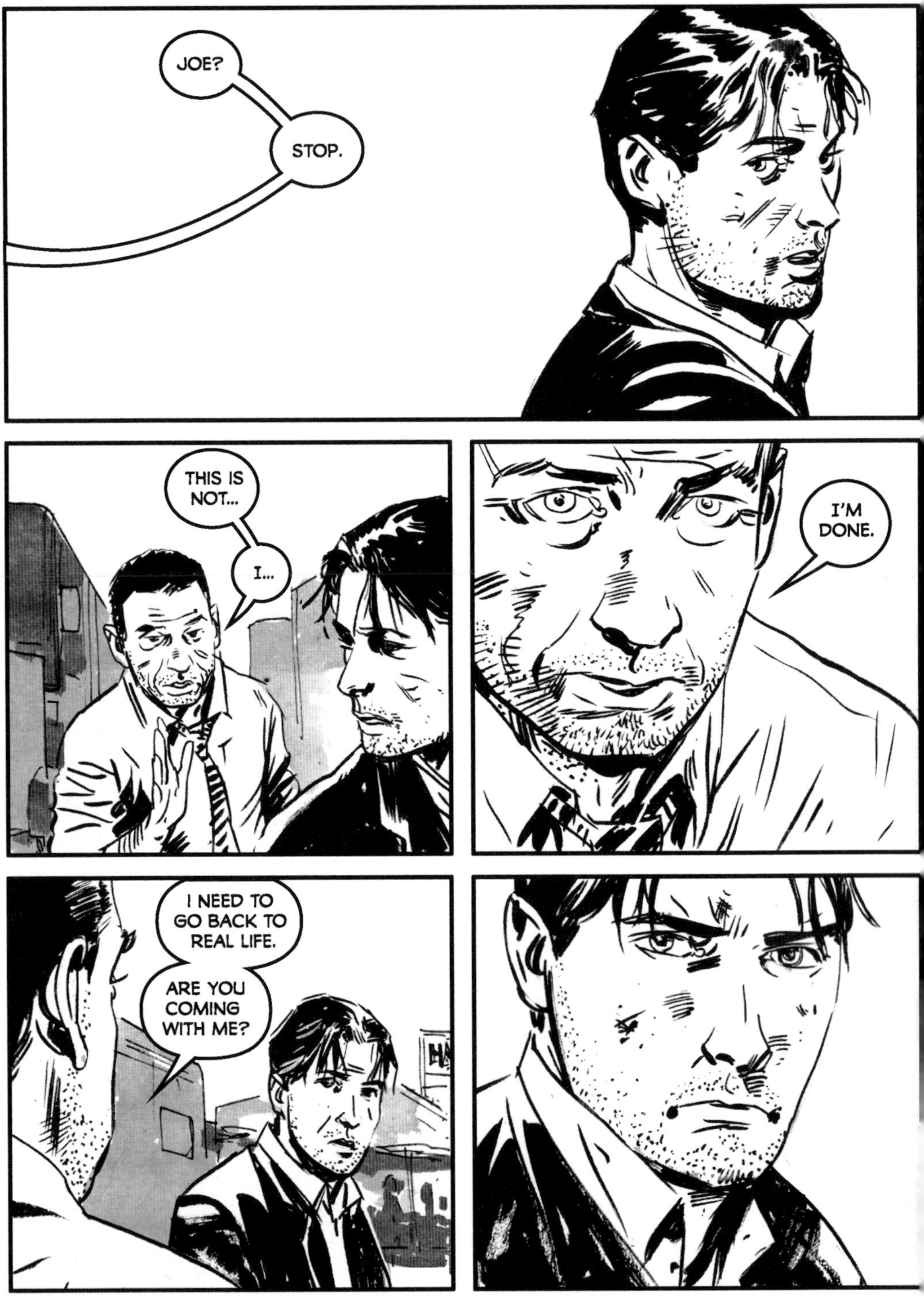

JOE?
STOP.
THIS IS NOT...
I...
I'M DONE.
I NEED TO GO BACK TO REAL LIFE.
ARE YOU COMING WITH ME?

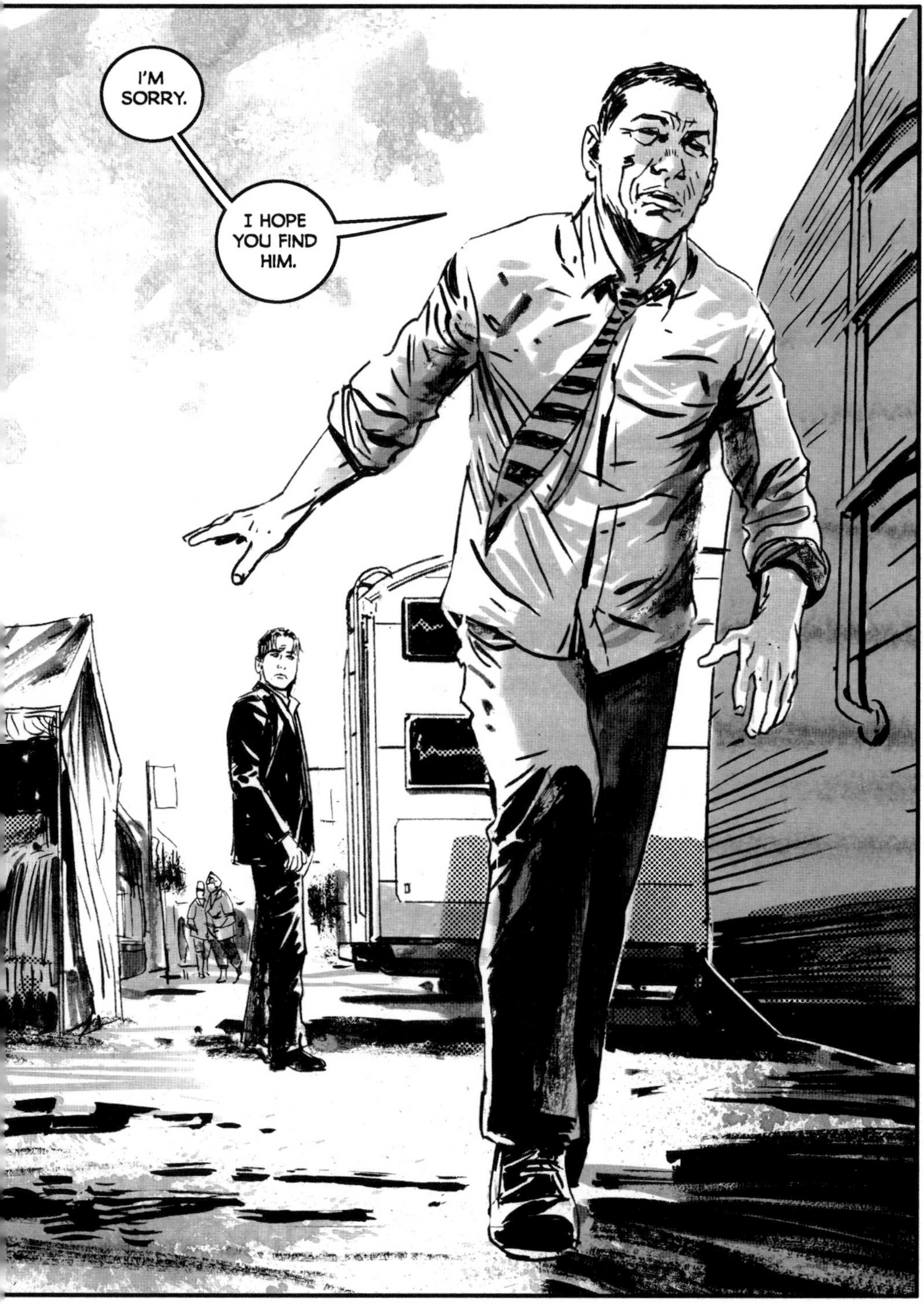
I'M SORRY.
I HOPE YOU FIND HIM.

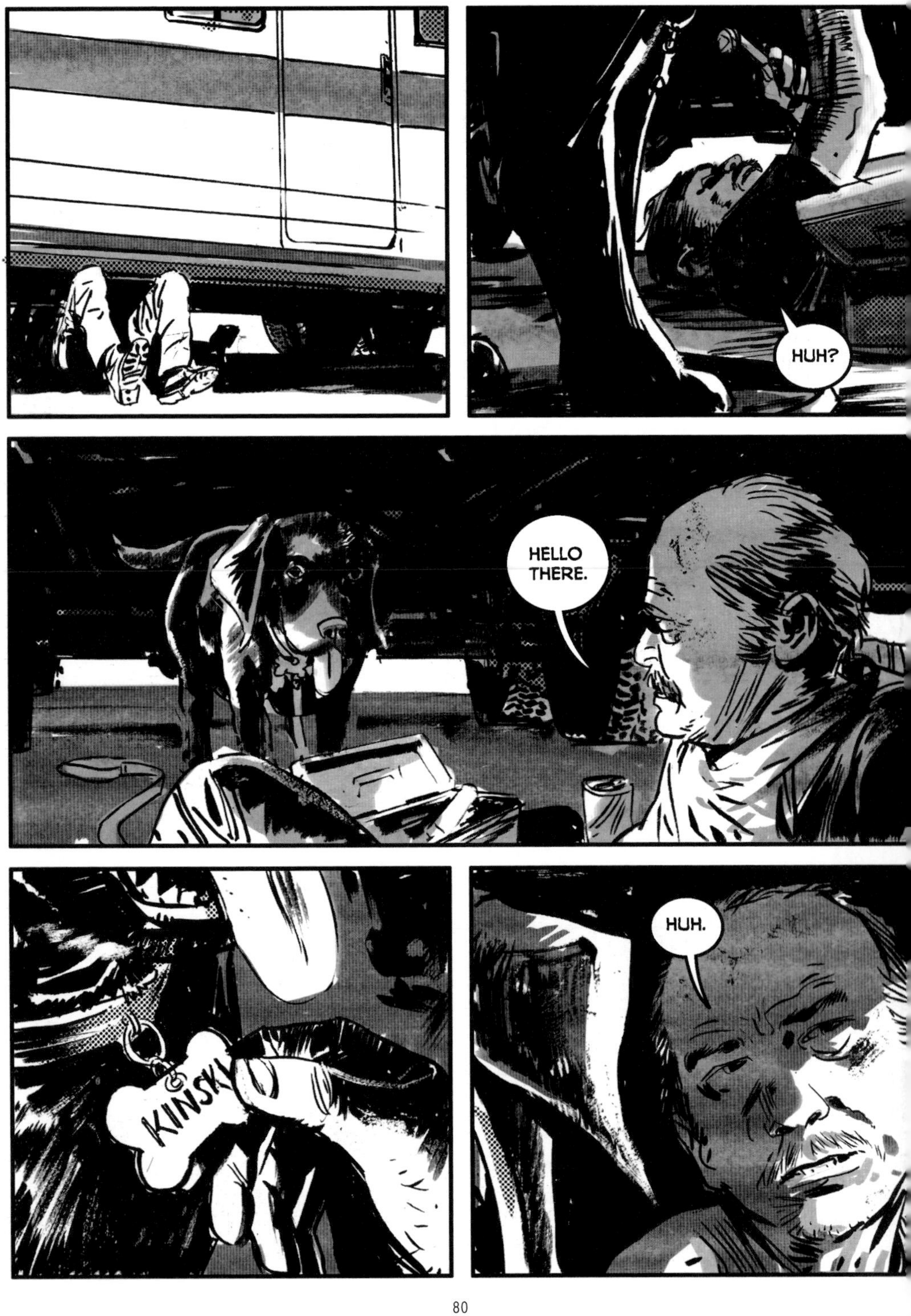
HUH?
HELLO THERE.
KINSKI
HUH.

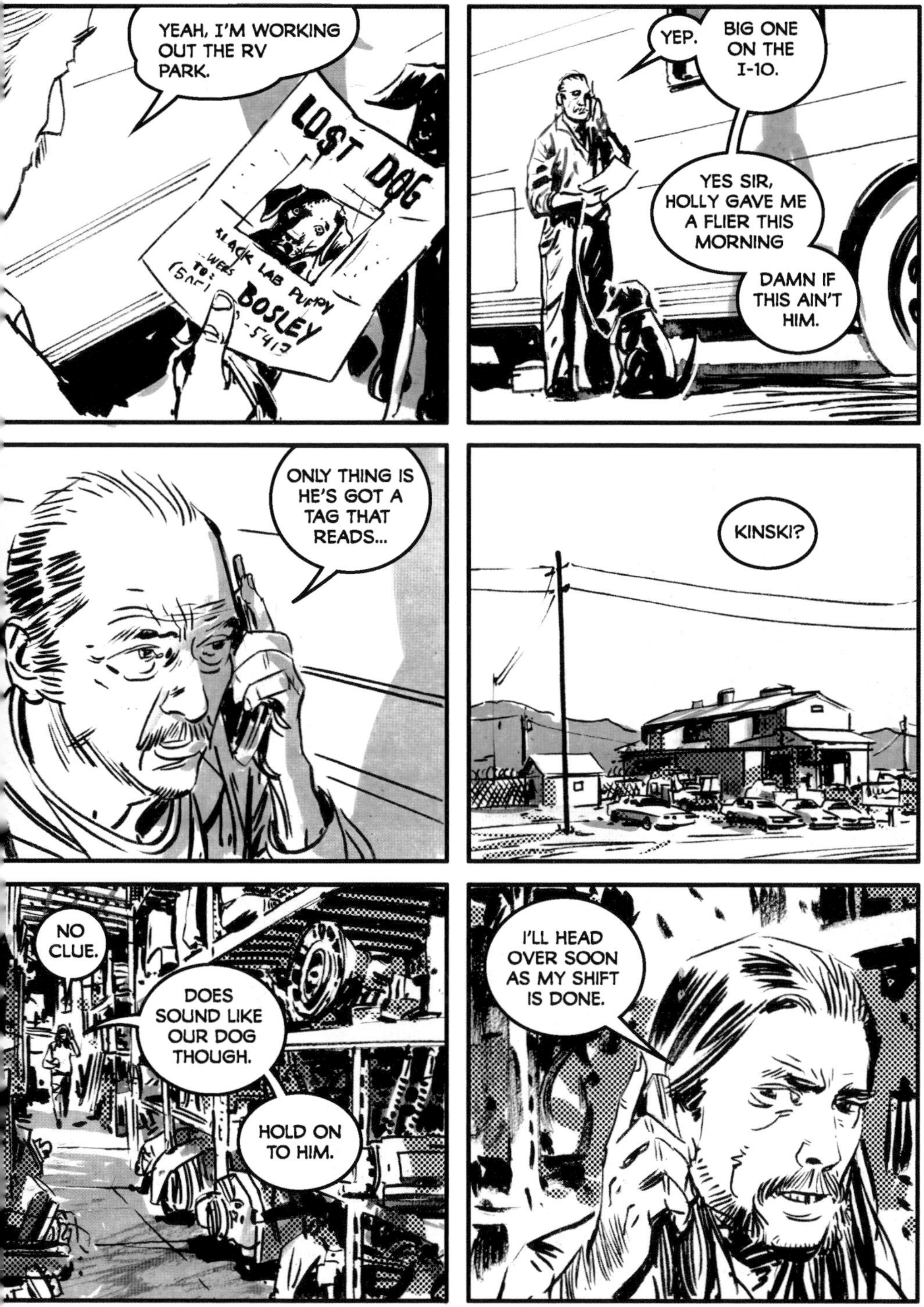
YEAH, I'M WORKING OUT THE RV PARK.
LOST DOG
BLACK LAB PUPPY
BOSLEY
YEP.
BIG ONE ON THE I-10.
YES SIR, HOLLY GAVE ME A FLIER THIS MORNING
DAMN IF THIS AIN'T HIM.
ONLY THING IS HE'S GOT A TAG THAT READS...
KINSKI?
NO CLUE.
DOES SOUND LIKE OUR DOG THOUGH.
HOLD ON TO HIM.
I'LL HEAD OVER SOON AS MY SHIFT IS DONE.

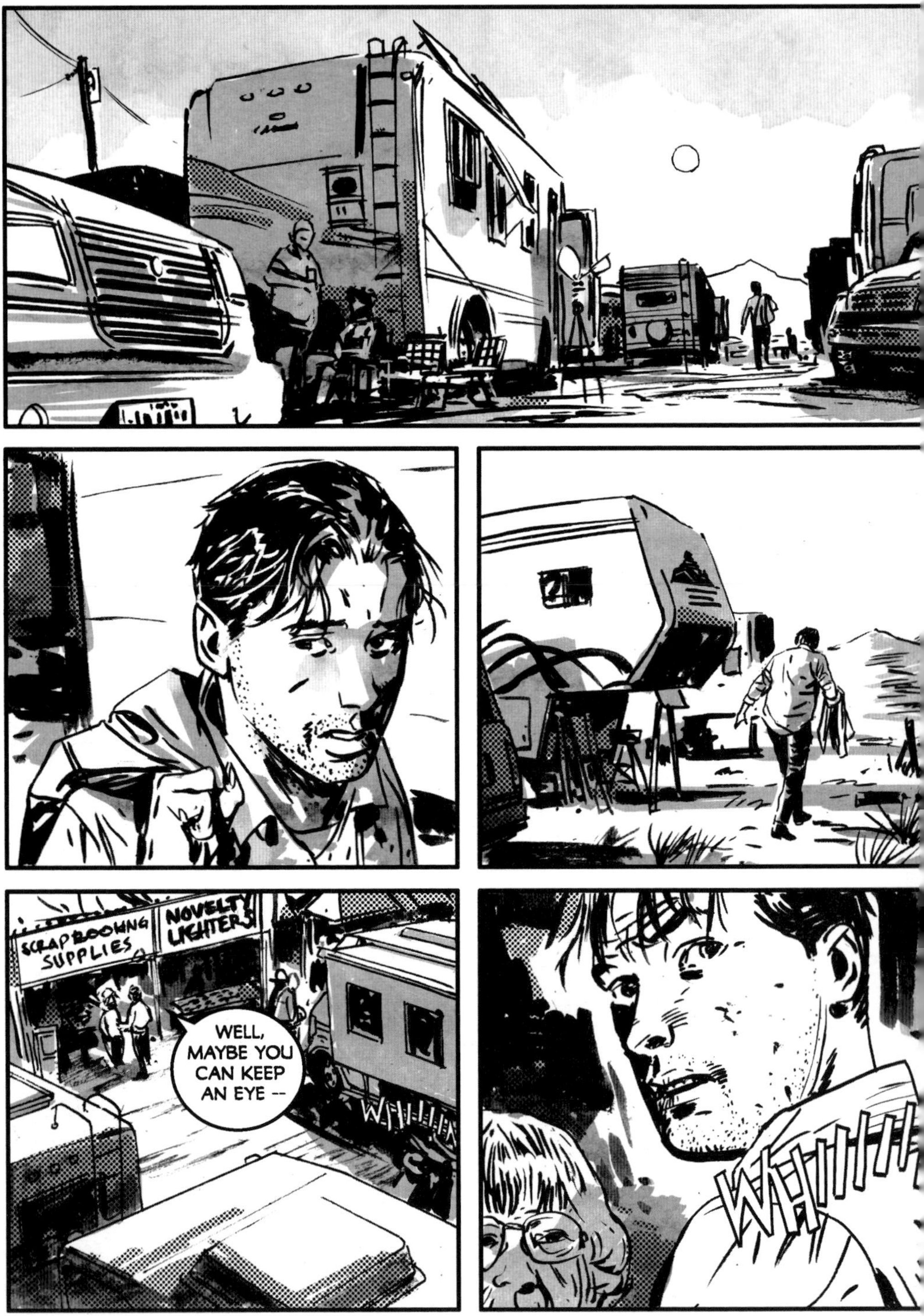
SCRAPBOOKING SUPPLIES
NOVELTY LIGHTERS
WELL, MAYBE YOU CAN KEEP AN EYE --
WHIIIII
WHIIIII

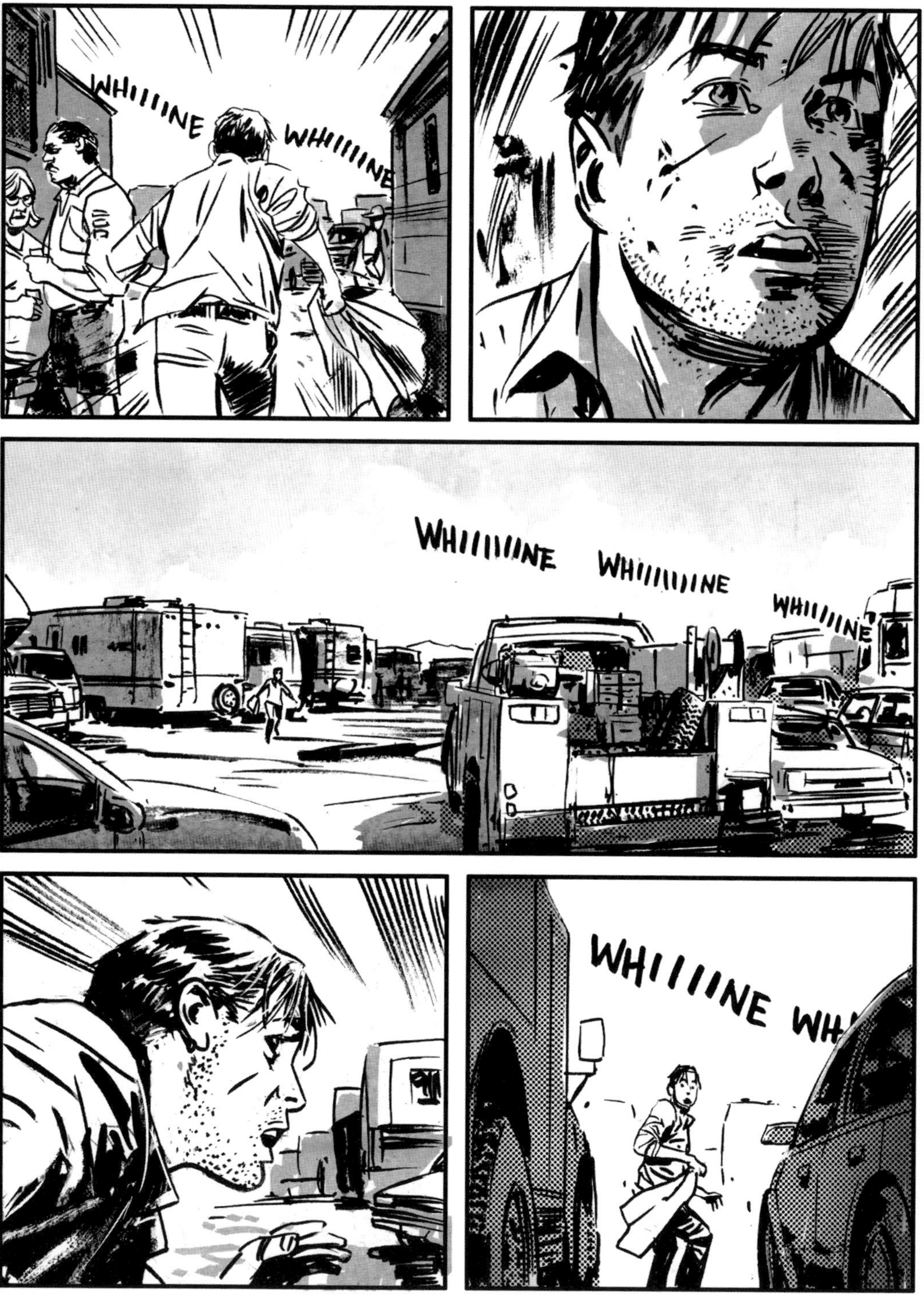
WHIIIINE
WHIIIIINE
WHIIIIIINE
WHIIIIIIINE
WHIIIINE
WHIIIINE
WH

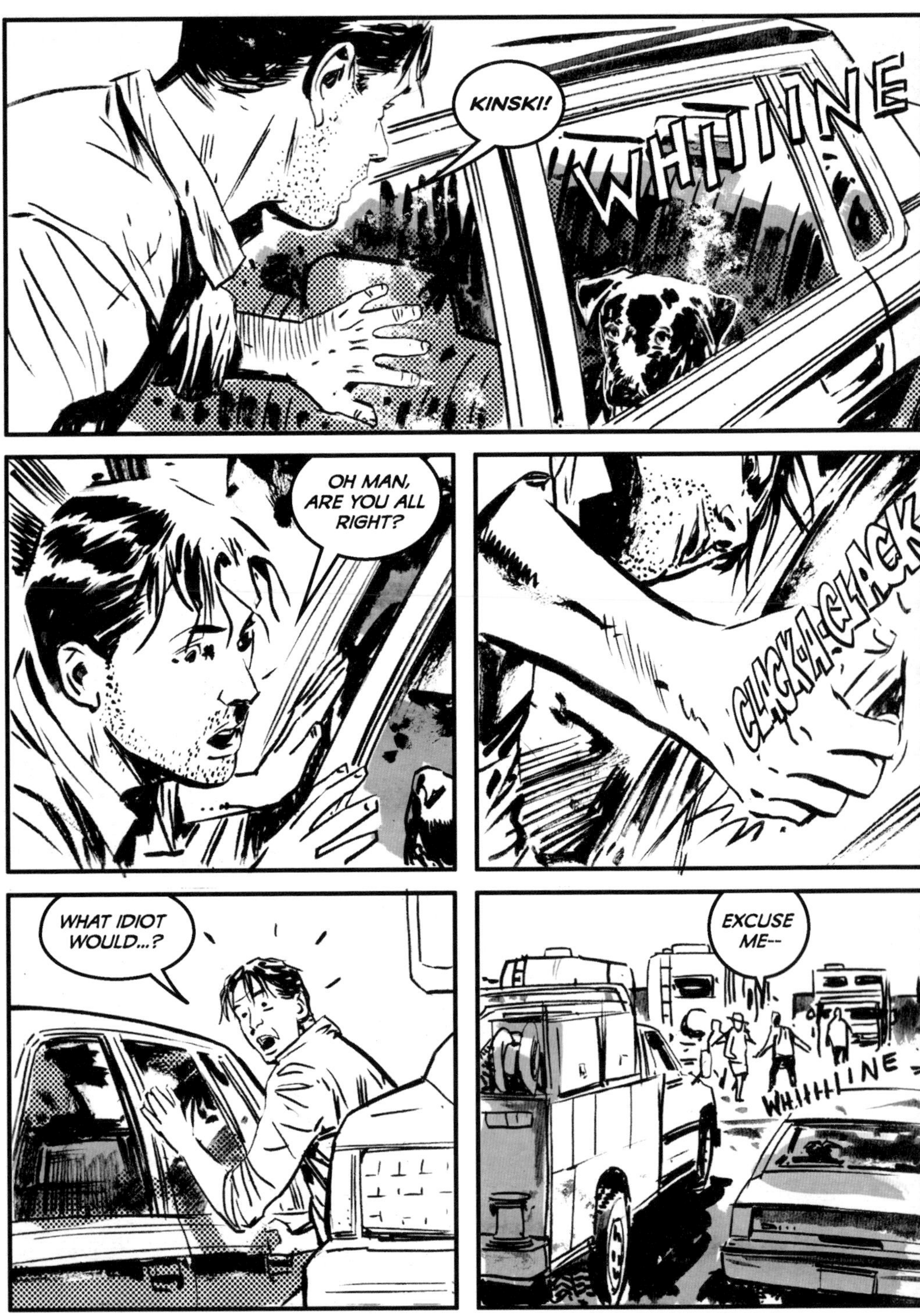
KINSKI!
WHIIIINE
OH MAN, ARE YOU ALL RIGHT?
CLICK-A-CLACK
WHAT IDIOT WOULD...?
EXCUSE ME--
WHIIIILINE

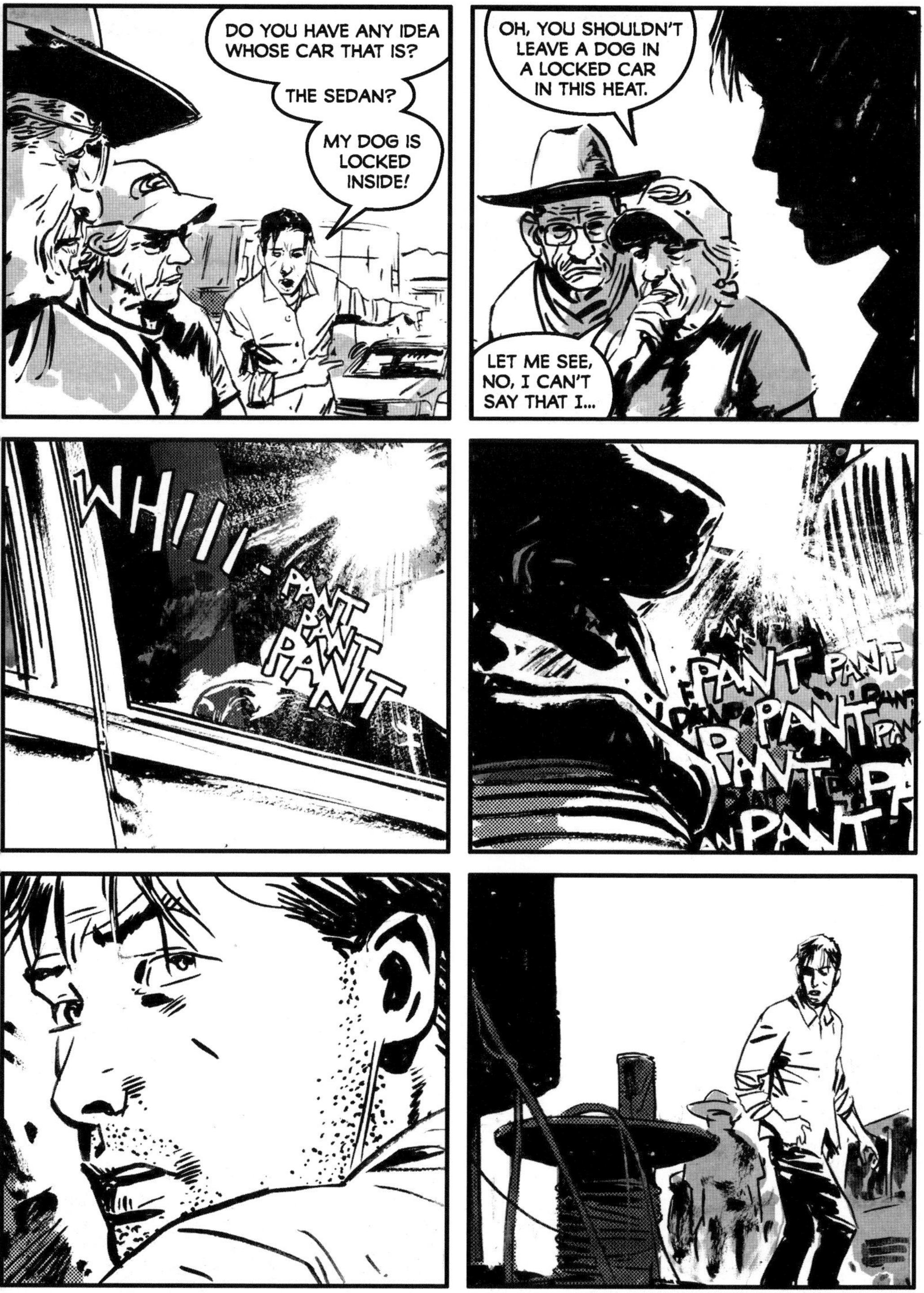
DO YOU HAVE ANY IDEA WHOSE CAR THAT IS?
THE SEDAN?
MY DOG IS LOCKED INSIDE!
OH, YOU SHOULDN'T LEAVE A DOG IN A LOCKED CAR IN THIS HEAT.
LET ME SEE, NO, I CAN'T SAY THAT I...
WHIII-
PANT PANT PANT
PANT PANT
PANT
PANT
PANT

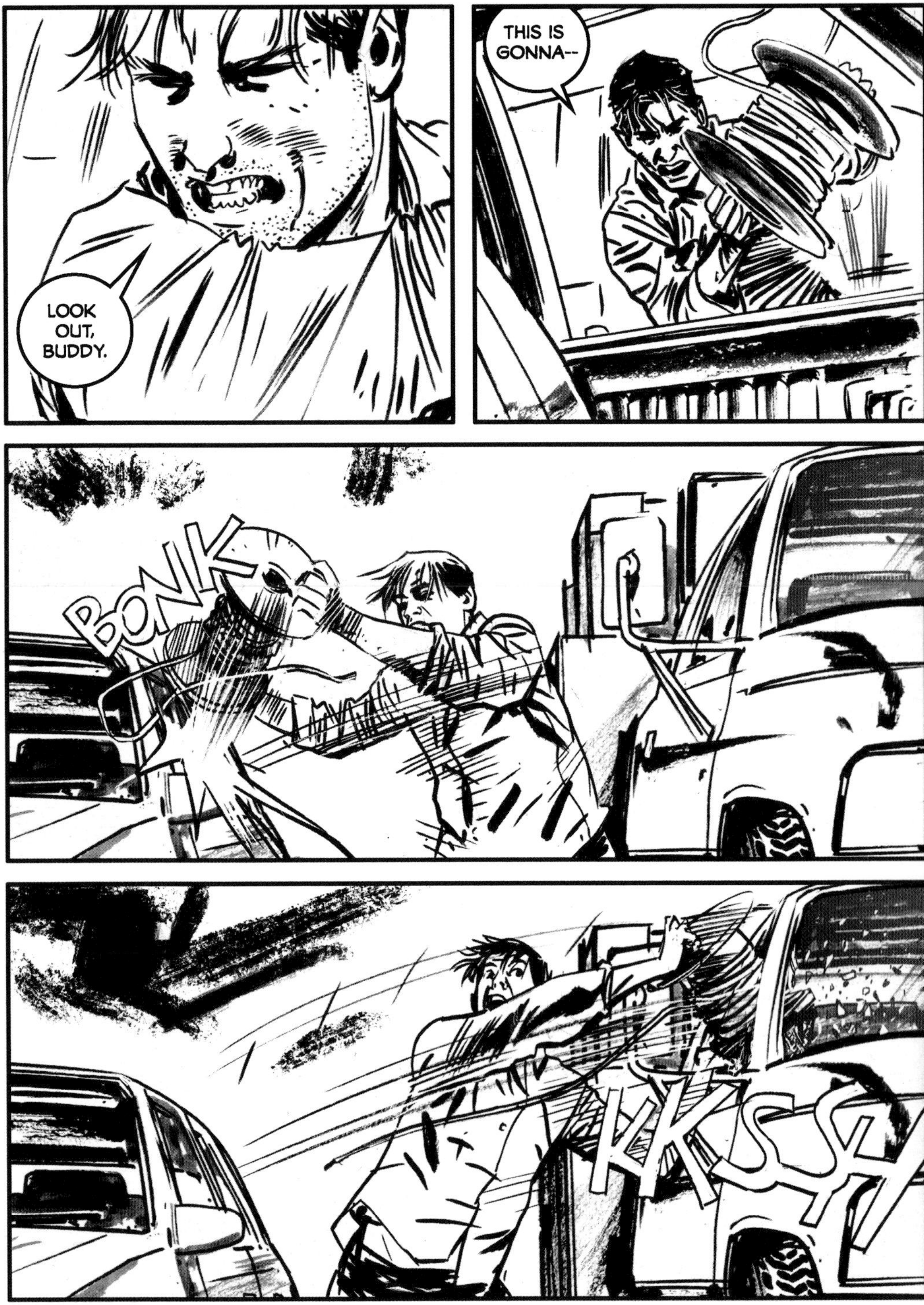
LOOK OUT, BUDDY.
THIS IS GONNA--
BONK
KKSSSH

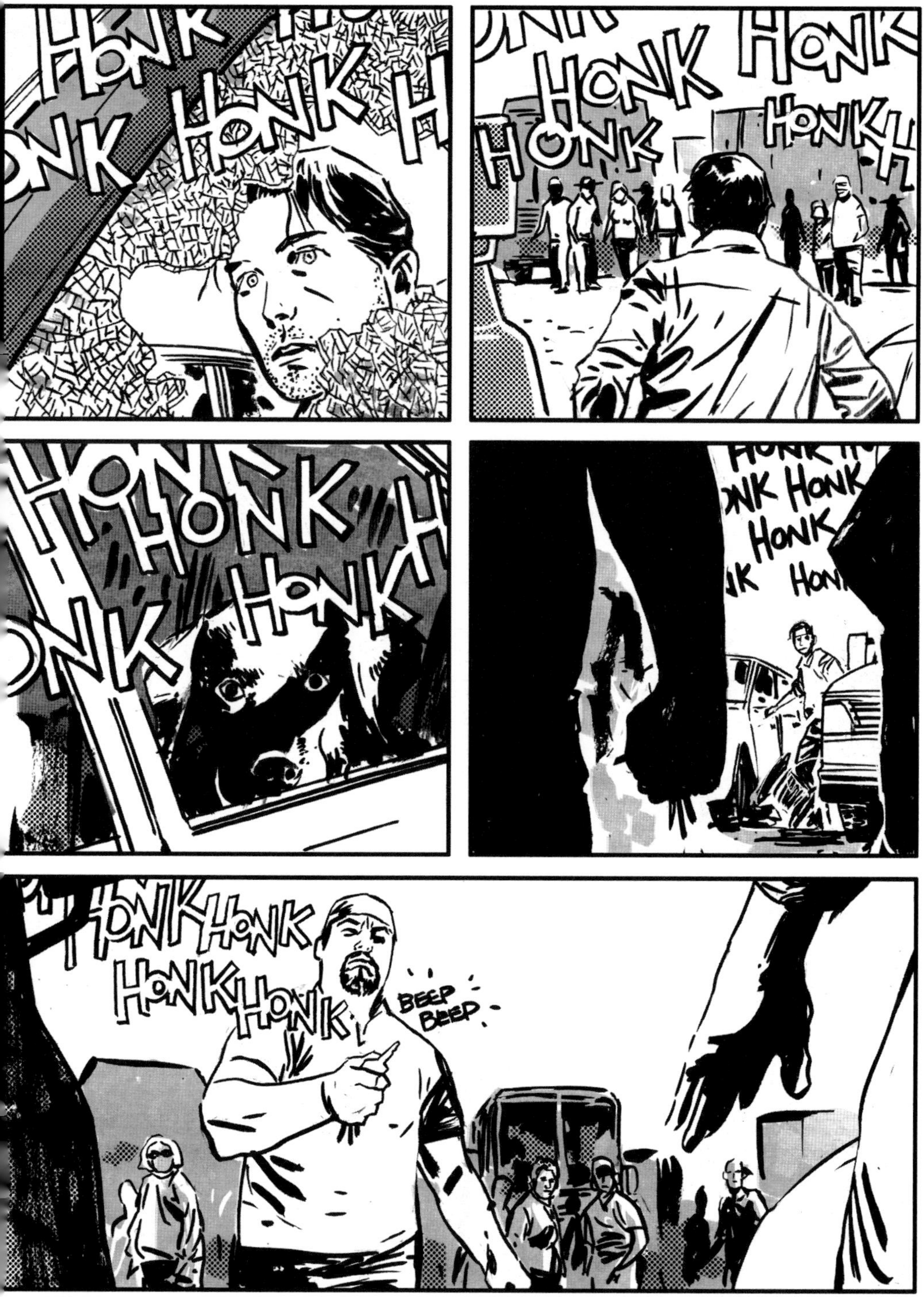
HONK
HONK HONK
HONK HONK
HONK
HONK
HONK
HONK
HONK
HONK HONK
HONK HONK
HONK HONK
HONK
BEEP
BEEP

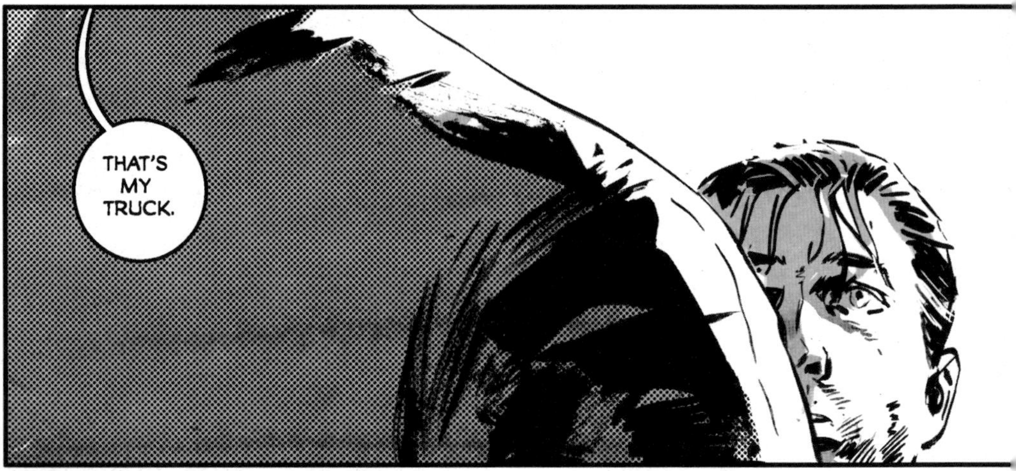
THAT'S MY TRUCK.
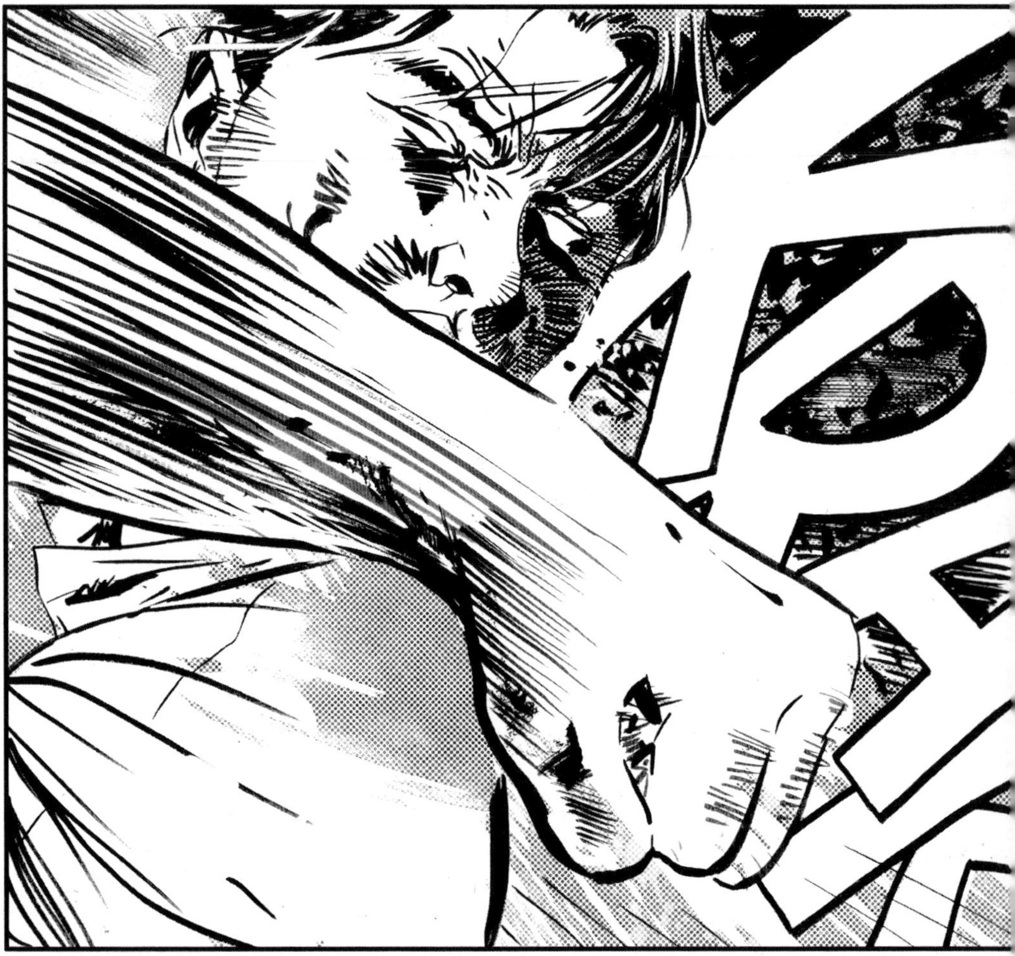

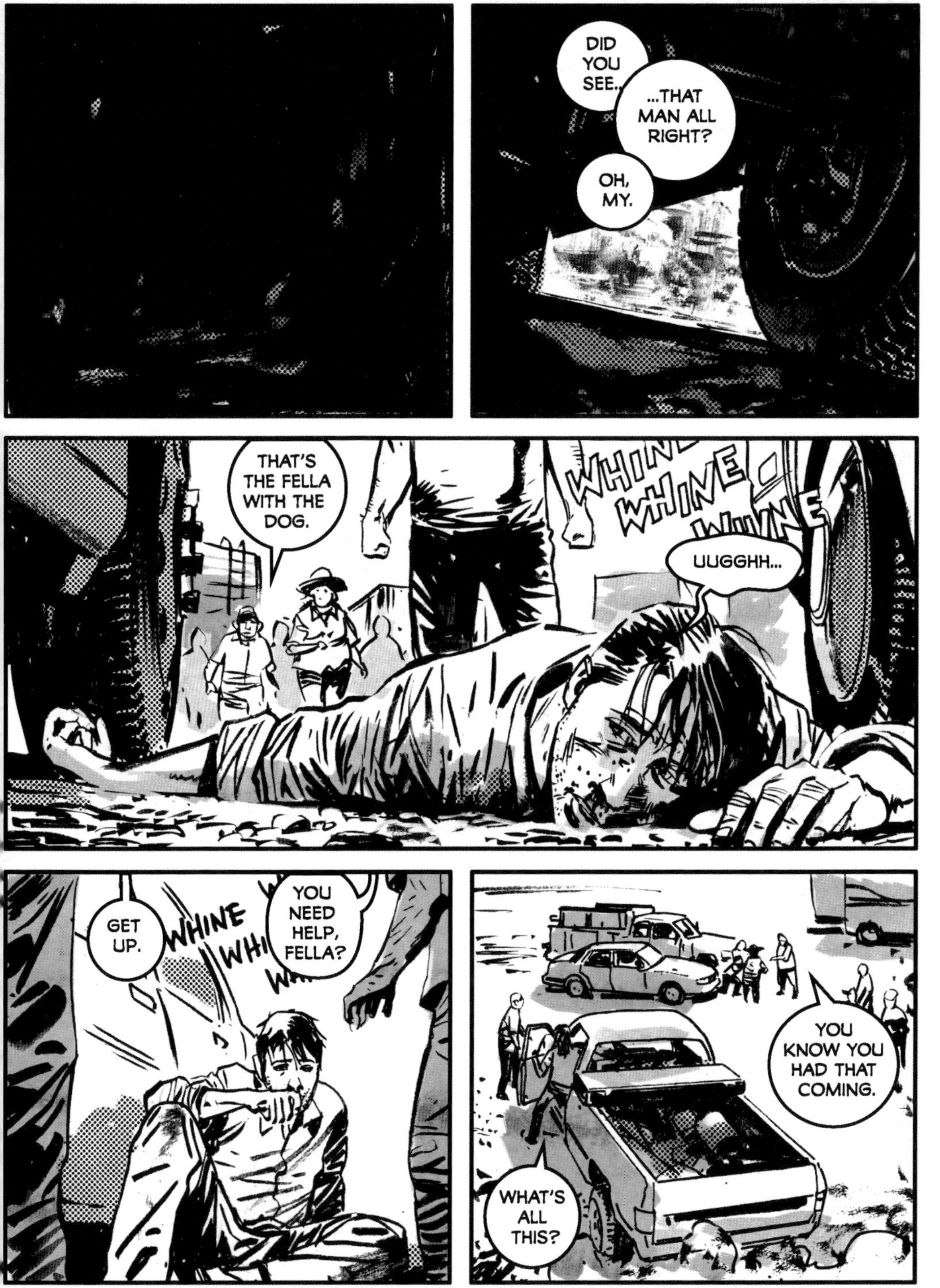
DID YOU SEE...
...THAT MAN ALL RIGHT?
OH, MY.
THAT'S THE FELLA WITH THE DOG.
WHINE WHINE WHINE
UUGGHH...
GET UP.
WHINE WHI
YOU NEED HELP, FELLA?
YOU KNOW YOU HAD THAT COMING.
WHAT'S ALL THIS?

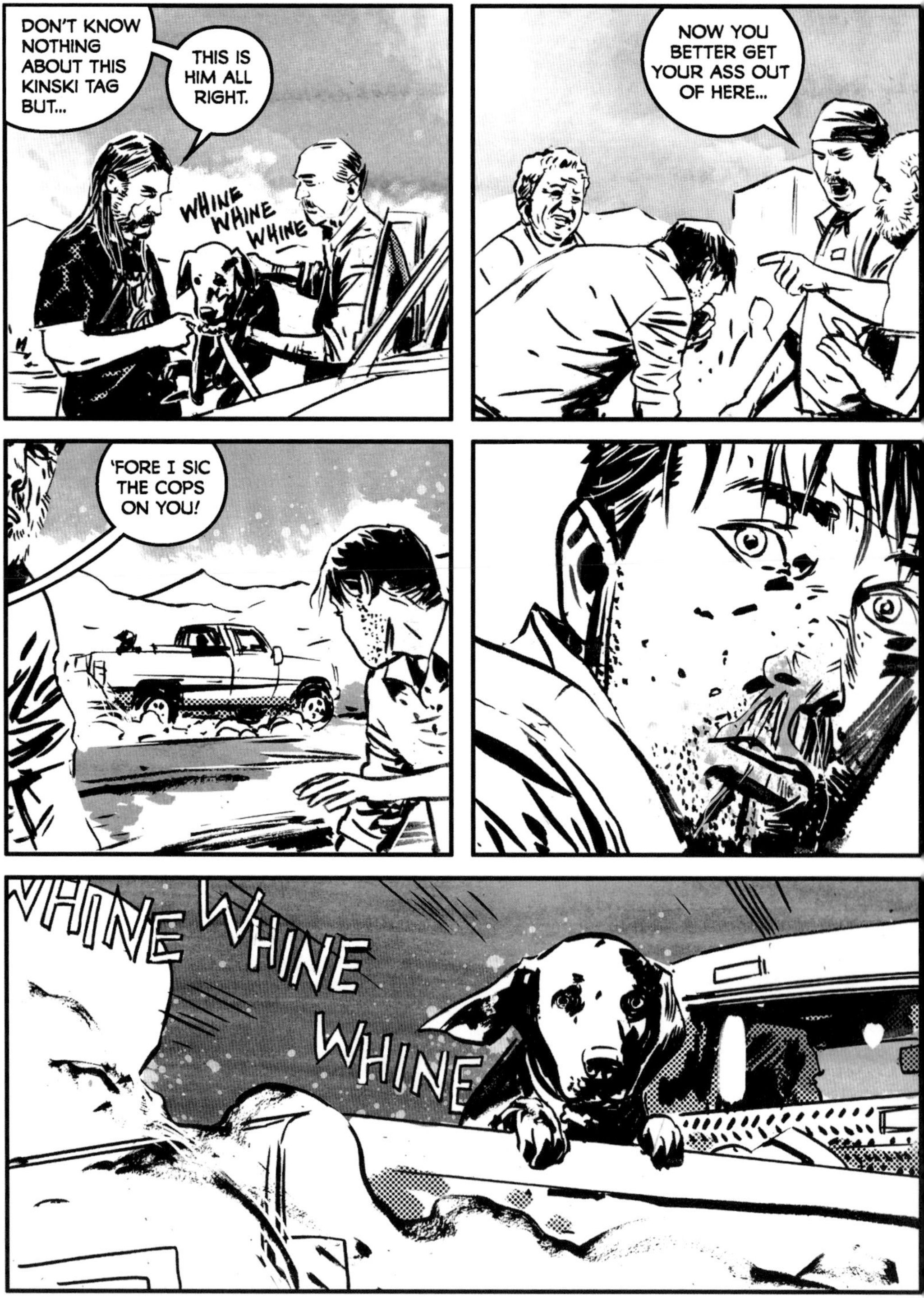
DON'T KNOW NOTHING ABOUT THIS KINSKI TAG BUT...
THIS IS HIM ALL RIGHT.
WHINE WHINE WHINE
NOW YOU BETTER GET YOUR ASS OUT OF HERE...
'FORE I SIC THE COPS ON YOU!
WHINE WHINE WHINE

FIVE

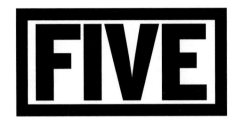

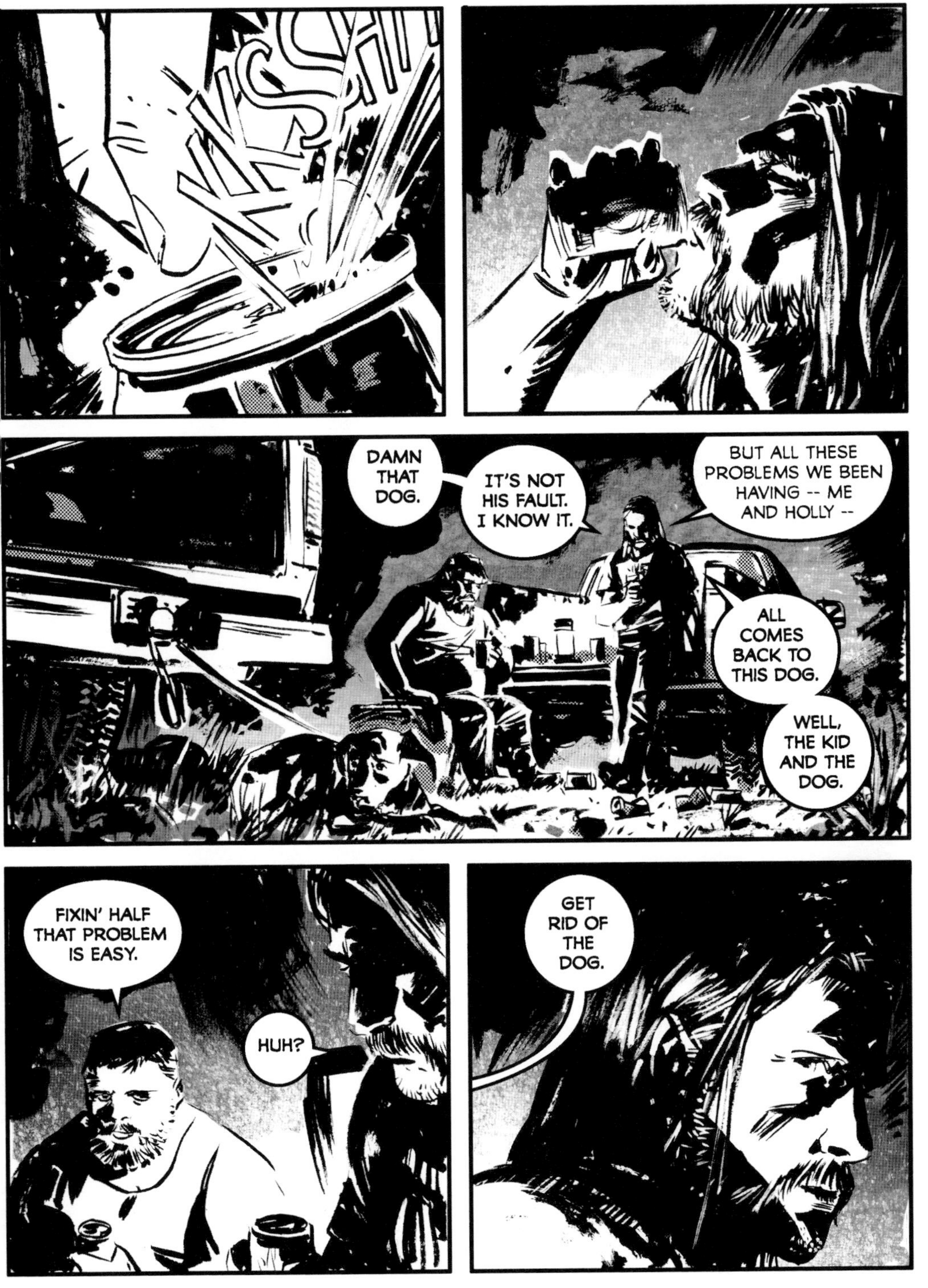
DAMN THAT DOG.
IT'S NOT HIS FAULT. I KNOW IT.
BUT ALL THESE PROBLEMS WE BEEN HAVING -- ME AND HOLLY --
ALL COMES BACK TO THIS DOG.
WELL, THE KID AND THE DOG.
FIXIN' HALF THAT PROBLEM IS EASY.
HUH?
GET RID OF THE DOG.

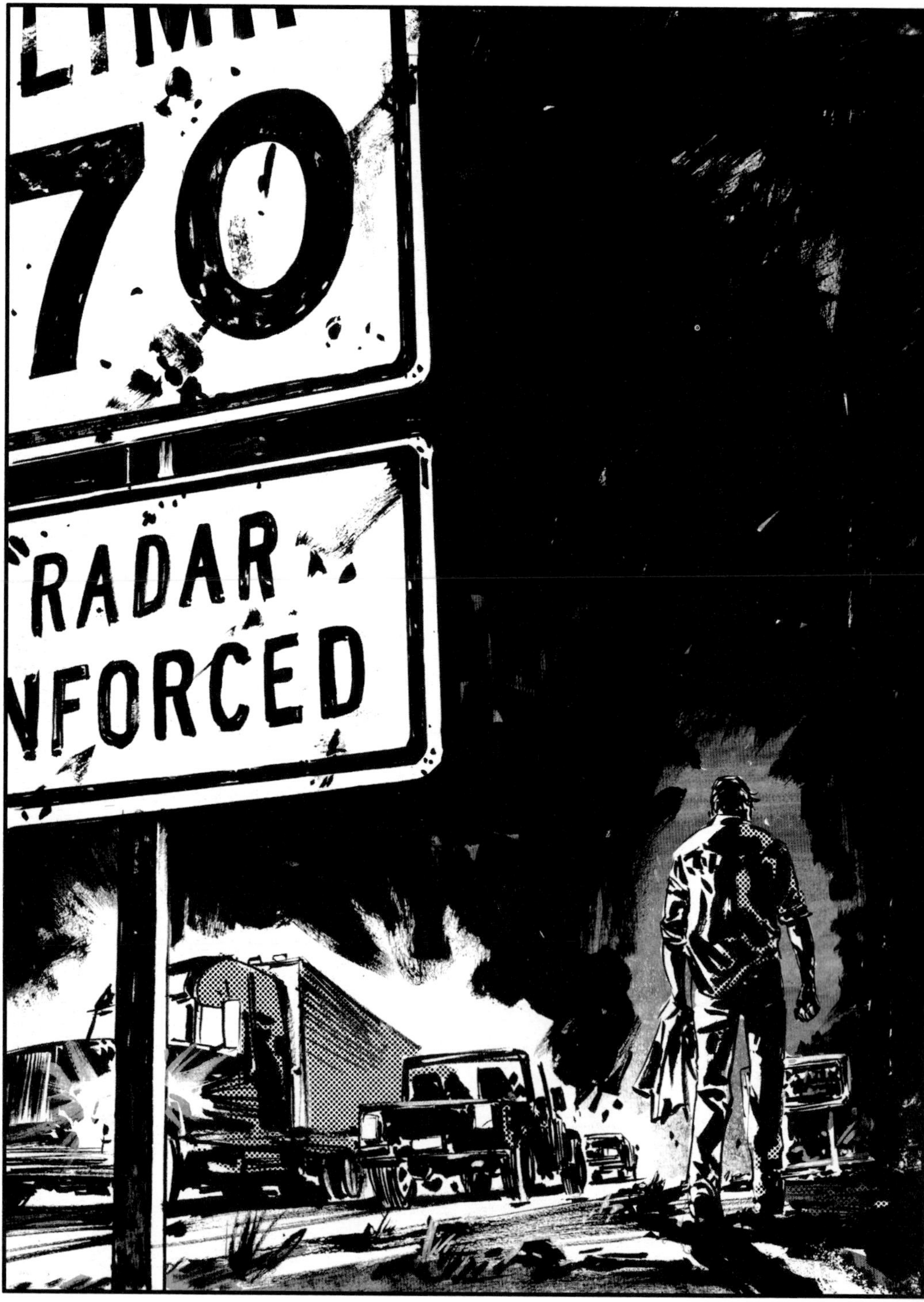
70
RADAR
NFORCED

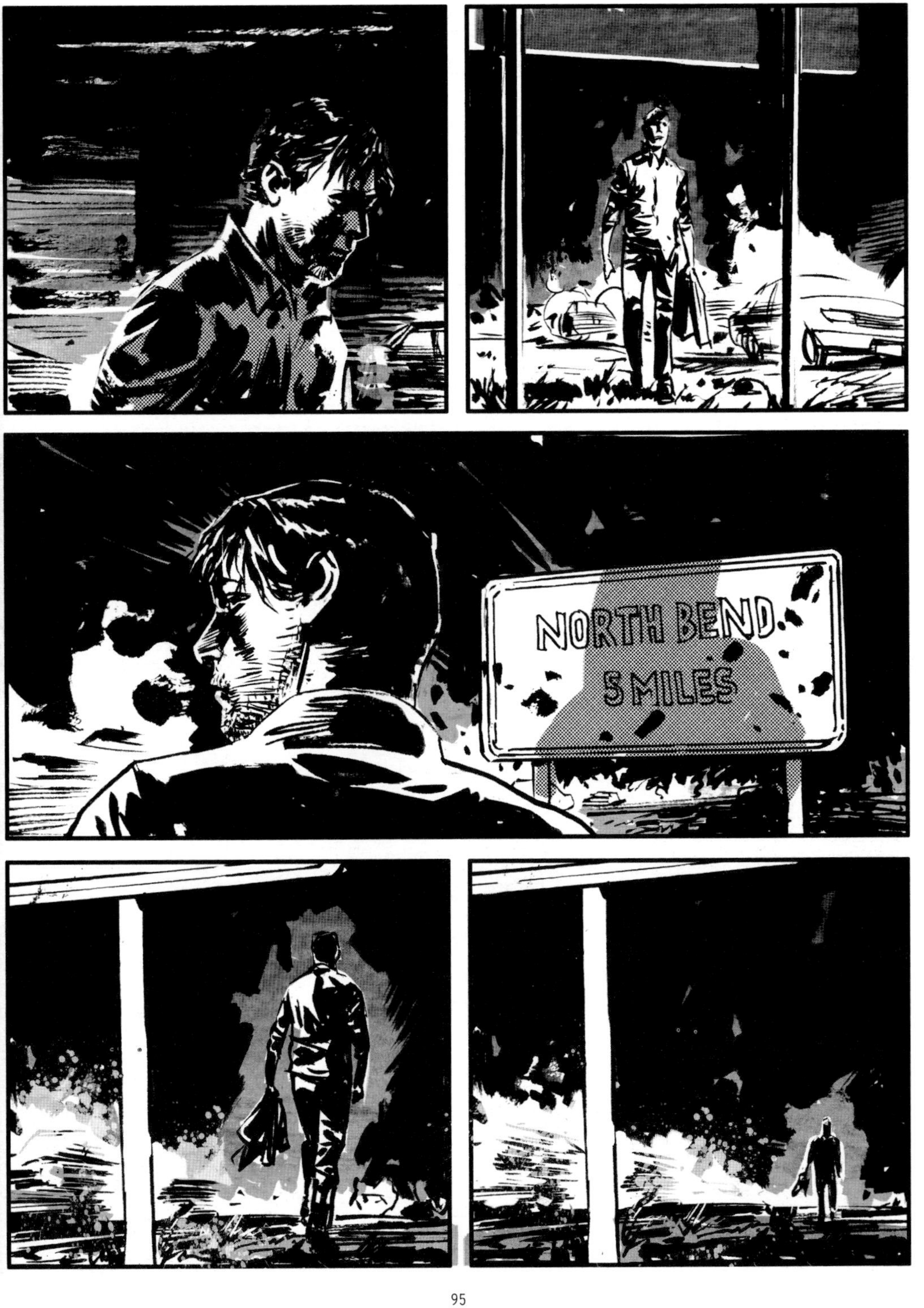
NORTH BEND
5 MILES

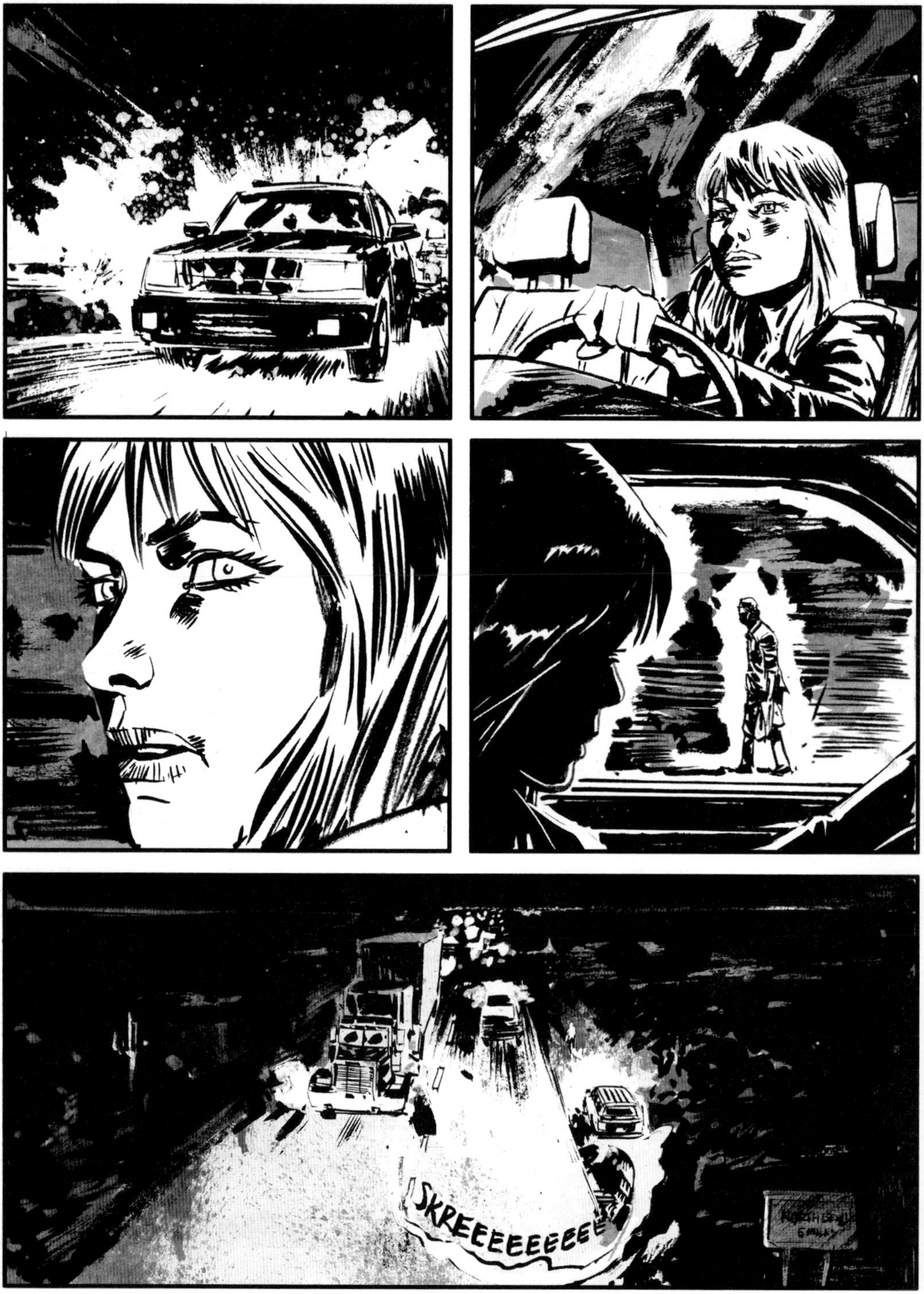
SKREEEEEEEEEEEE

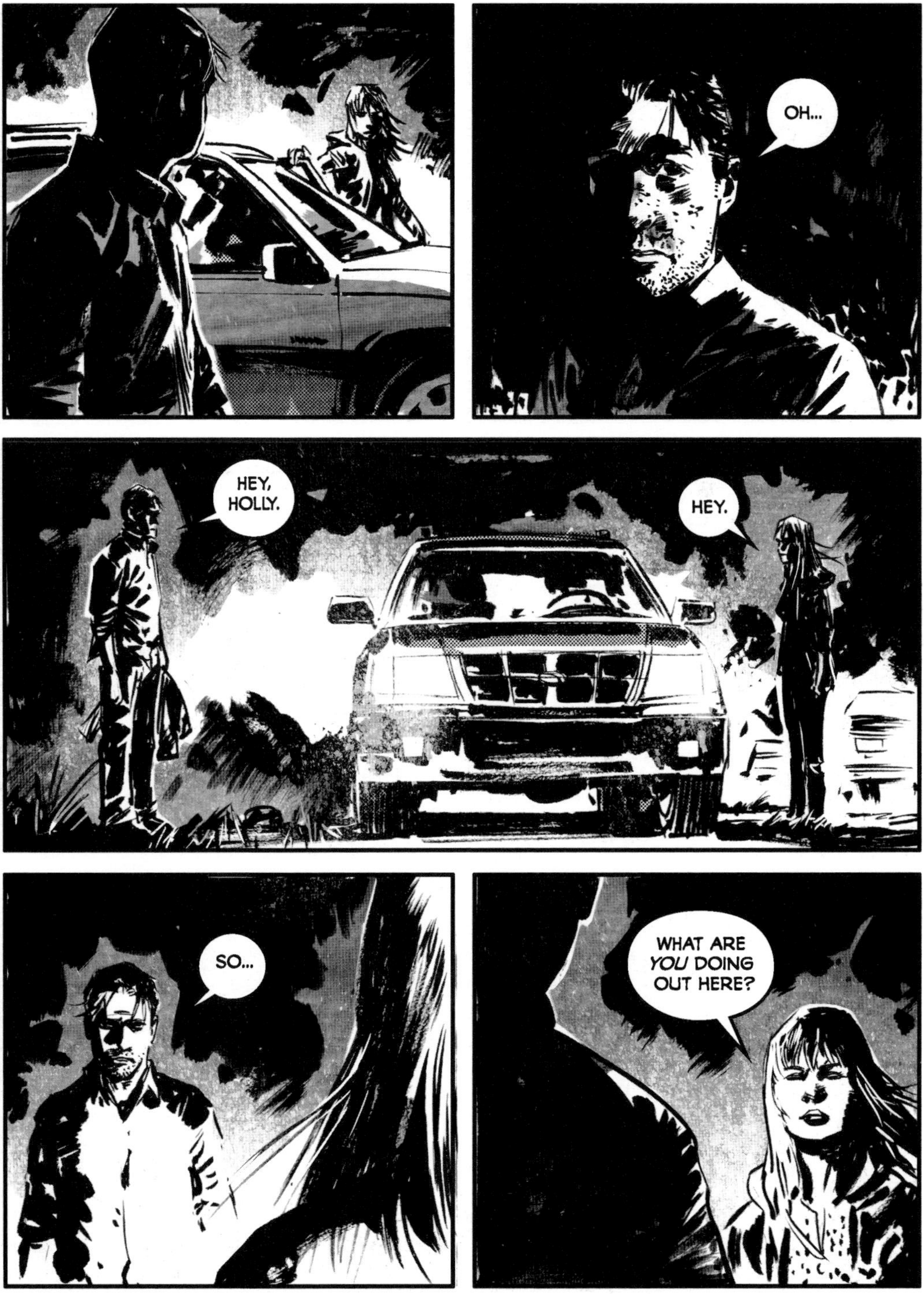
OH...
HEY, HOLLY.
HEY.
SO...
WHAT ARE *YOU* DOING OUT HERE?

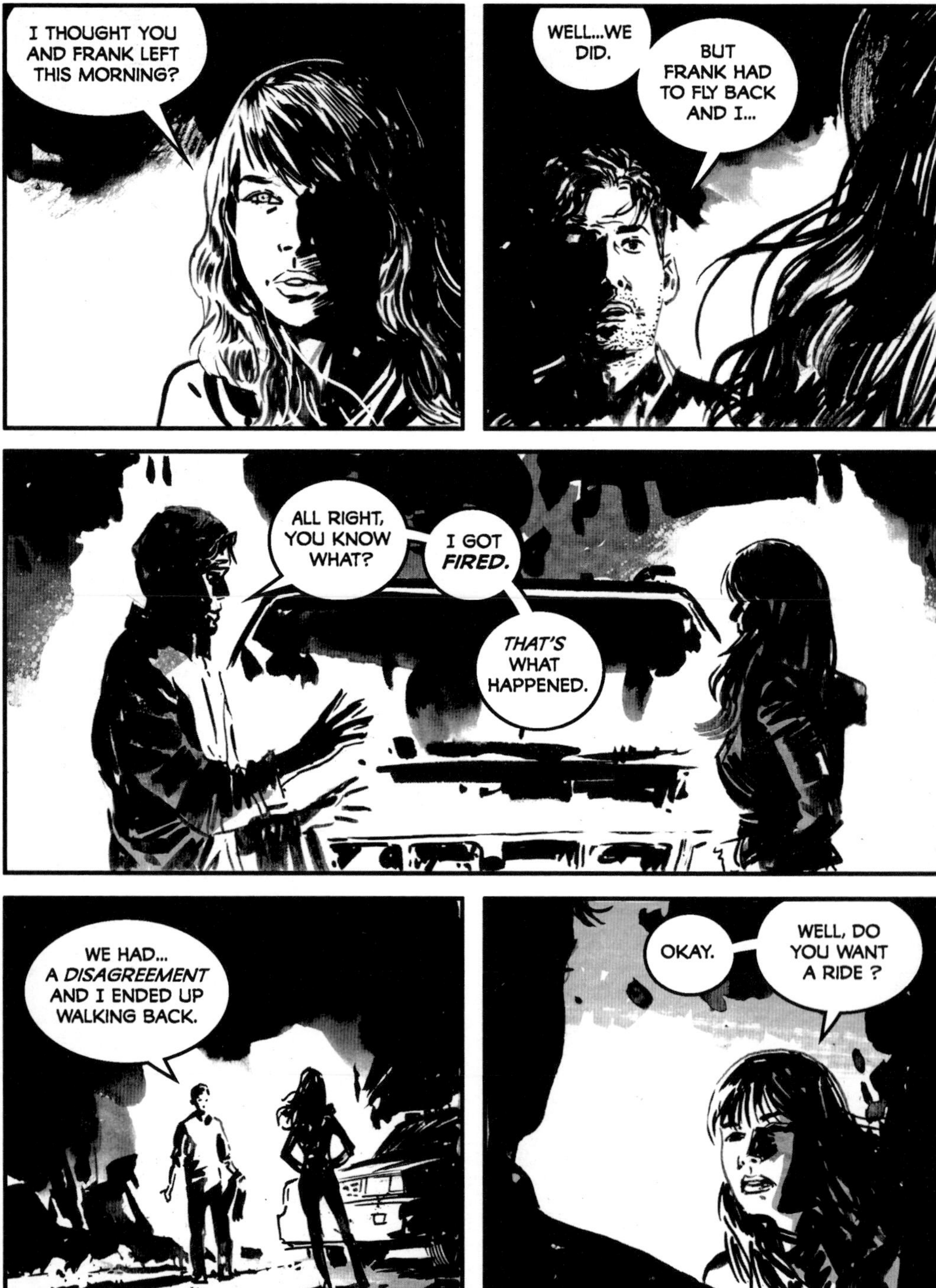
I THOUGHT YOU AND FRANK LEFT THIS MORNING?
WELL...WE DID.
BUT FRANK HAD TO FLY BACK AND I...
ALL RIGHT, YOU KNOW WHAT?
I GOT *FIRED.*
THAT'S WHAT HAPPENED.
WE HAD... A *DISAGREEMENT* AND I ENDED UP WALKING BACK.
OKAY.
WELL, DO YOU WANT A RIDE ?

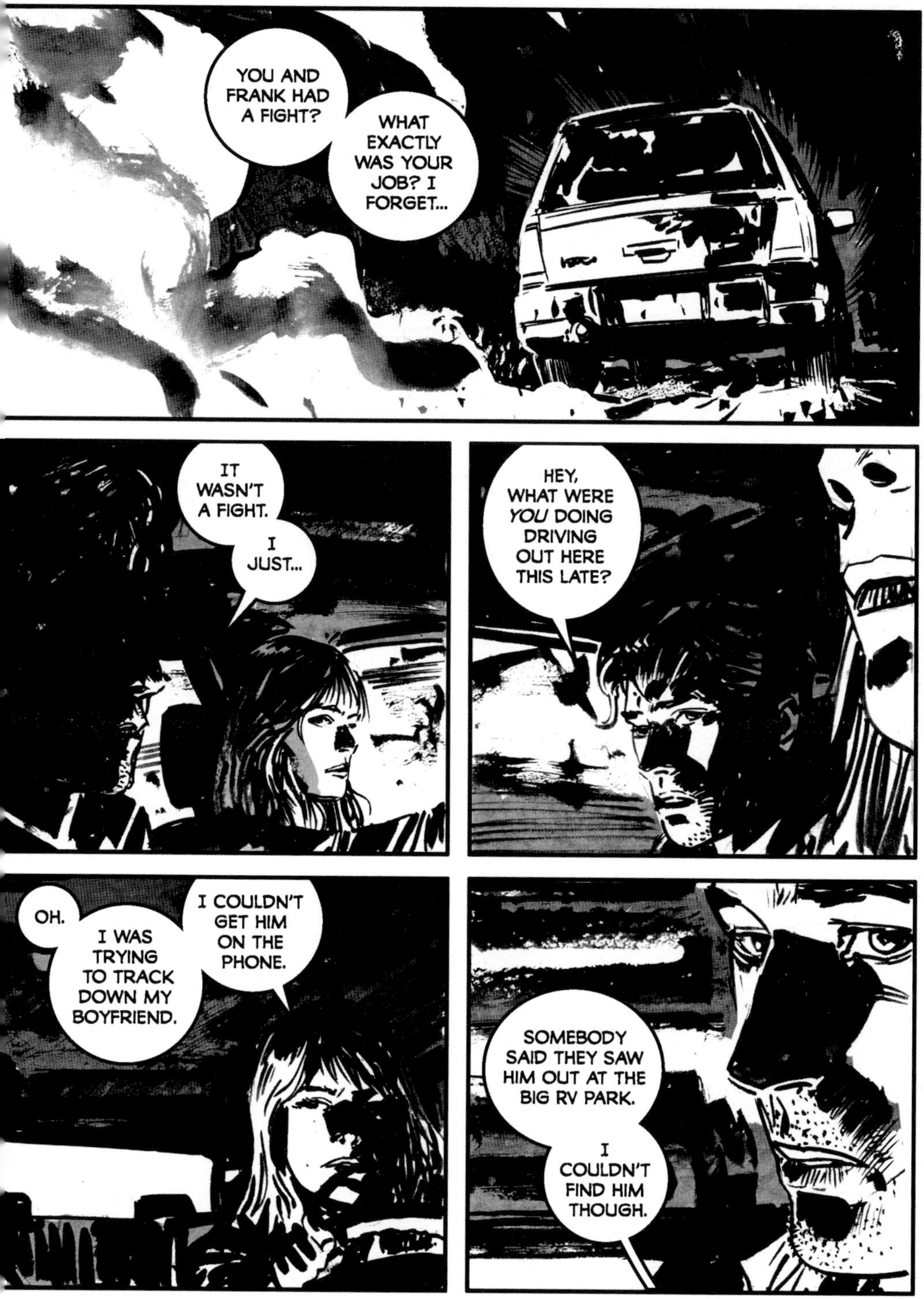
YOU AND FRANK HAD A FIGHT?
WHAT EXACTLY WAS YOUR JOB? I FORGET...
IT WASN'T A FIGHT.
I JUST...
HEY, WHAT WERE *YOU* DOING DRIVING OUT HERE THIS LATE?
OH.
I WAS TRYING TO TRACK DOWN MY BOYFRIEND.
I COULDN'T GET HIM ON THE PHONE.
SOMEBODY SAID THEY SAW HIM OUT AT THE BIG RV PARK.
I COULDN'T FIND HIM THOUGH.

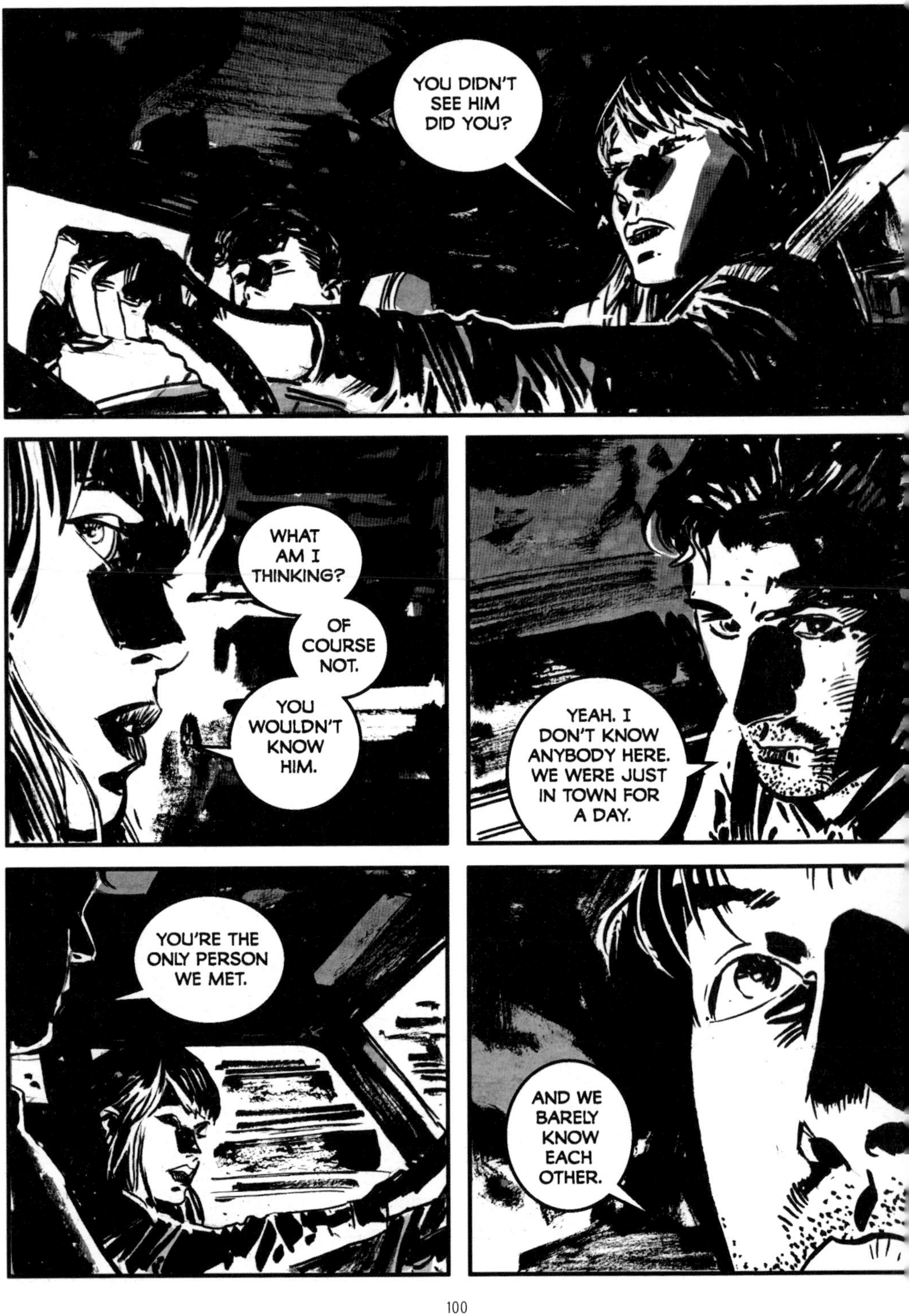
YOU DIDN'T SEE HIM DID YOU?
WHAT AM I THINKING?
OF COURSE NOT.
YOU WOULDN'T KNOW HIM.
YEAH. I DON'T KNOW ANYBODY HERE. WE WERE JUST IN TOWN FOR A DAY.
YOU'RE THE ONLY PERSON WE MET.
AND WE BARELY KNOW EACH OTHER.

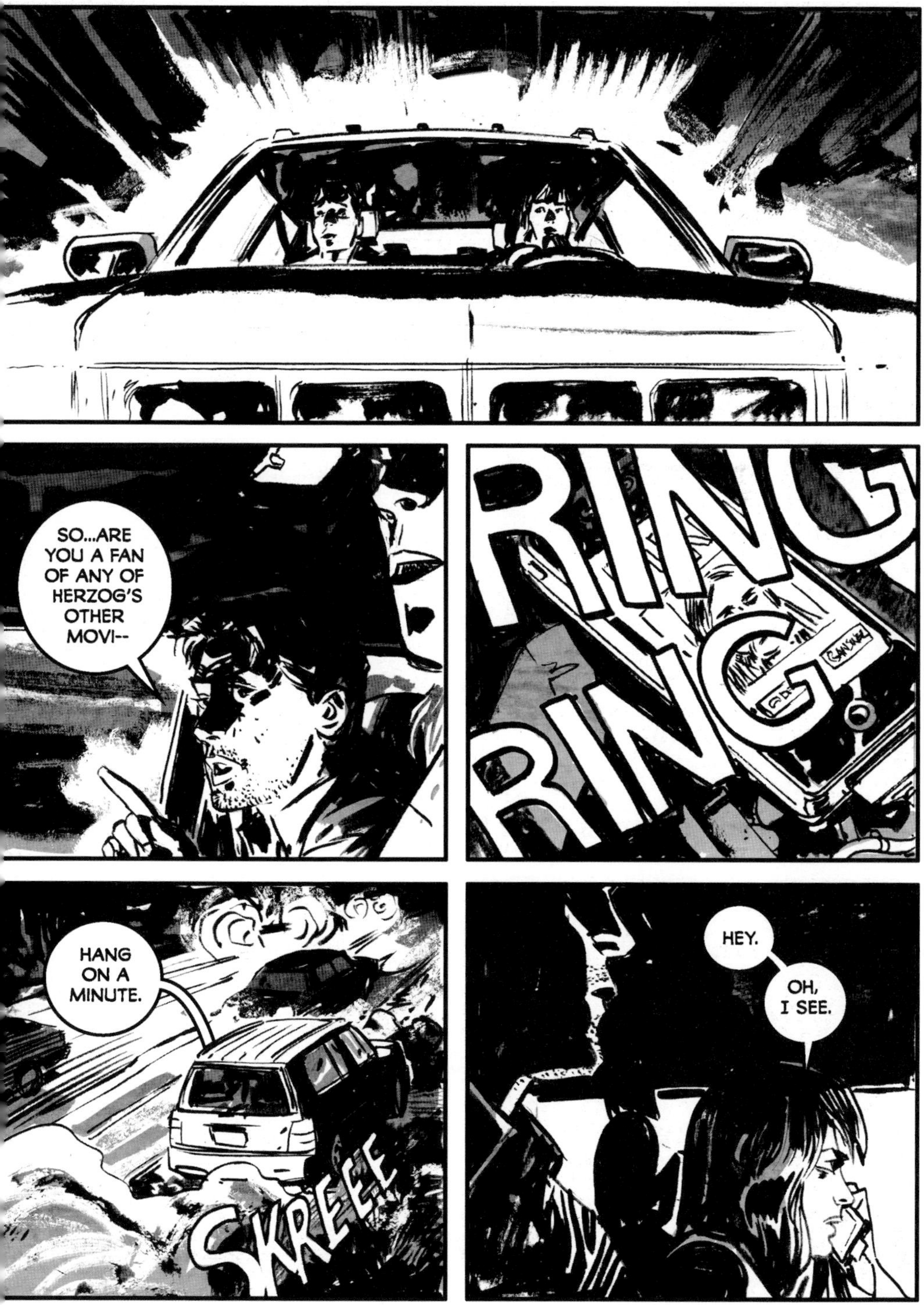
SO...ARE YOU A FAN OF ANY OF HERZOG'S OTHER MOVI--
RING RING
HANG ON A MINUTE.
SKREEE
HEY.
OH, I SEE.

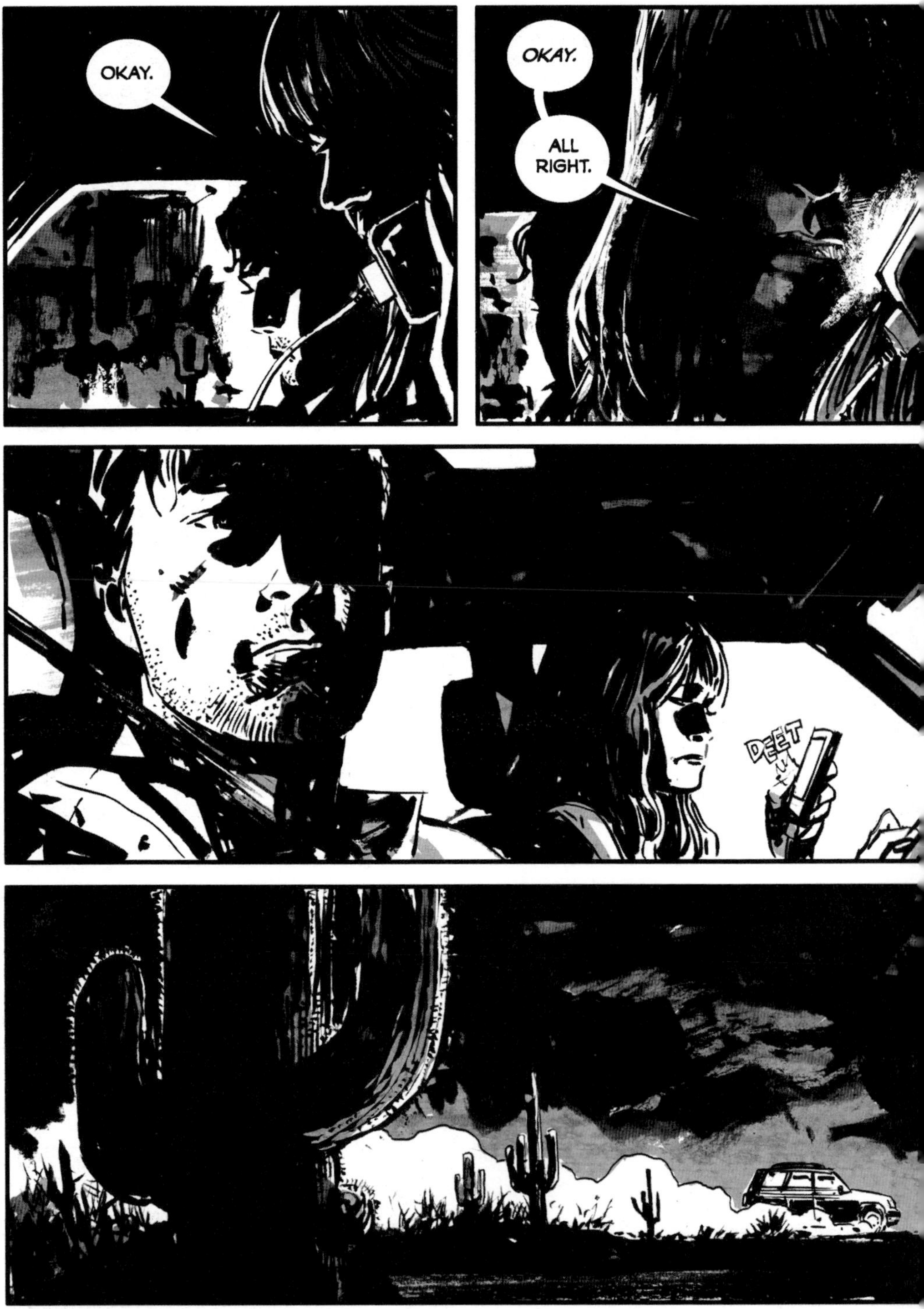
OKAY.
OKAY.
ALL RIGHT.
DEET

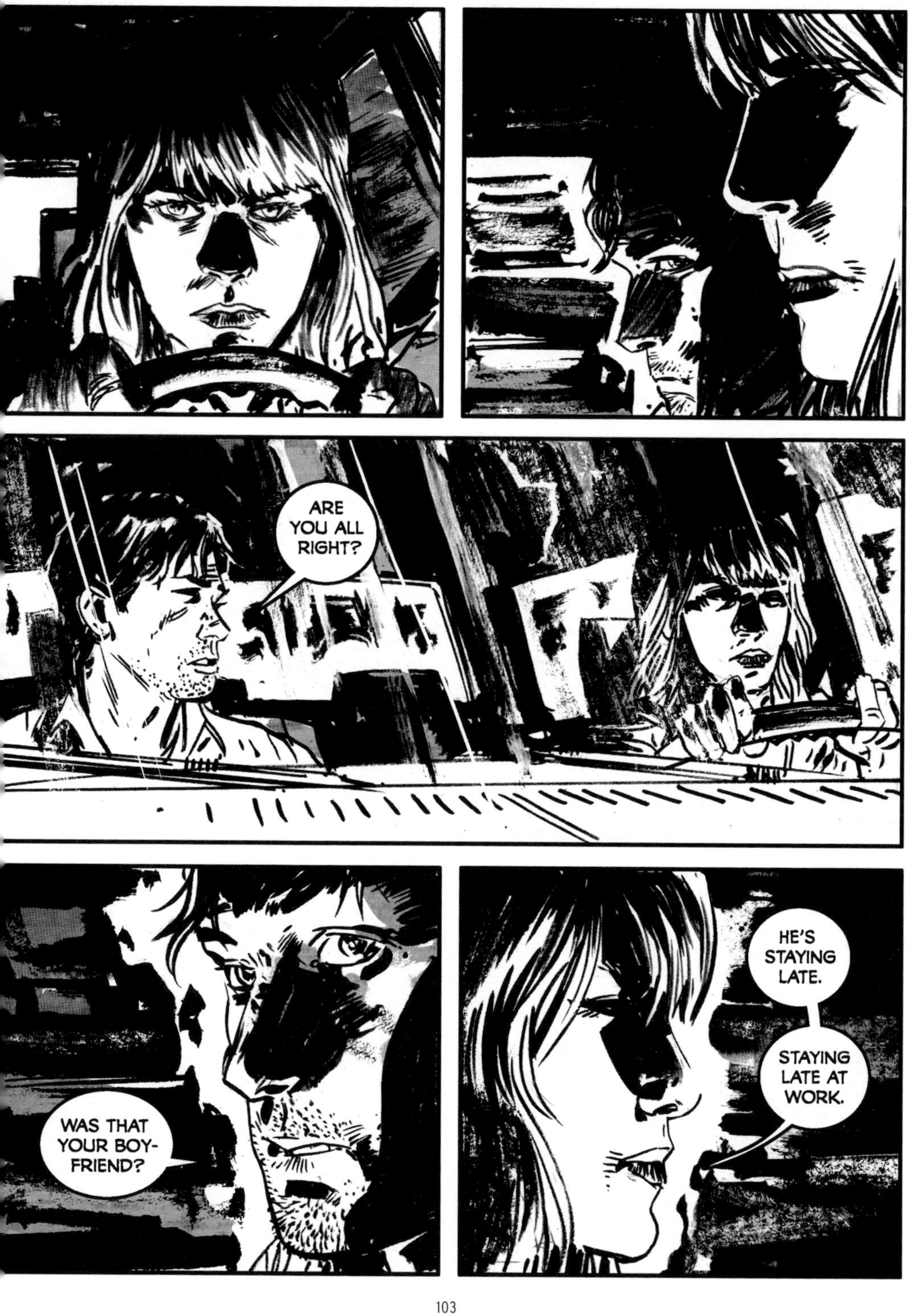
ARE YOU ALL RIGHT?
WAS THAT YOUR BOY-FRIEND?
HE'S STAYING LATE.
STAYING LATE AT WORK.

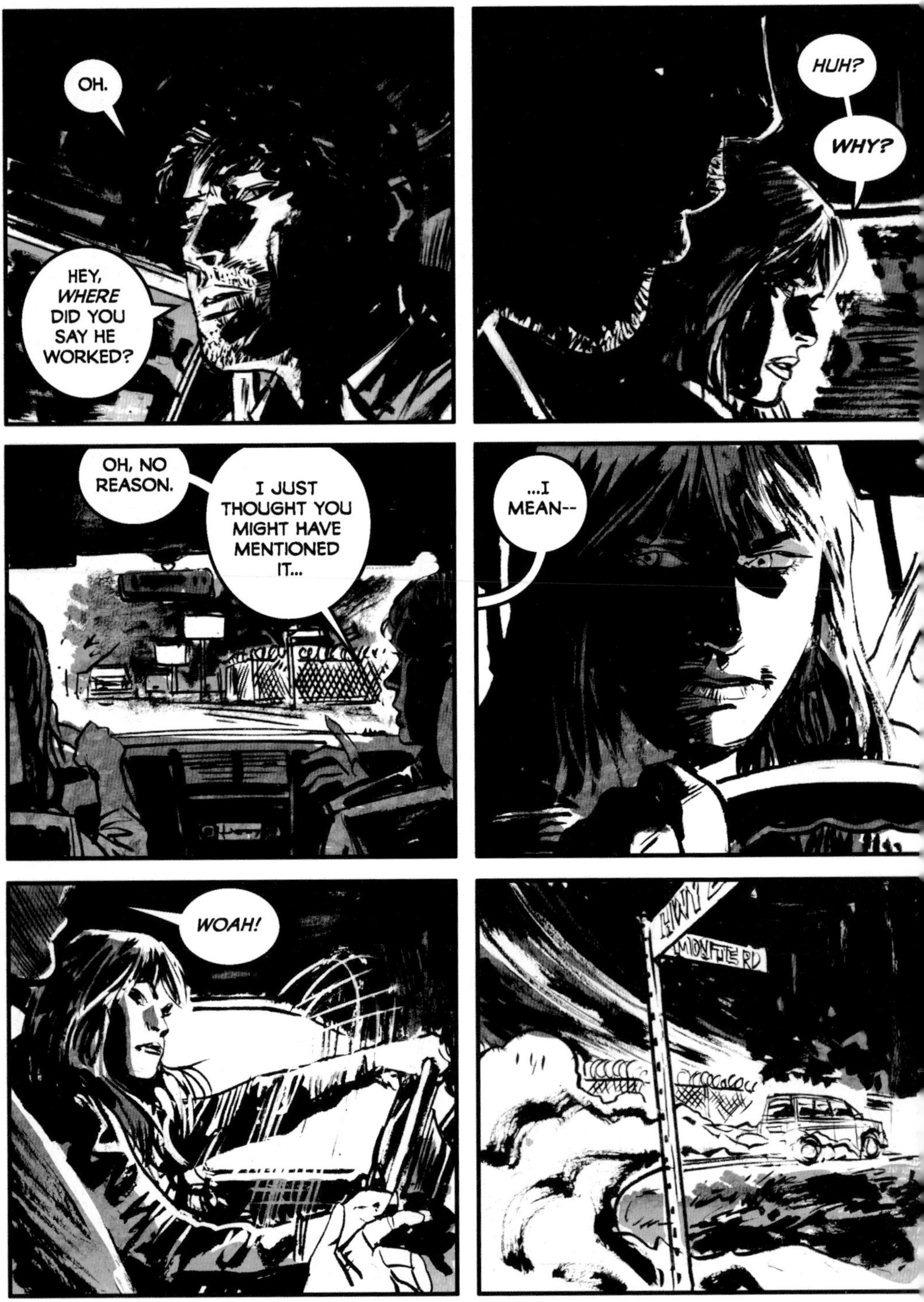
OH.
HEY, *WHERE* DID YOU SAY HE WORKED?
HUH?
WHY?
OH, NO REASON.
I JUST THOUGHT YOU MIGHT HAVE MENTIONED IT...
...I MEAN--
WOAH!

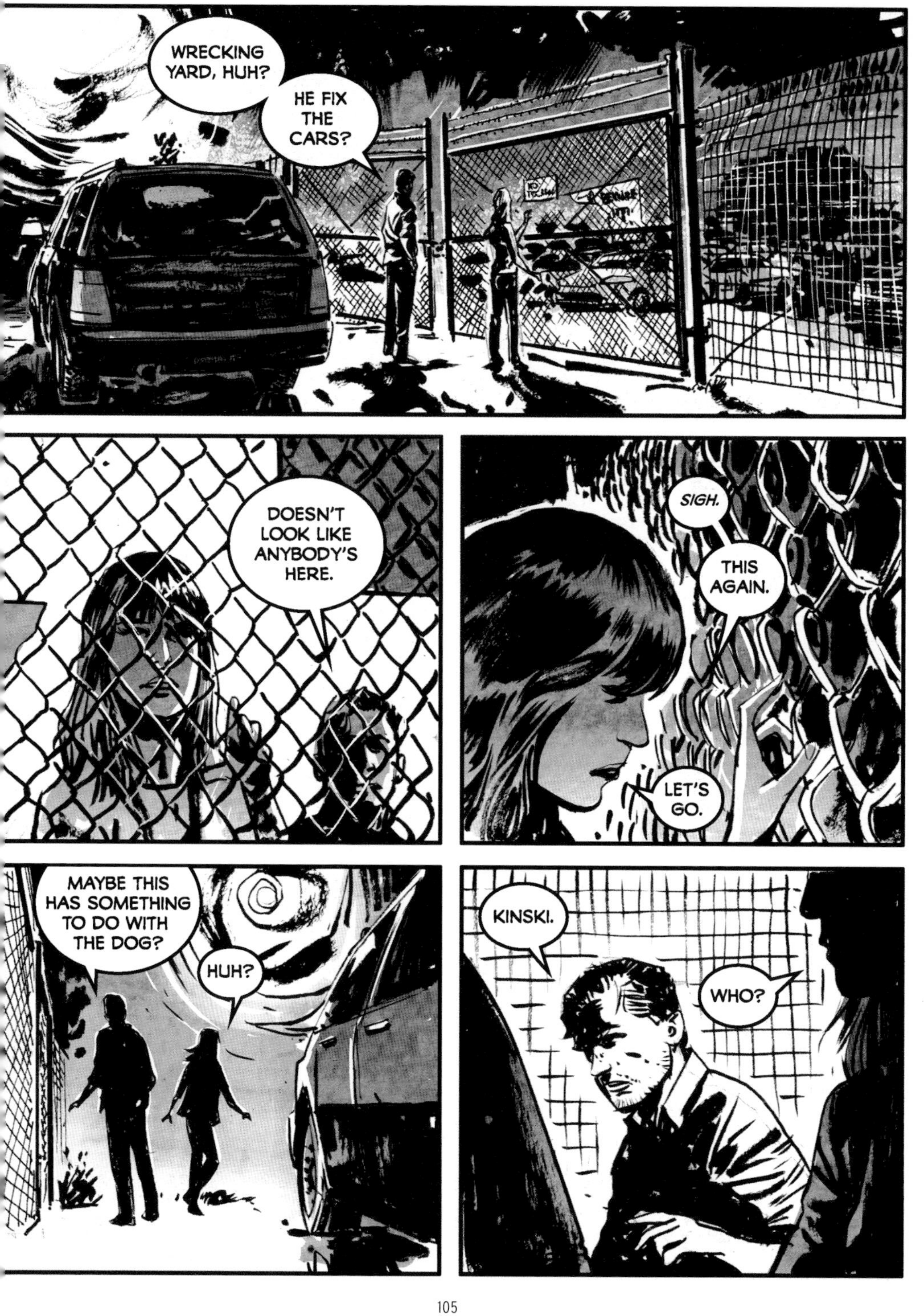
WRECKING YARD, HUH?
HE FIX THE CARS?
DOESN'T LOOK LIKE ANYBODY'S HERE.
SIGH.
THIS AGAIN.
LET'S GO.
MAYBE THIS HAS SOMETHING TO DO WITH THE DOG?
HUH?
KINSKI.
WHO?

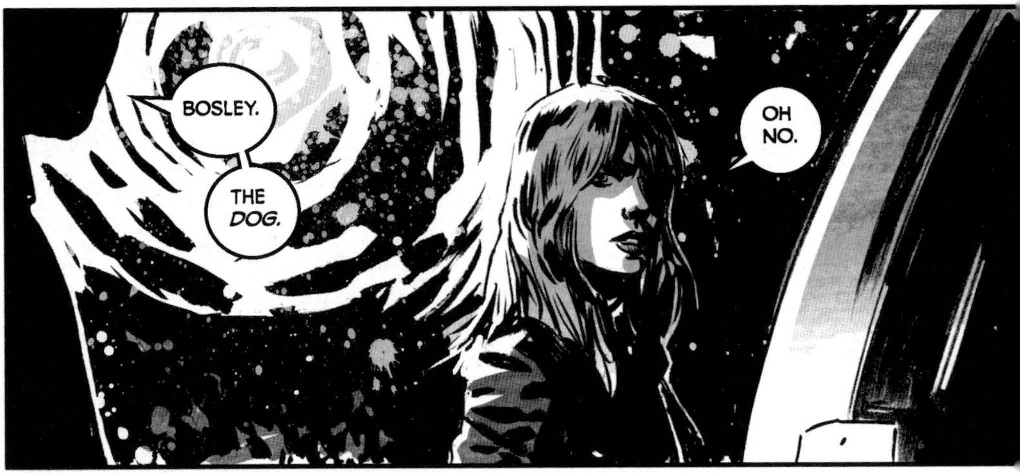
BOSLEY.
THE *DOG.*
OH NO.

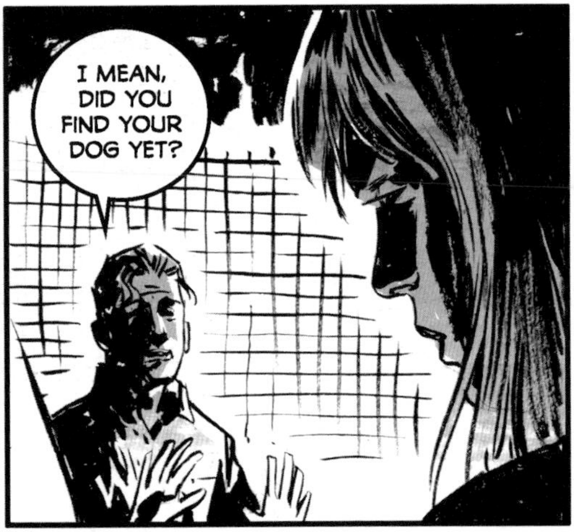
I MEAN, DID YOU FIND YOUR DOG YET?

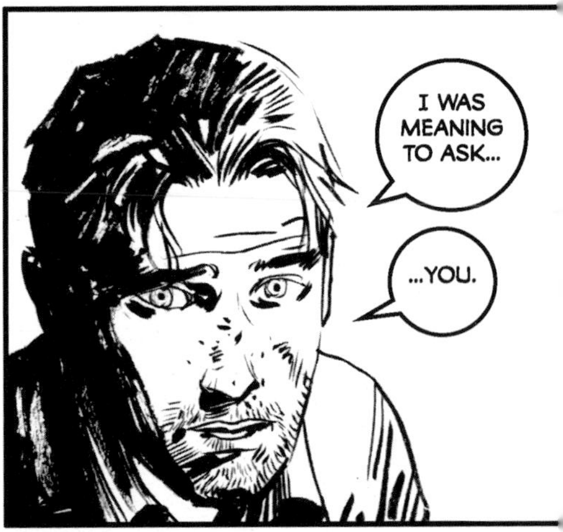
I WAS MEANING TO ASK...
...YOU.

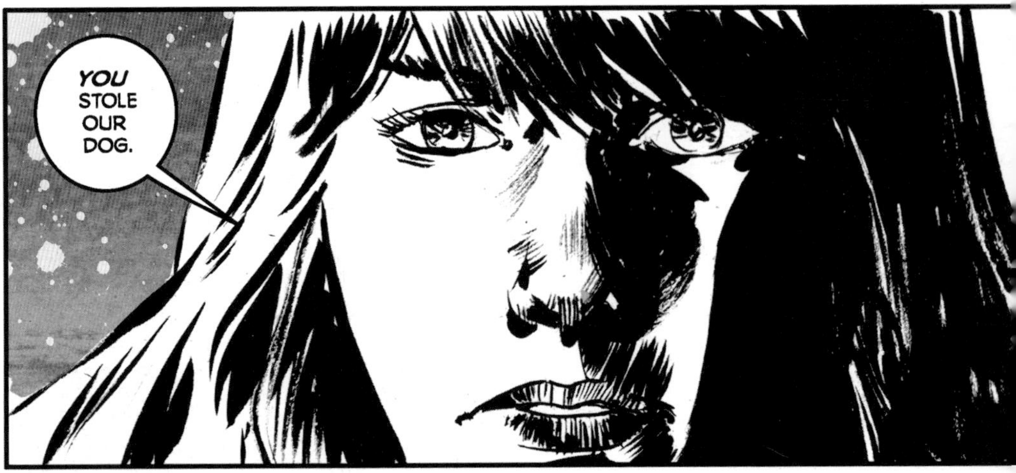
YOU STOLE OUR DOG.

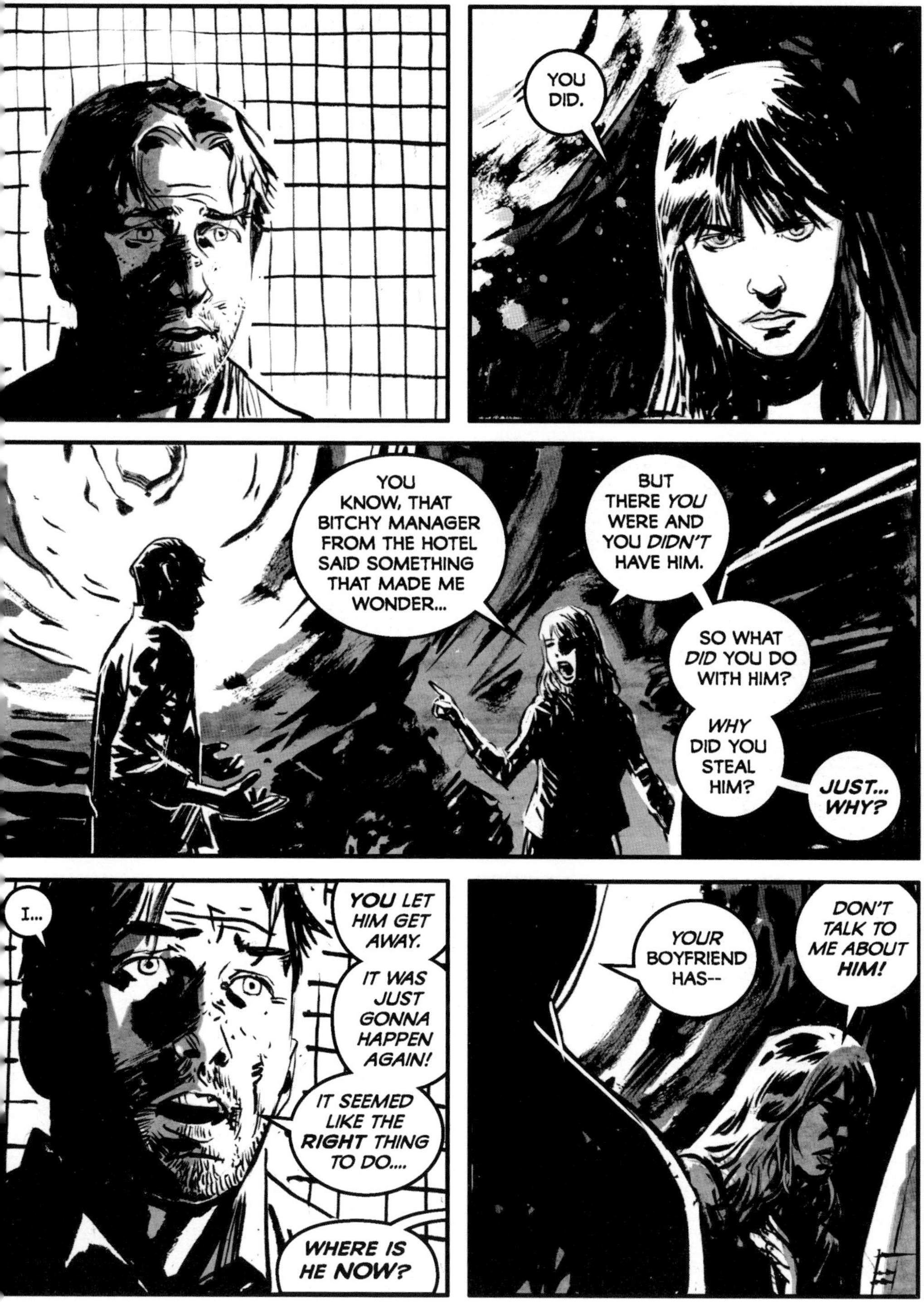
YOU DID.
YOU KNOW, THAT BITCHY MANAGER FROM THE HOTEL SAID SOMETHING THAT MADE ME WONDER...
BUT THERE *YOU* WERE AND YOU *DIDN'T* HAVE HIM.
SO WHAT *DID* YOU DO WITH HIM?
WHY DID YOU STEAL HIM?
JUST... WHY?
I...
***YOU** LET HIM GET AWAY.*
IT WAS JUST GONNA HAPPEN AGAIN!
*IT SEEMED LIKE THE **RIGHT** THING TO DO....*
WHERE IS HE NOW?
YOUR BOYFRIEND HAS--
DON'T TALK TO ME ABOUT HIM!

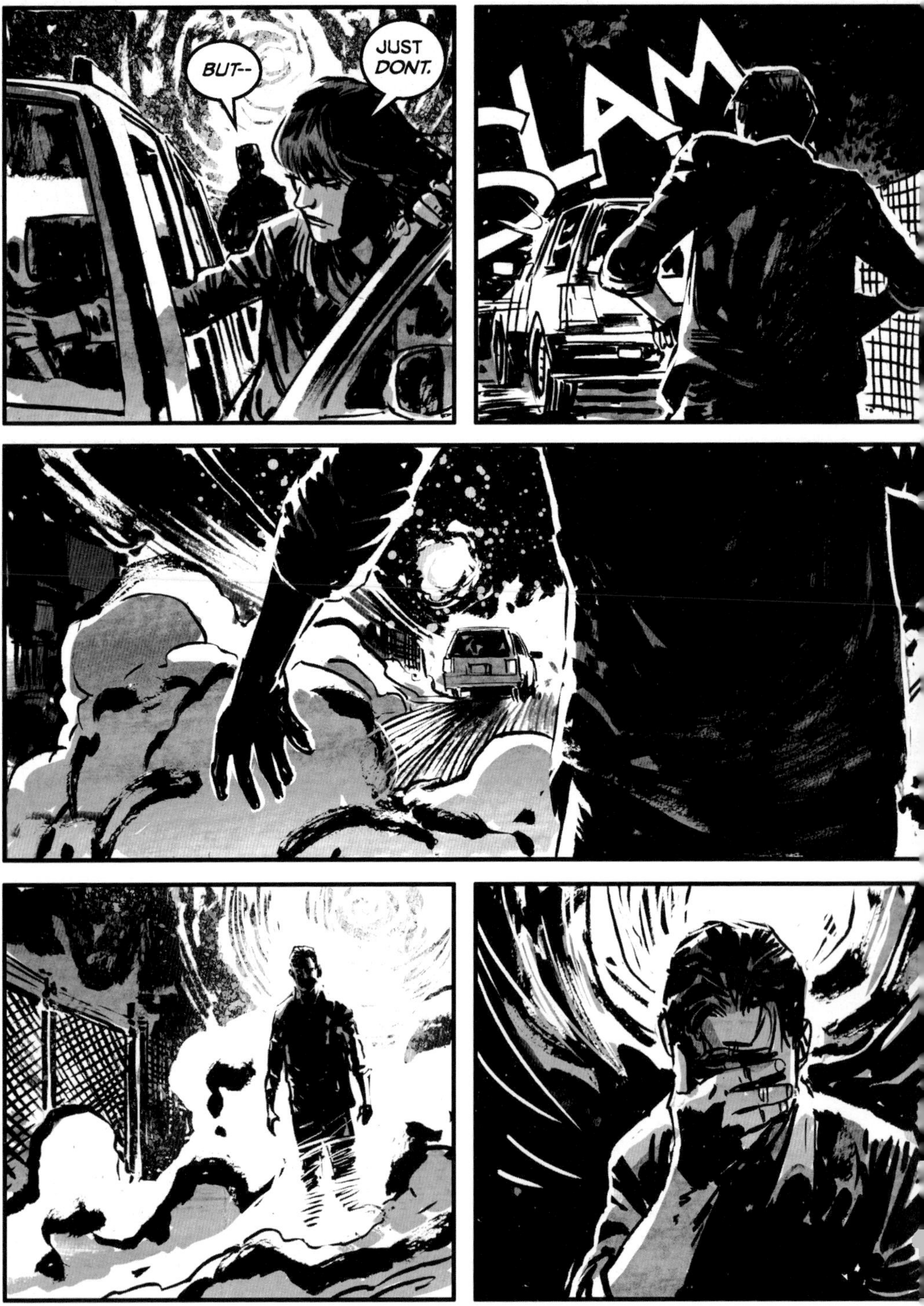
BUT--
JUST DONT.

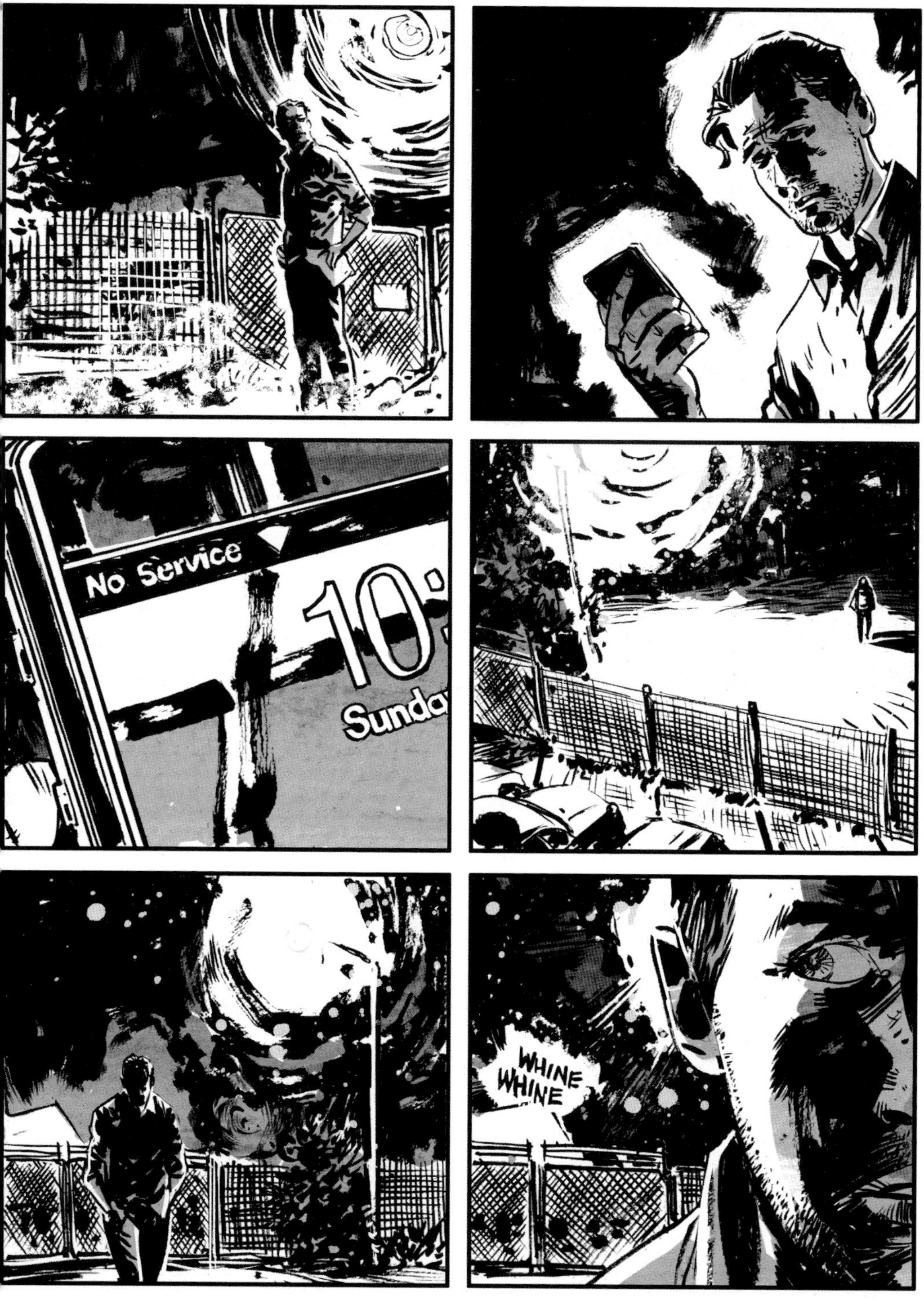
No Service
10:
Sunda
WHINE
WHINE

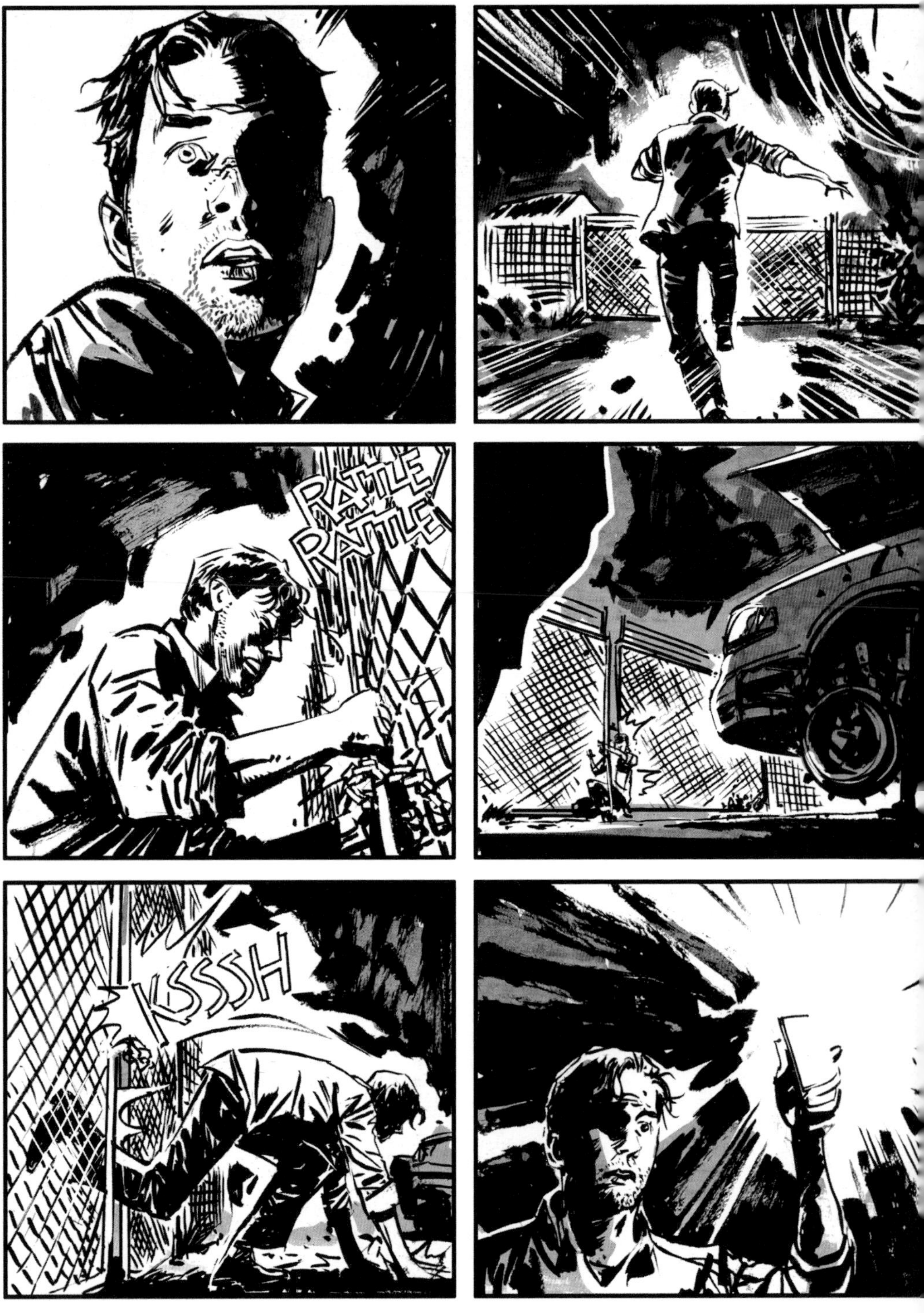
RATTLE
RATTLE
KSSSH

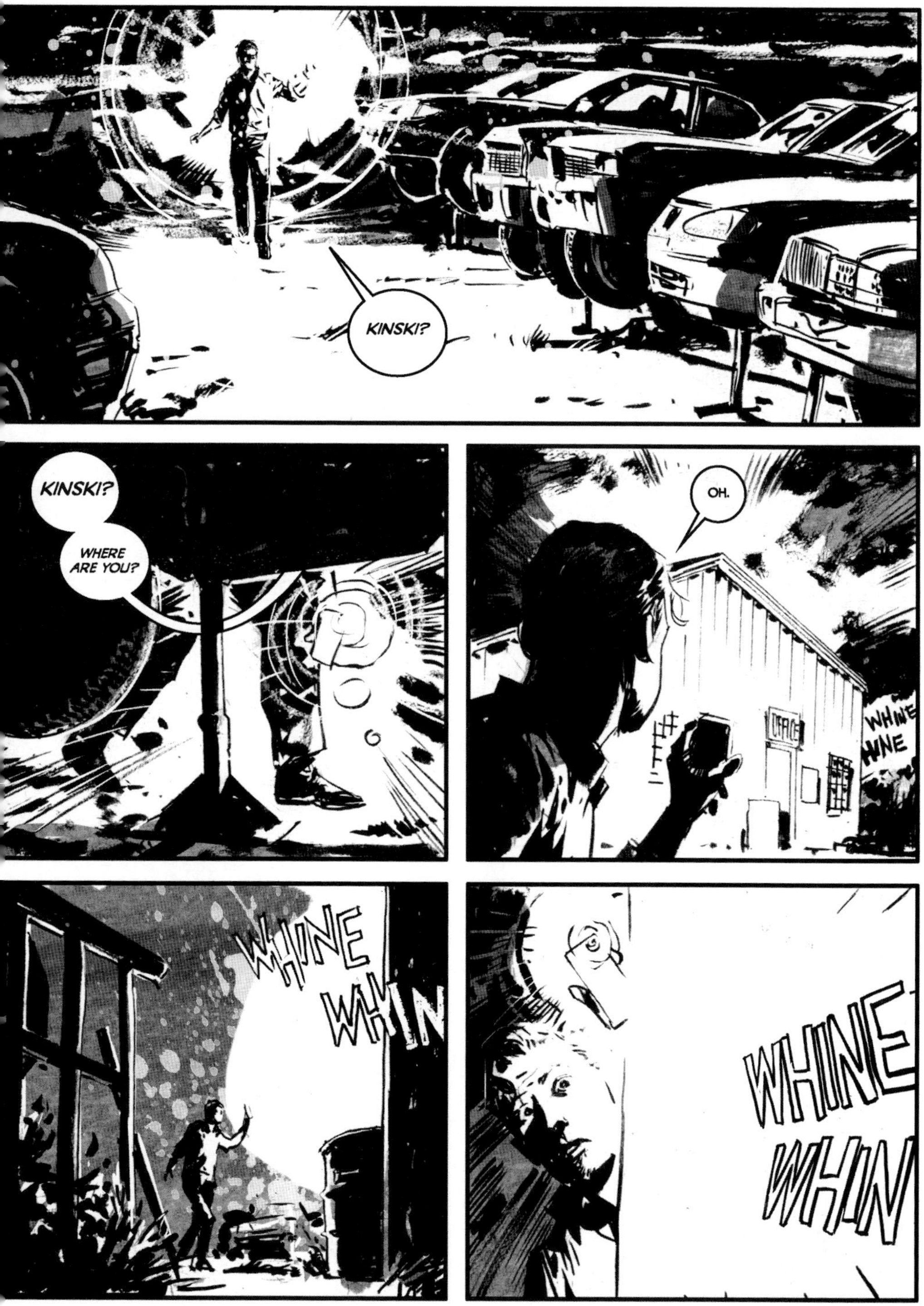
KINSKI?
KINSKI?
WHERE ARE YOU?
OH.
OFFICE
WHINE
WHINE
WHINE
WHIN
WHINE
WHIN

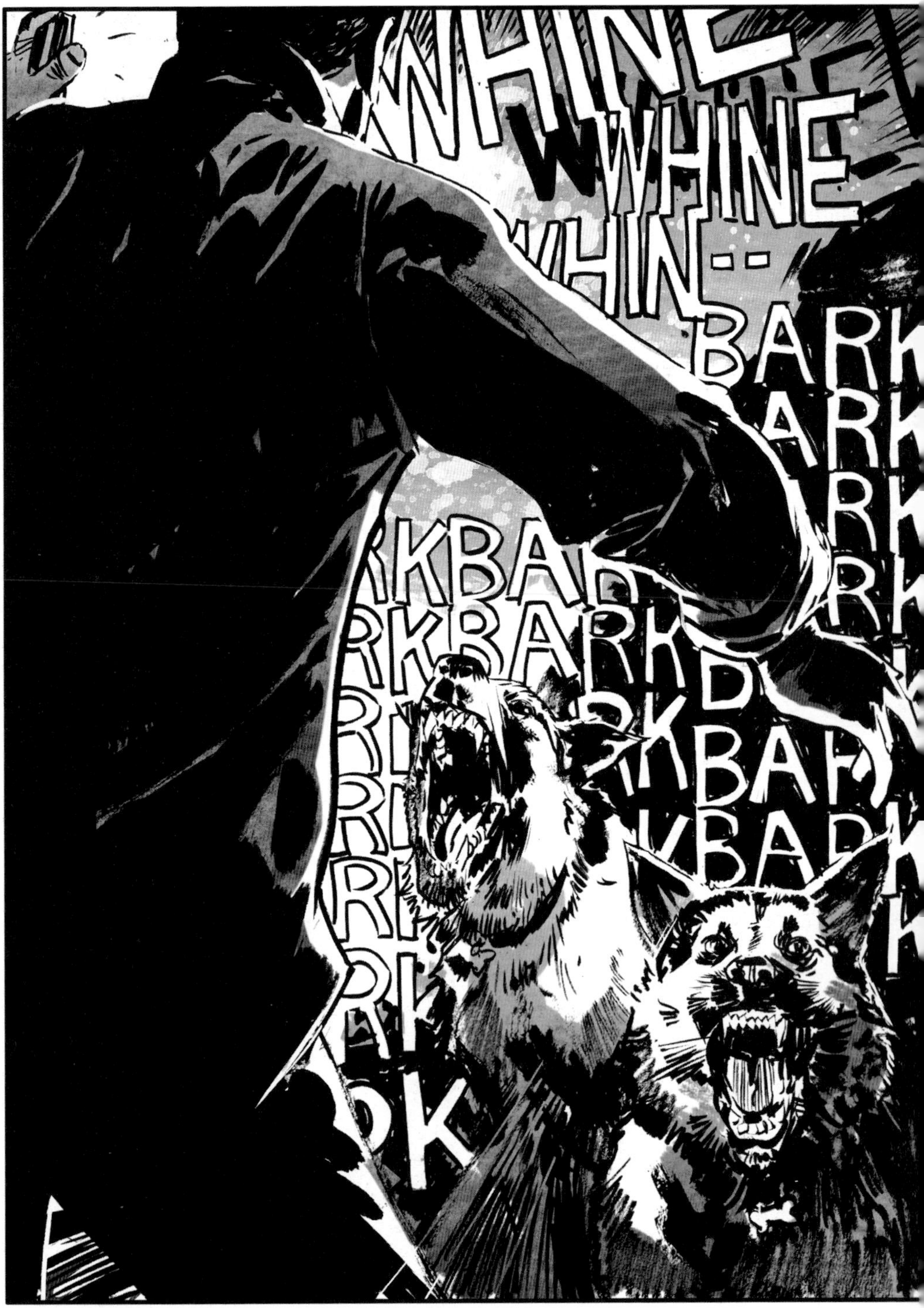
WHINE
WHINE
WHIN--
BARK
BARK
BARK

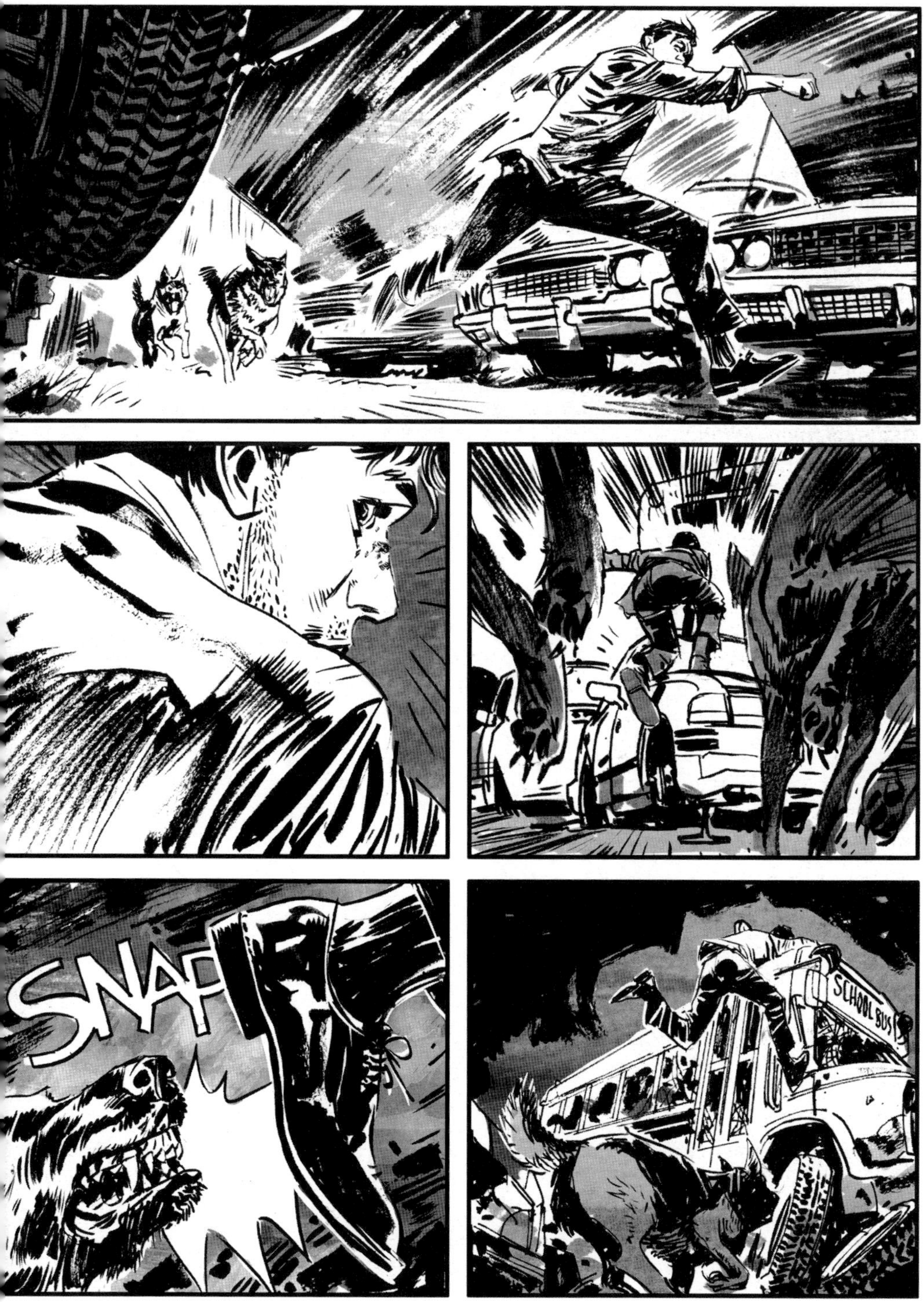
SNAP
SCHOOL BUS

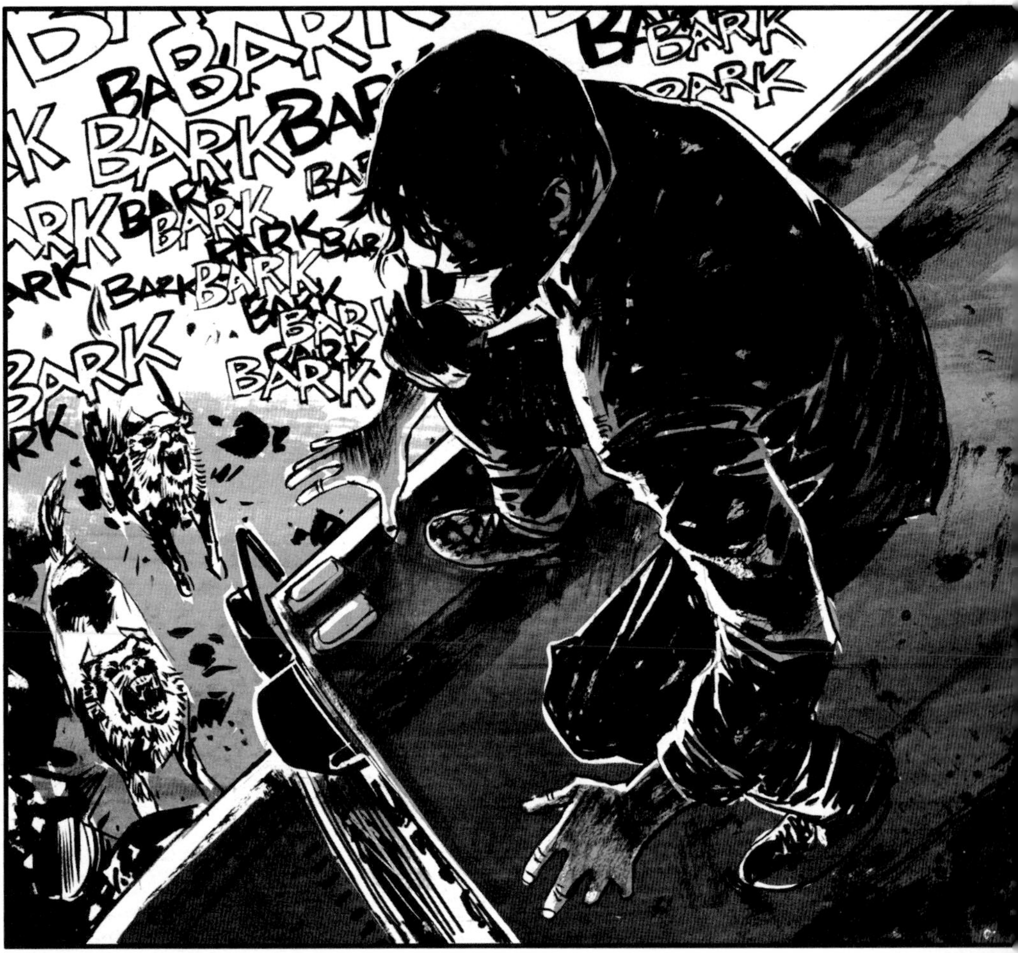
BARK
BARK
BARK
BARK
BARK
BARK
BARK
BARK
BARK
BARK
BARK
BARK
BARK
BARK
BARK

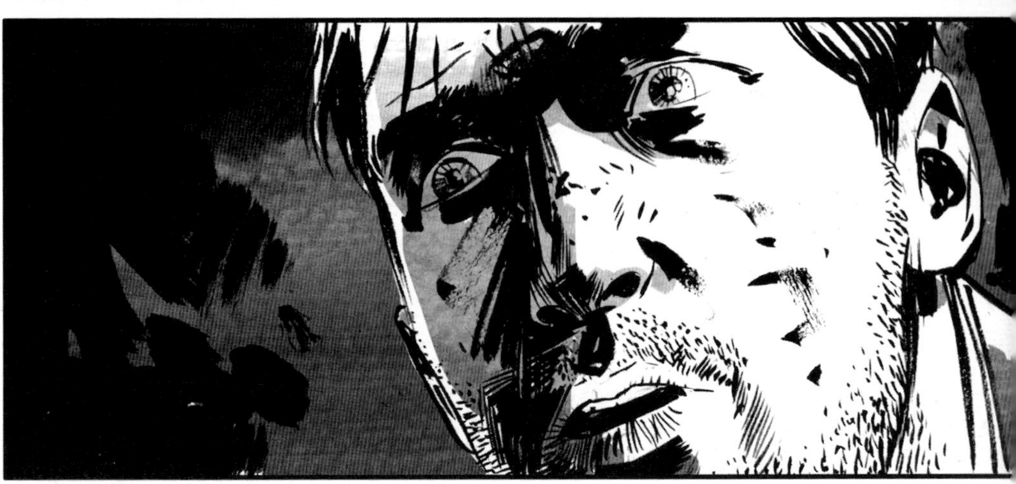

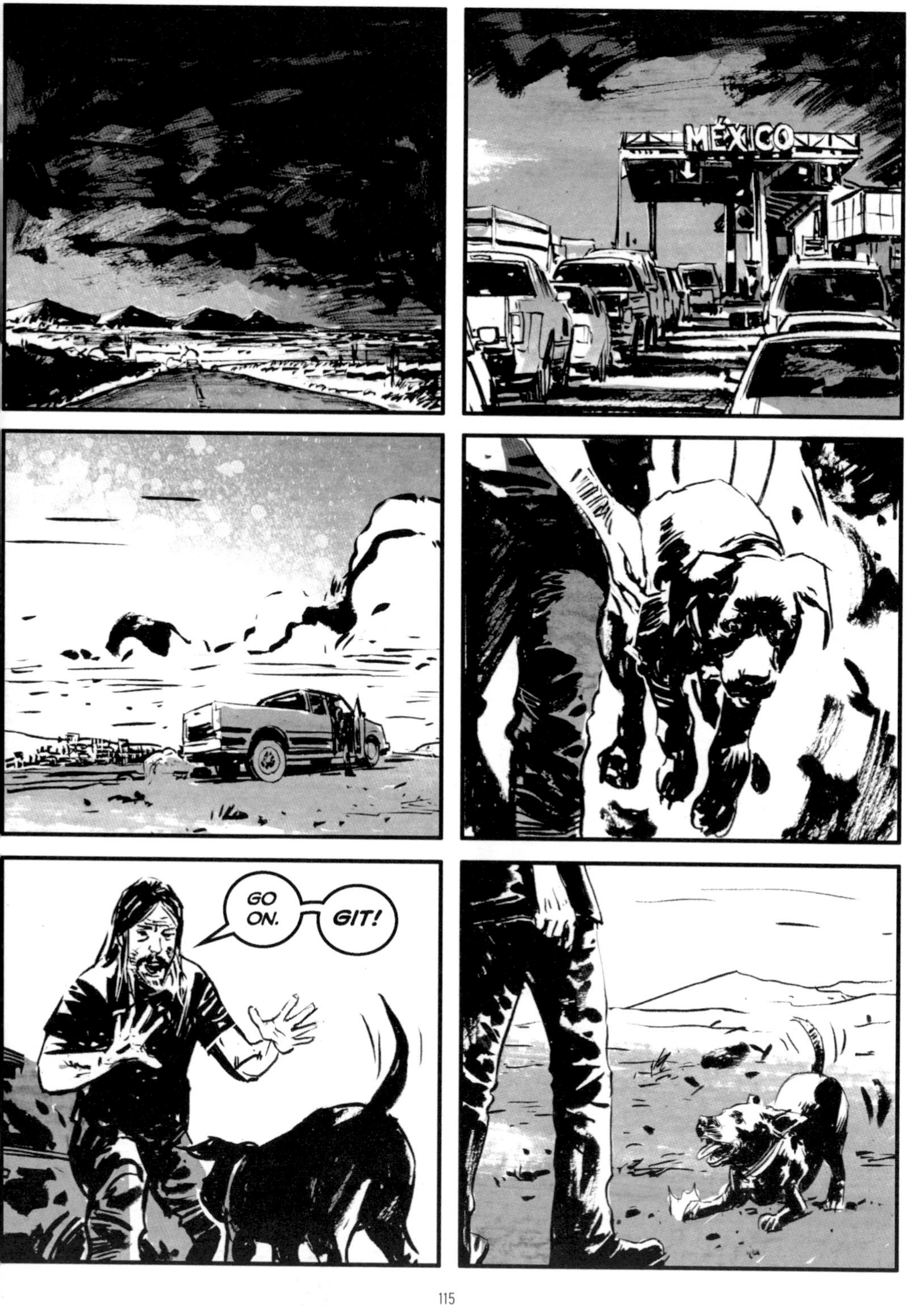
MÉXICO
GO ON.
GIT!

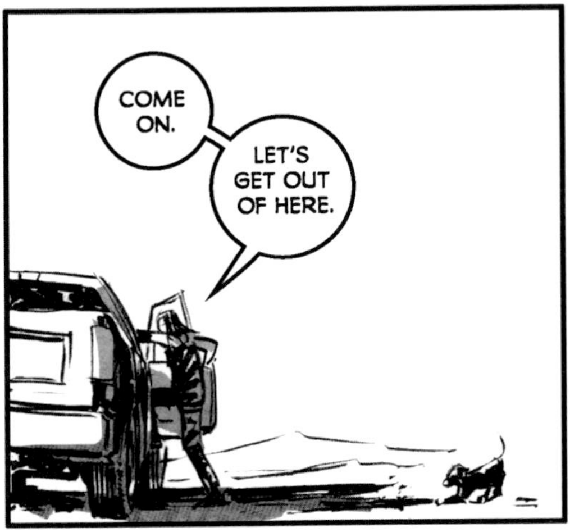
COME ON.
LET'S GET OUT OF HERE.
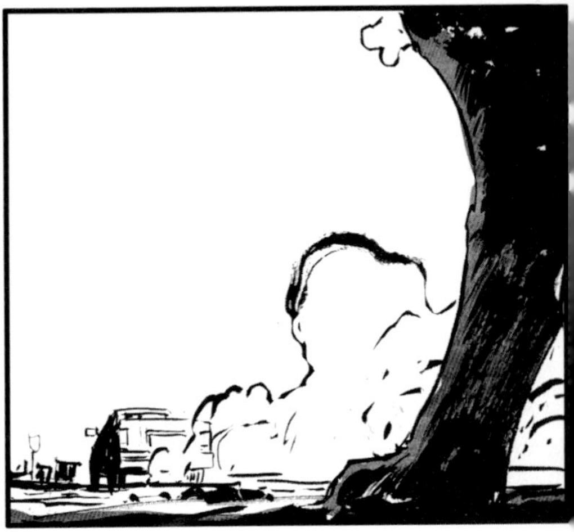
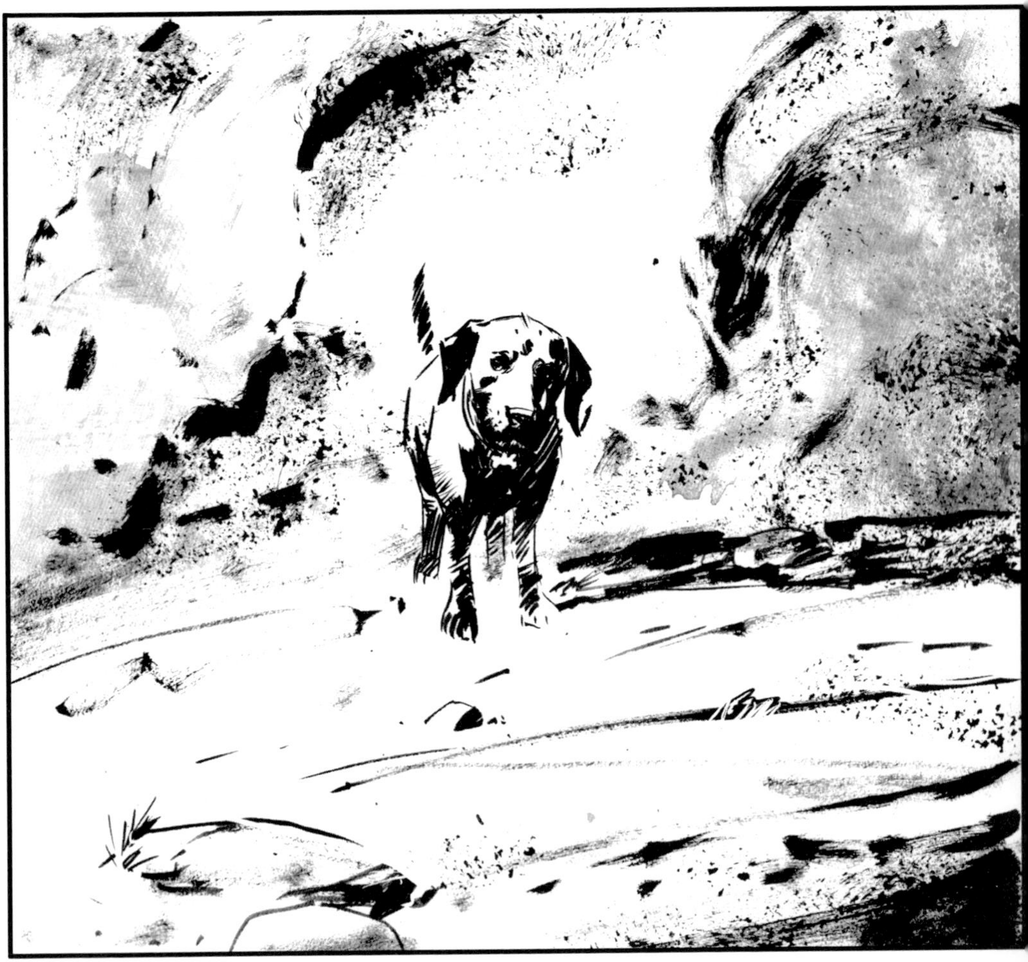

SIX

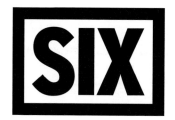

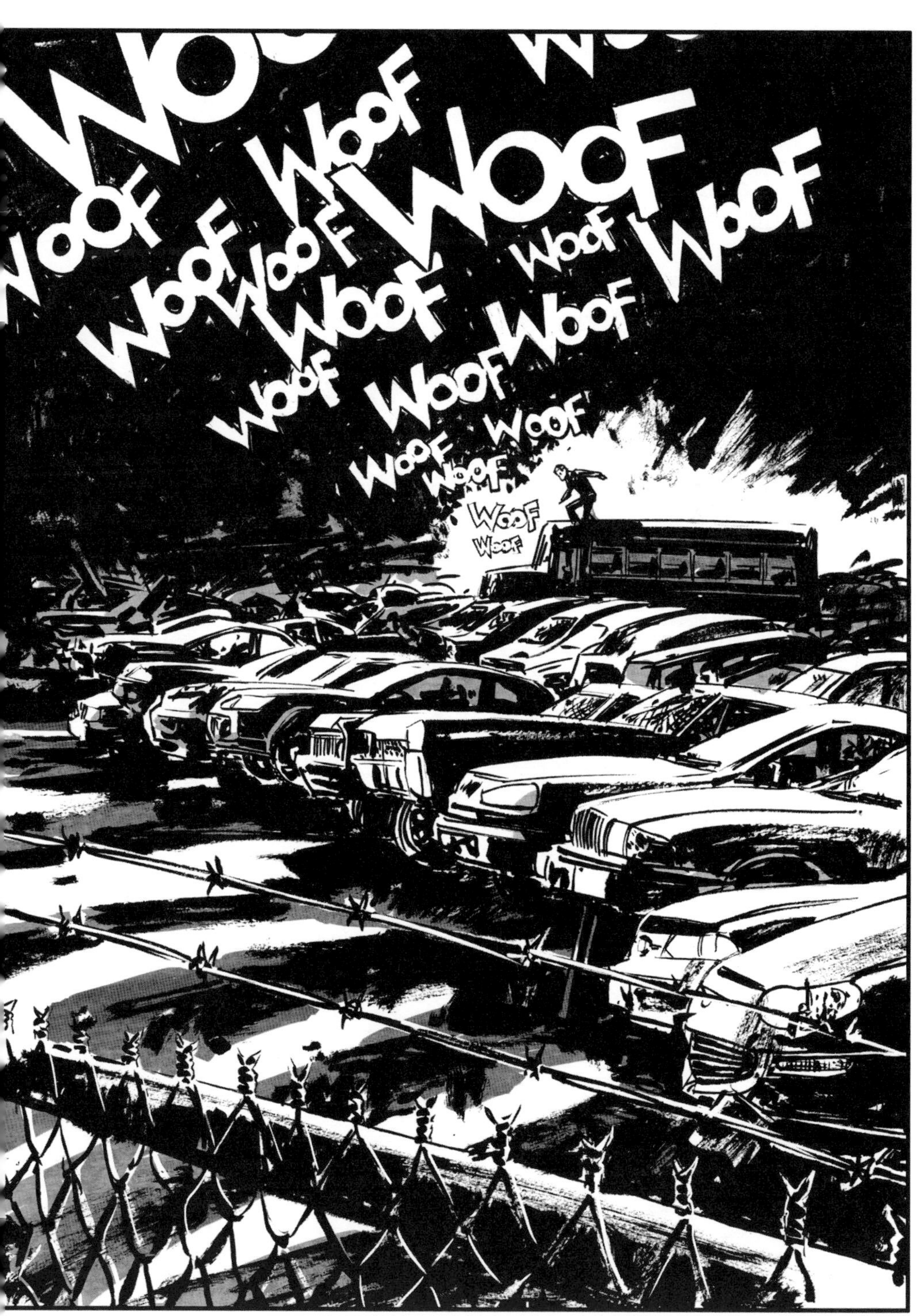
WOOF
WOOF
WOOF
WOOF
WOOF
WOOF
WOOF
WOOF
WOOF
WOOF
WOOF
WOOF
WOOF
WOOF
WOOF
WOOF
WOOF

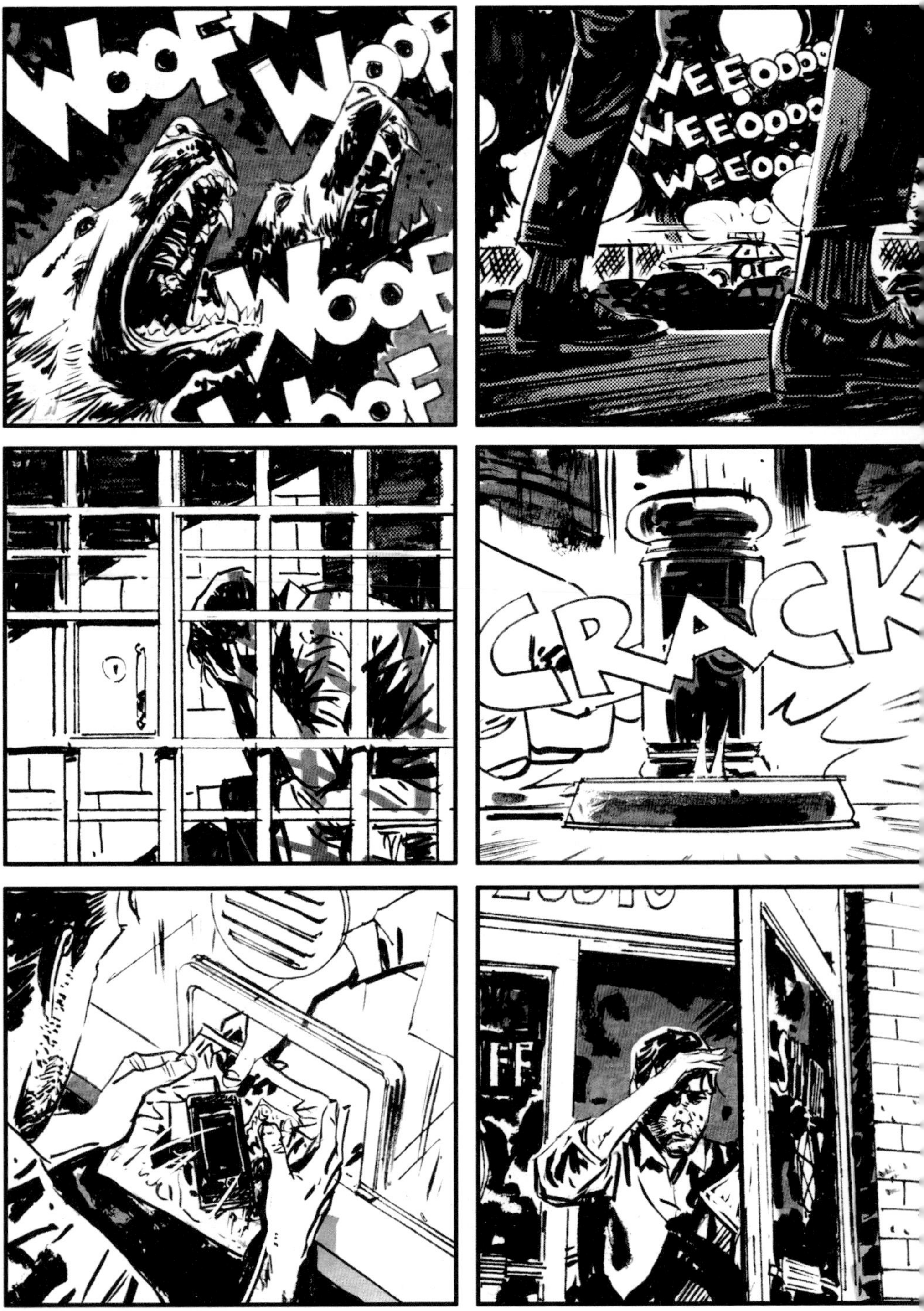
WOOF
WOOF
WOOF
WOOF
WEEOOO
WEEOOO
WEEOO
CRACK

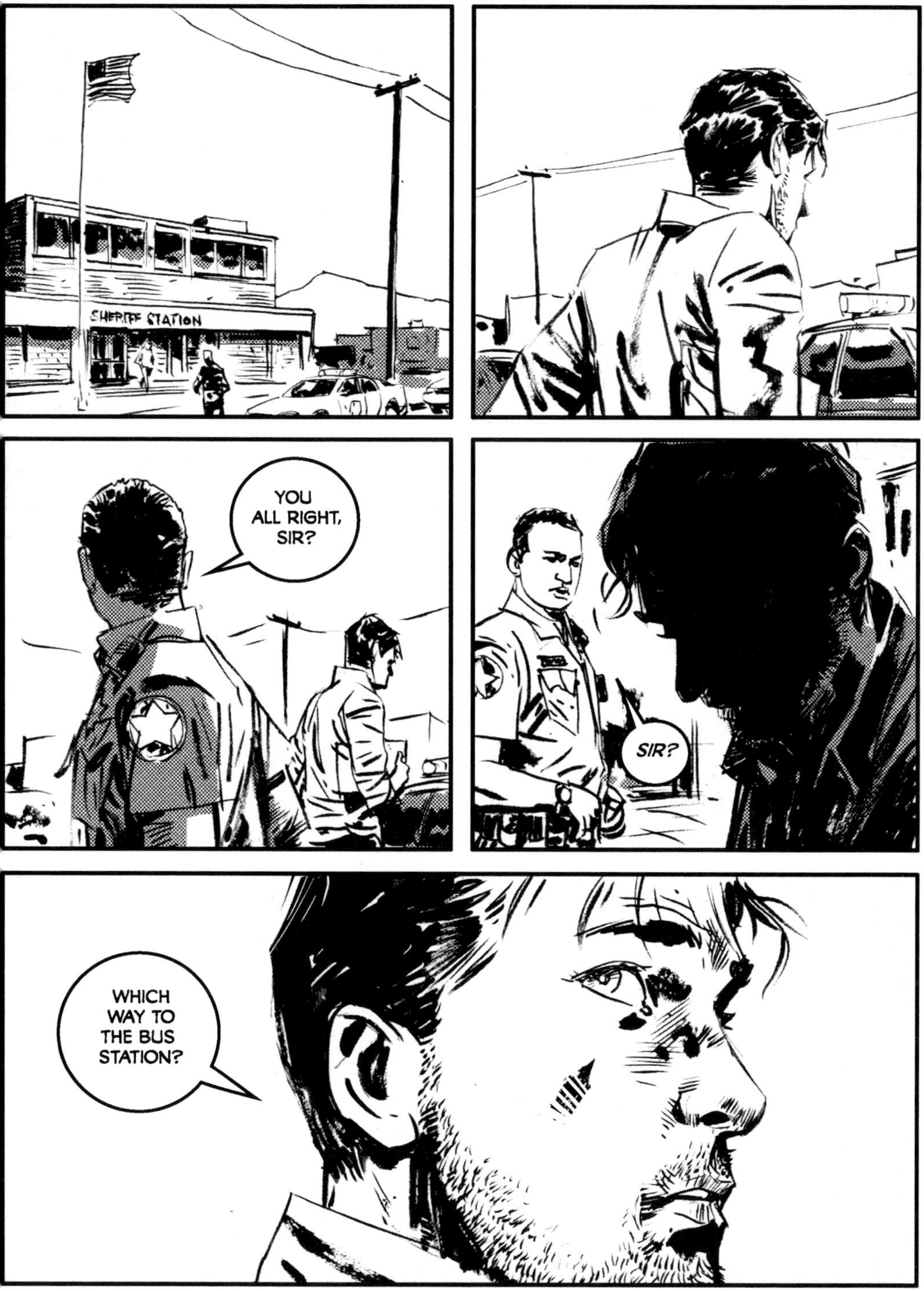
SHERIFF STATION
YOU ALL RIGHT, SIR?
SIR?
WHICH WAY TO THE BUS STATION?

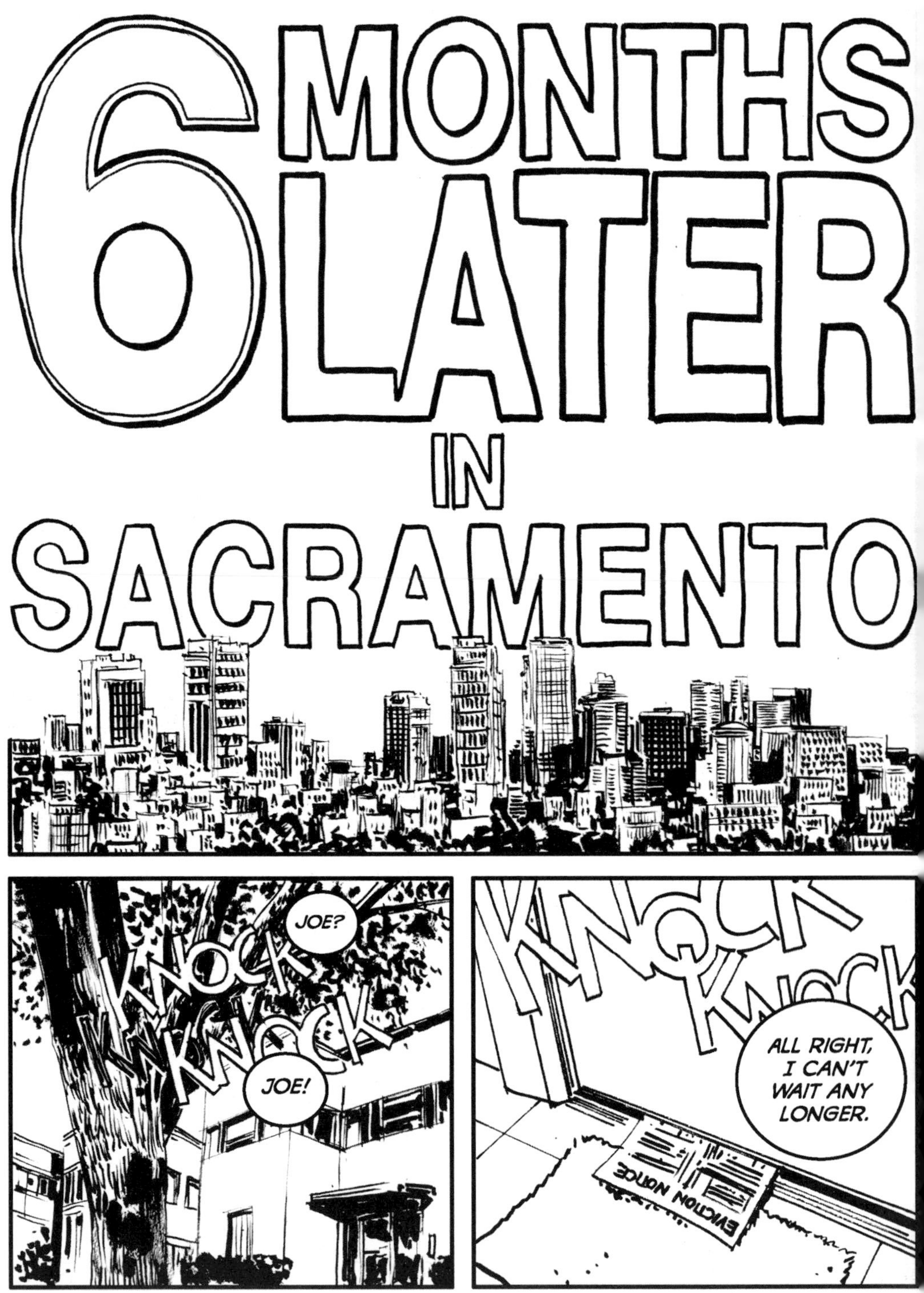
6 MONTHS LATER IN SACRAMENTO
JOE?
KNOCK KNOCK
JOE!
KNOCK KNOCK
ALL RIGHT, I CAN'T WAIT ANY LONGER.
EVICTION NOTICE

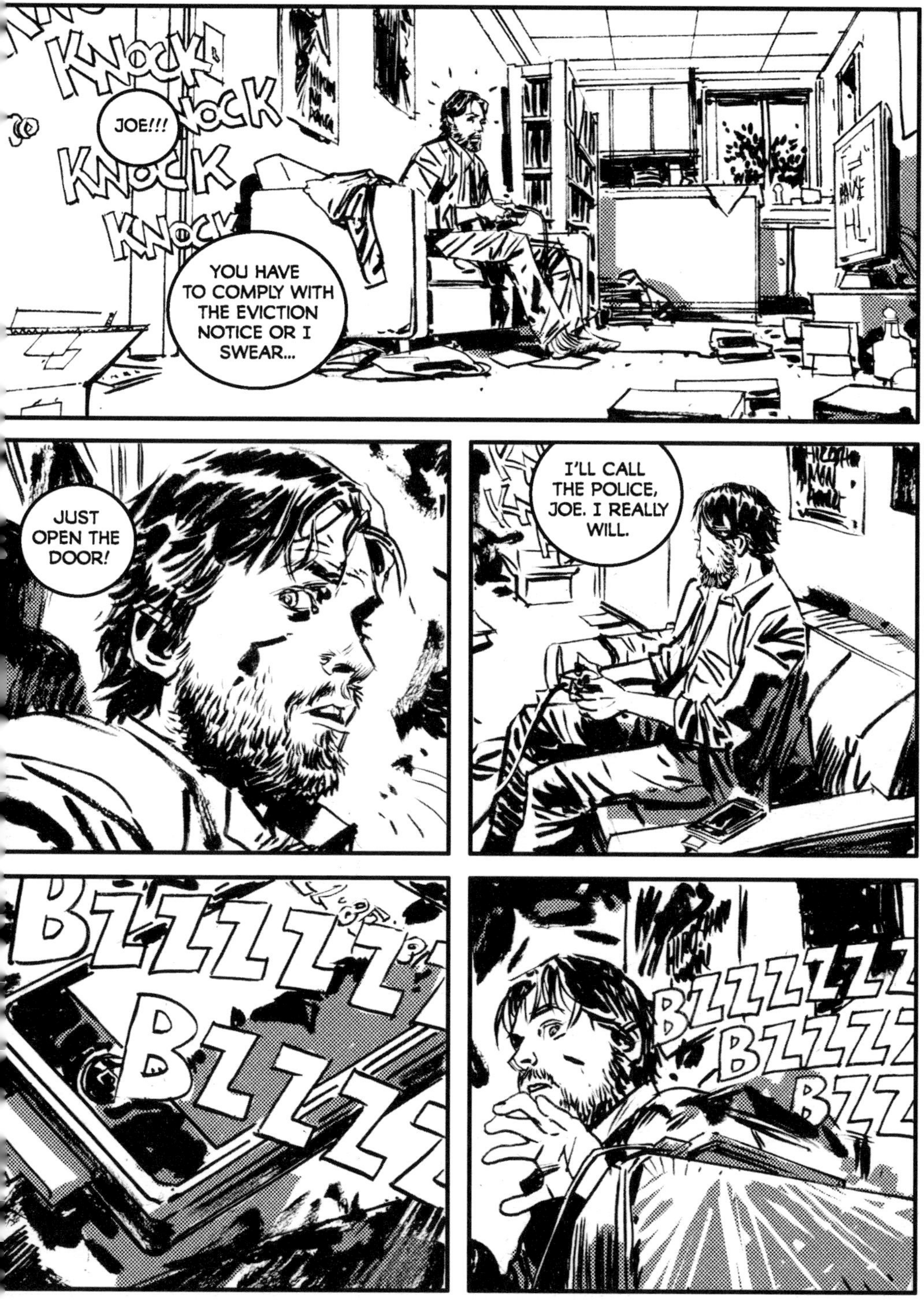
KNOCK!
KNOCK
JOE!!!
KNOCK
KNOCK
YOU HAVE TO COMPLY WITH THE EVICTION NOTICE OR I SWEAR...
JUST OPEN THE DOOR!
I'LL CALL THE POLICE, JOE. I REALLY WILL.
BZZZZZ
BZZZ
BZZZZZZ
BZZZZZ
BZZ

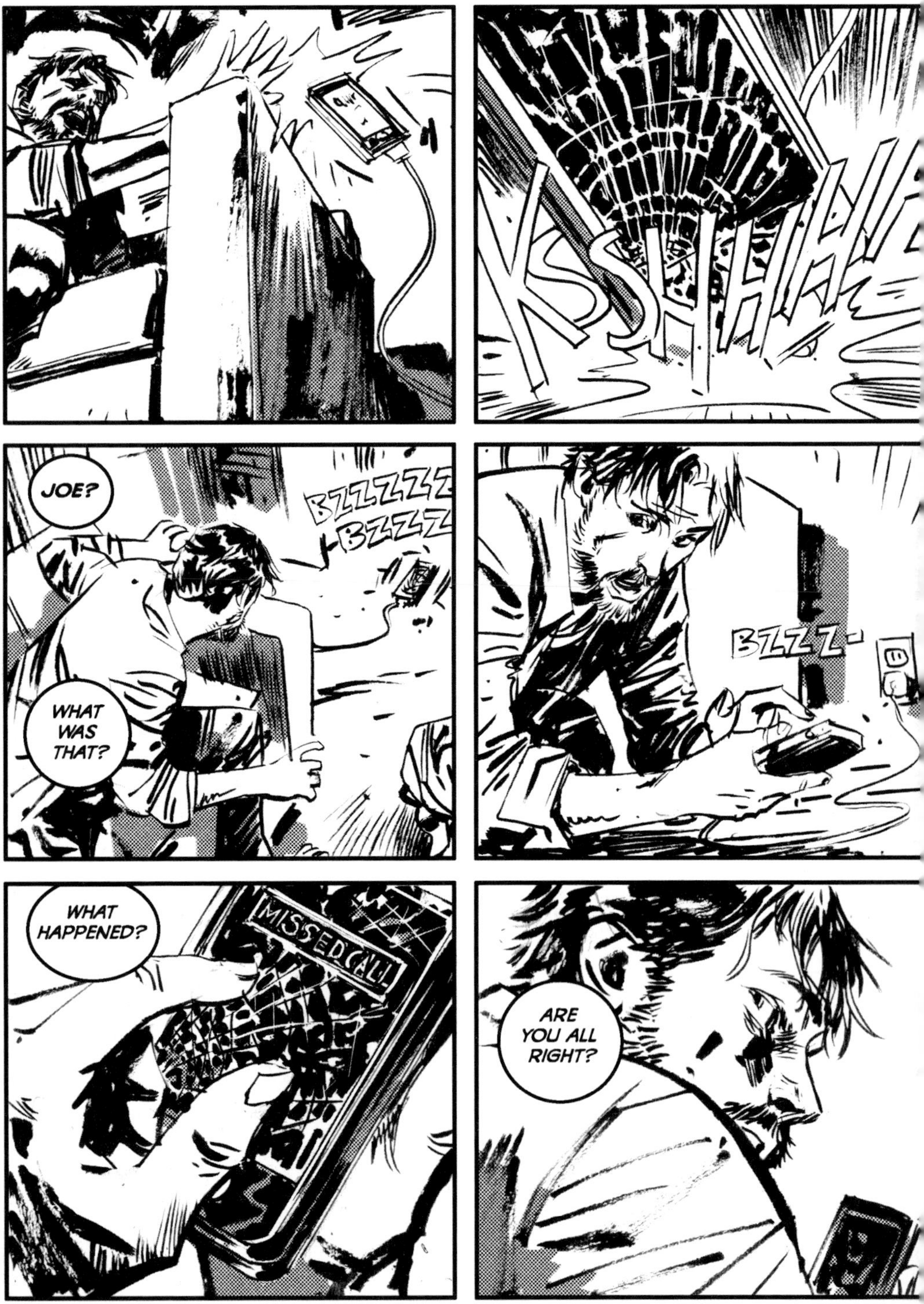
KSSHHH
JOE?
BZZZZZZ
BZZZZ
WHAT WAS THAT?
BZZZ-
WHAT HAPPENED?
MISSED CALL
ARE YOU ALL RIGHT?

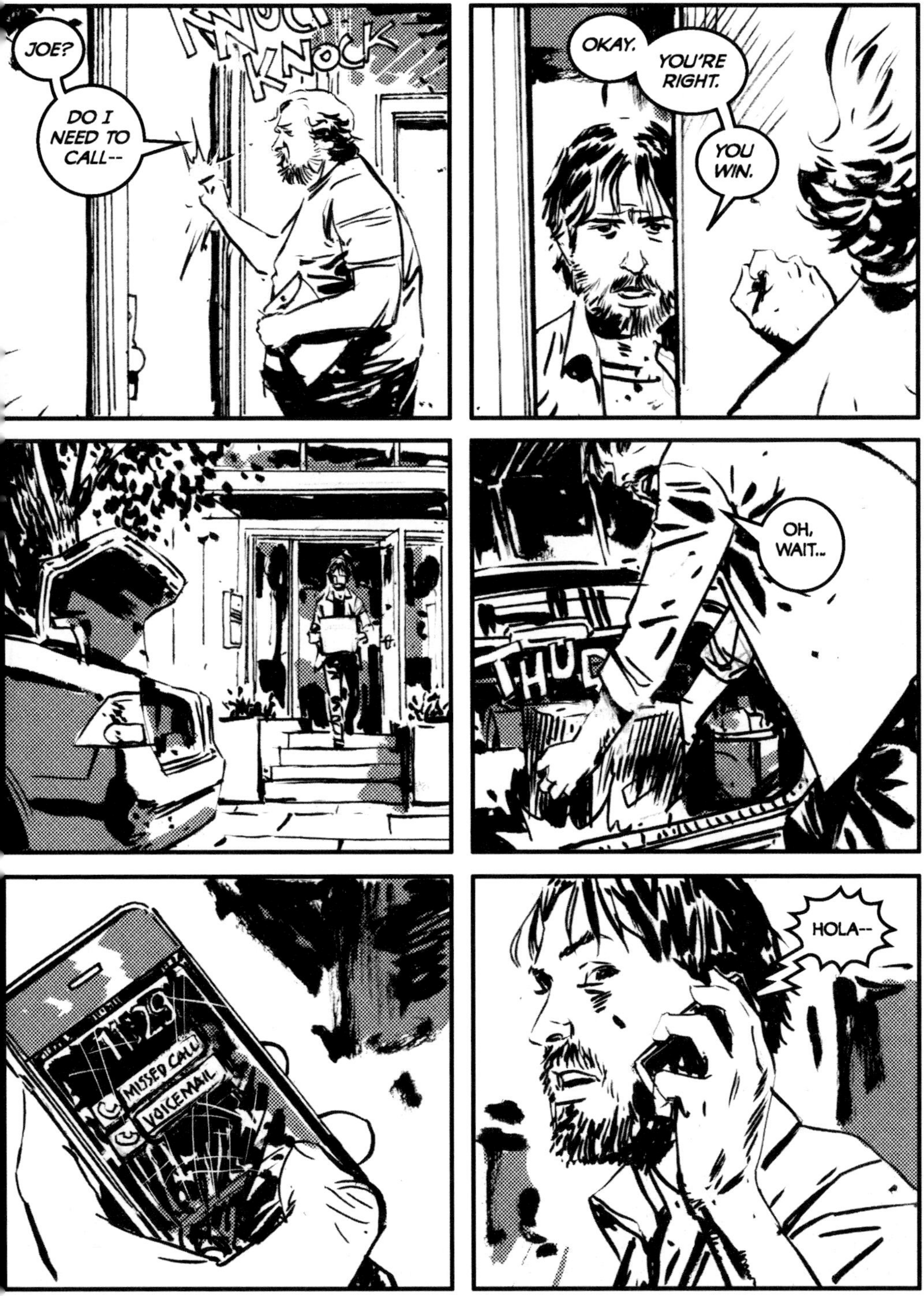
KNOCK KNOCK
JOE?
DO I NEED TO CALL--
OKAY.
YOU'RE RIGHT.
YOU WIN.
OH, WAIT...
THUD
MISSED CALL
VOICEMAIL
HOLA--

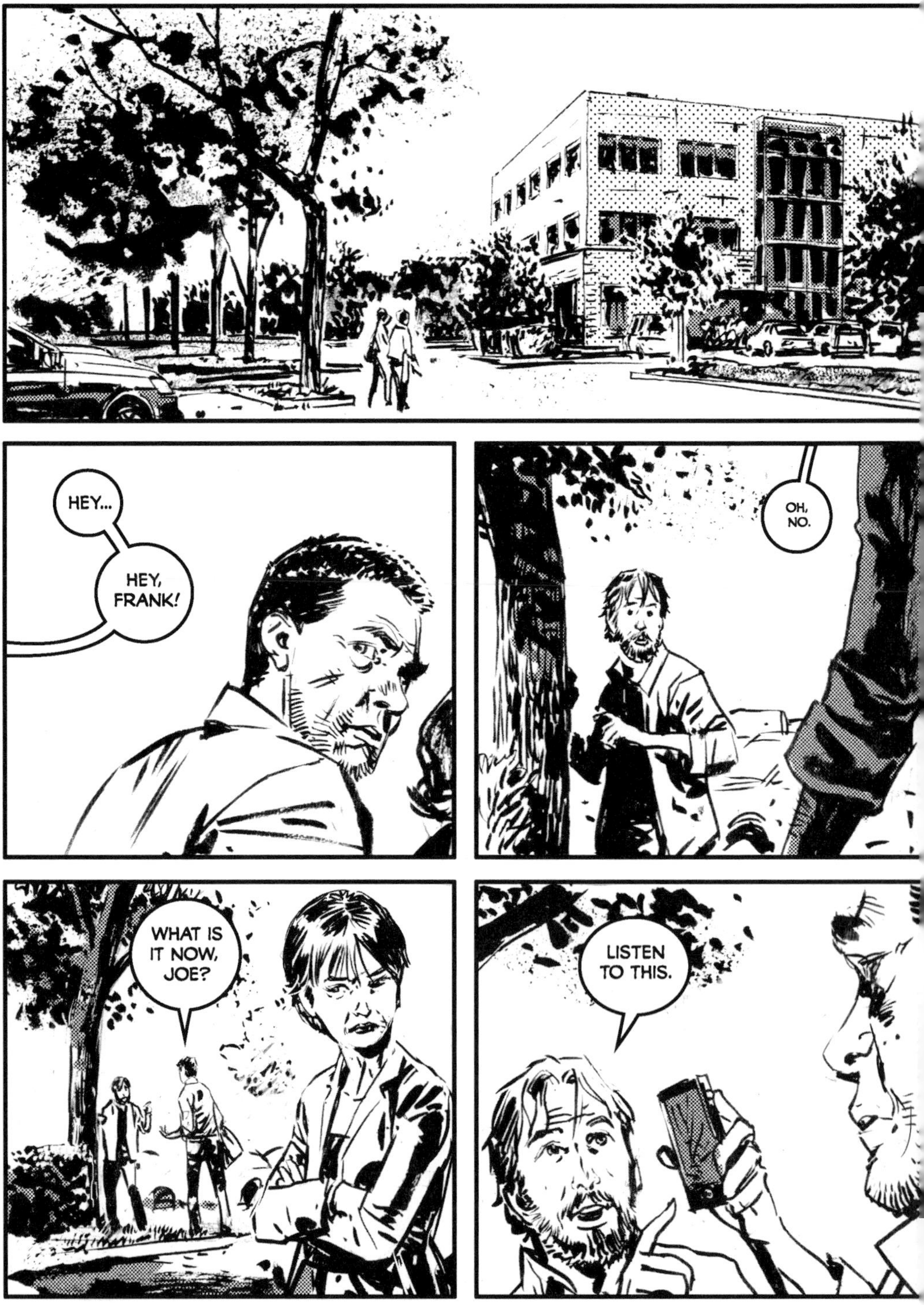
HEY...
HEY, FRANK!
OH, NO.
WHAT IS IT NOW, JOE?
LISTEN TO THIS.

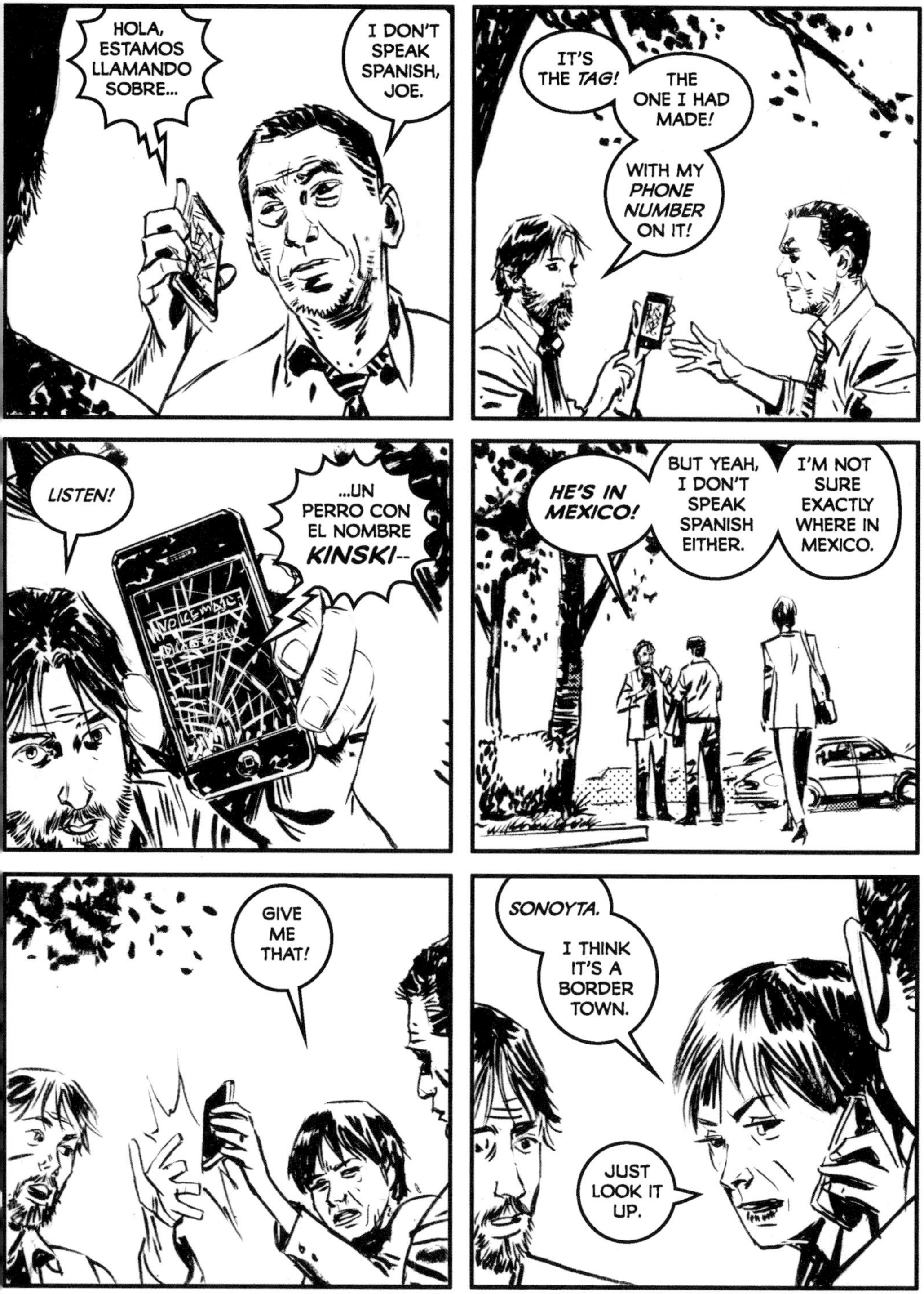
HOLA, ESTAMOS LLAMANDO SOBRE...
I DON'T SPEAK SPANISH, JOE.
IT'S THE *TAG!*
THE ONE I HAD MADE!
WITH MY *PHONE NUMBER* ON IT!
LISTEN!
...UN PERRO CON EL NOMBRE ***KINSKI***--
HE'S IN MEXICO!
BUT YEAH, I DON'T SPEAK SPANISH EITHER.
I'M NOT SURE EXACTLY WHERE IN MEXICO.
GIVE ME THAT!
SONOYTA.
I THINK IT'S A BORDER TOWN.
JUST LOOK IT UP.

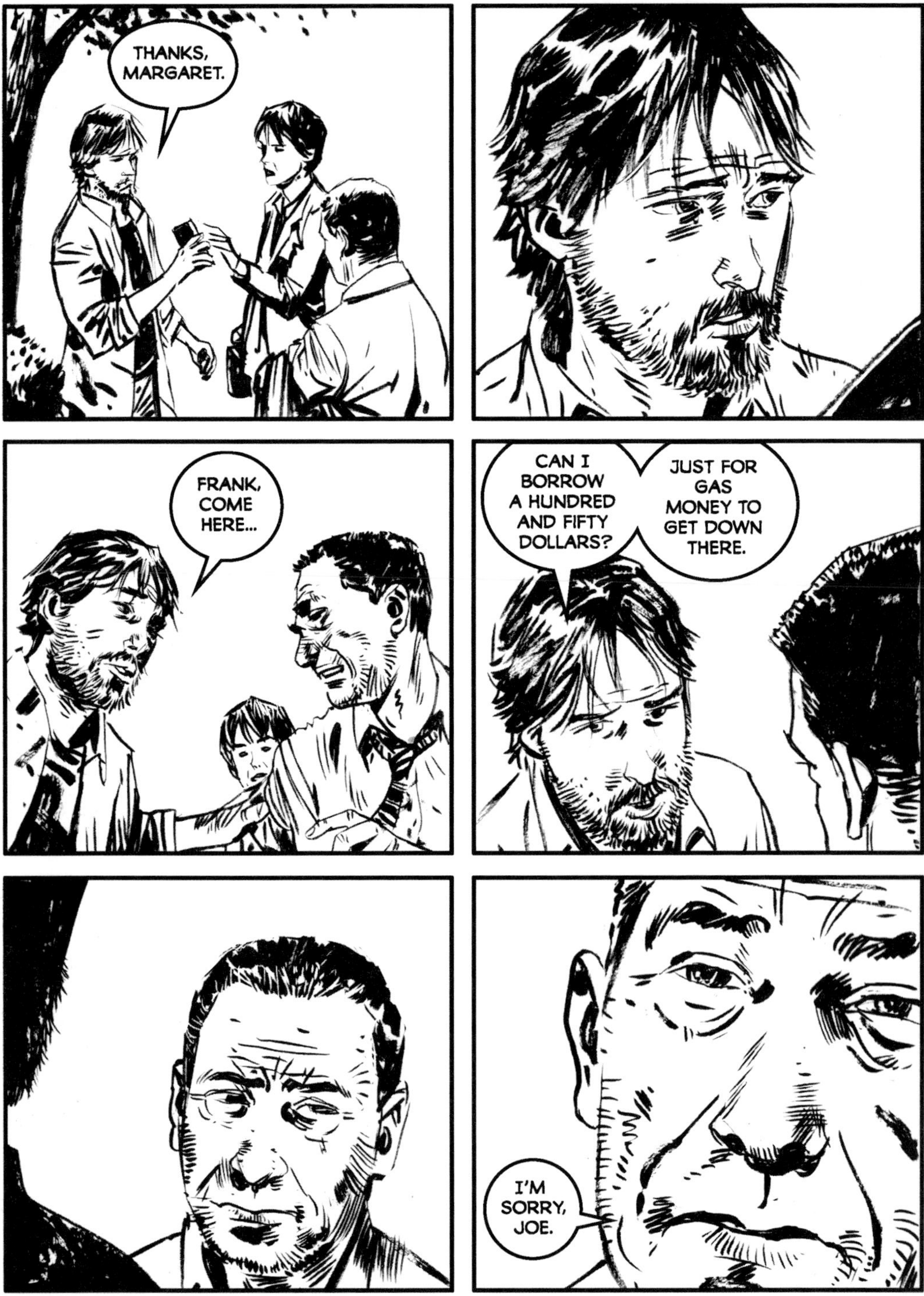
THANKS, MARGARET.
FRANK, COME HERE...
CAN I BORROW A HUNDRED AND FIFTY DOLLARS?
JUST FOR GAS MONEY TO GET DOWN THERE.
I'M SORRY, JOE.

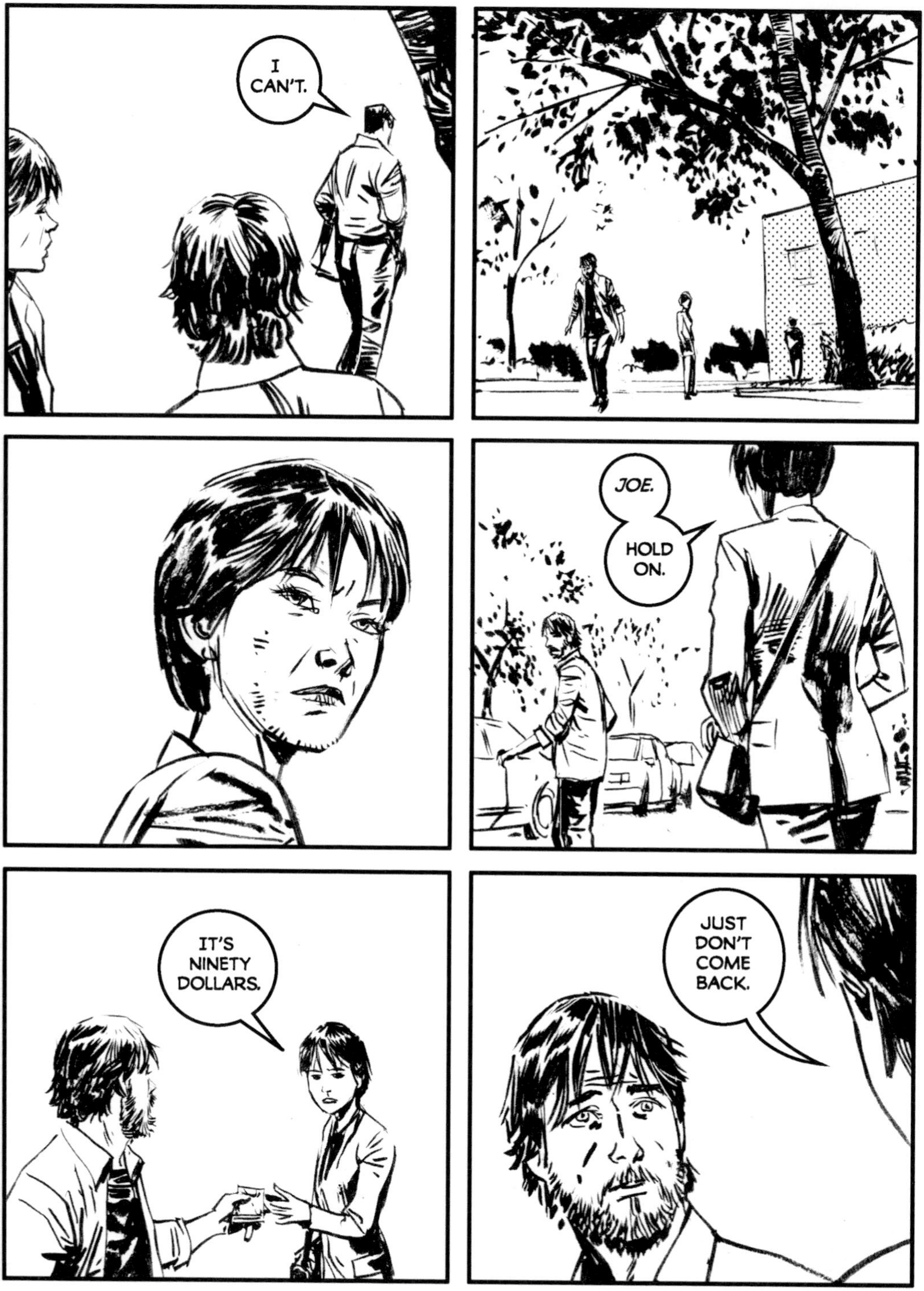
I CAN'T.
JOE.
HOLD ON.
IT'S NINETY DOLLARS.
JUST DON'T COME BACK.

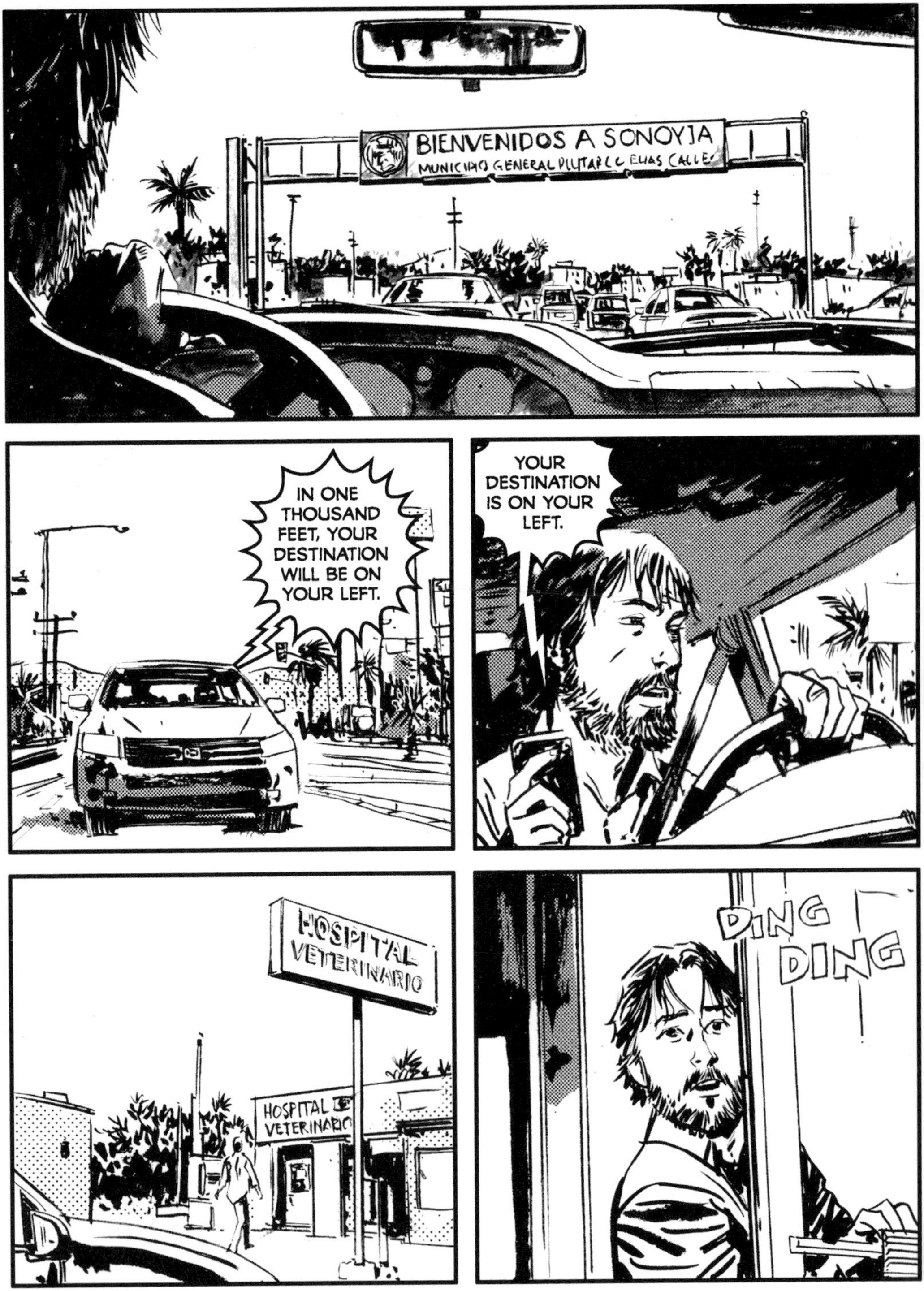
BIENVENIDOS A SONOYJA
IN ONE THOUSAND FEET, YOUR DESTINATION WILL BE ON YOUR LEFT.
YOUR DESTINATION IS ON YOUR LEFT.
HOSPITAL VETERINARIO
HOSPITAL VETERINARIO
DING DING

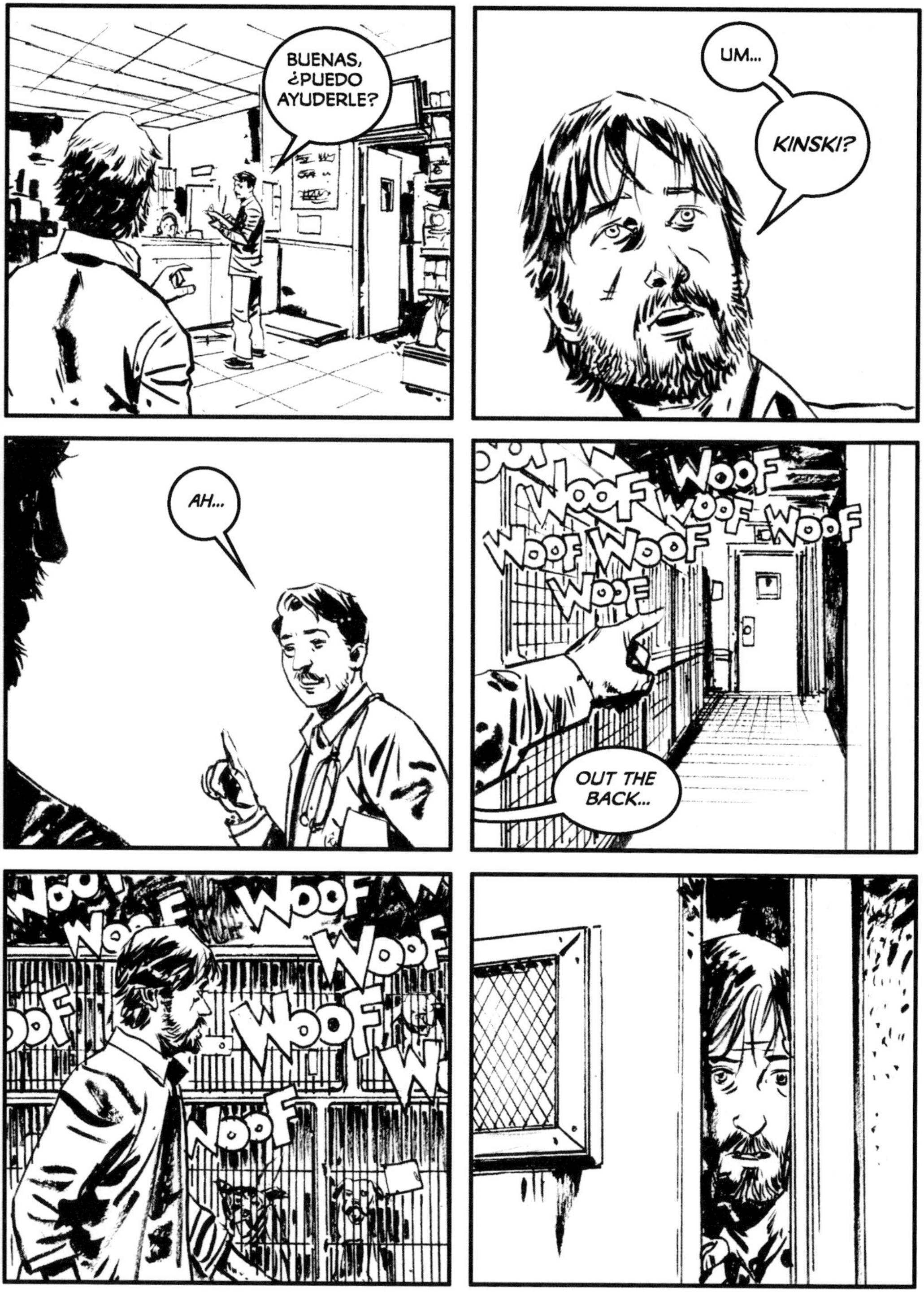
BUENAS, ¿PUEDO AYUDERLE?
UM...
KINSKI?
AH...
WOOF WOOF WOOF WOOF WOOF WOOF
OUT THE BACK...
WOOF WOOF WOOF WOOF WOOF

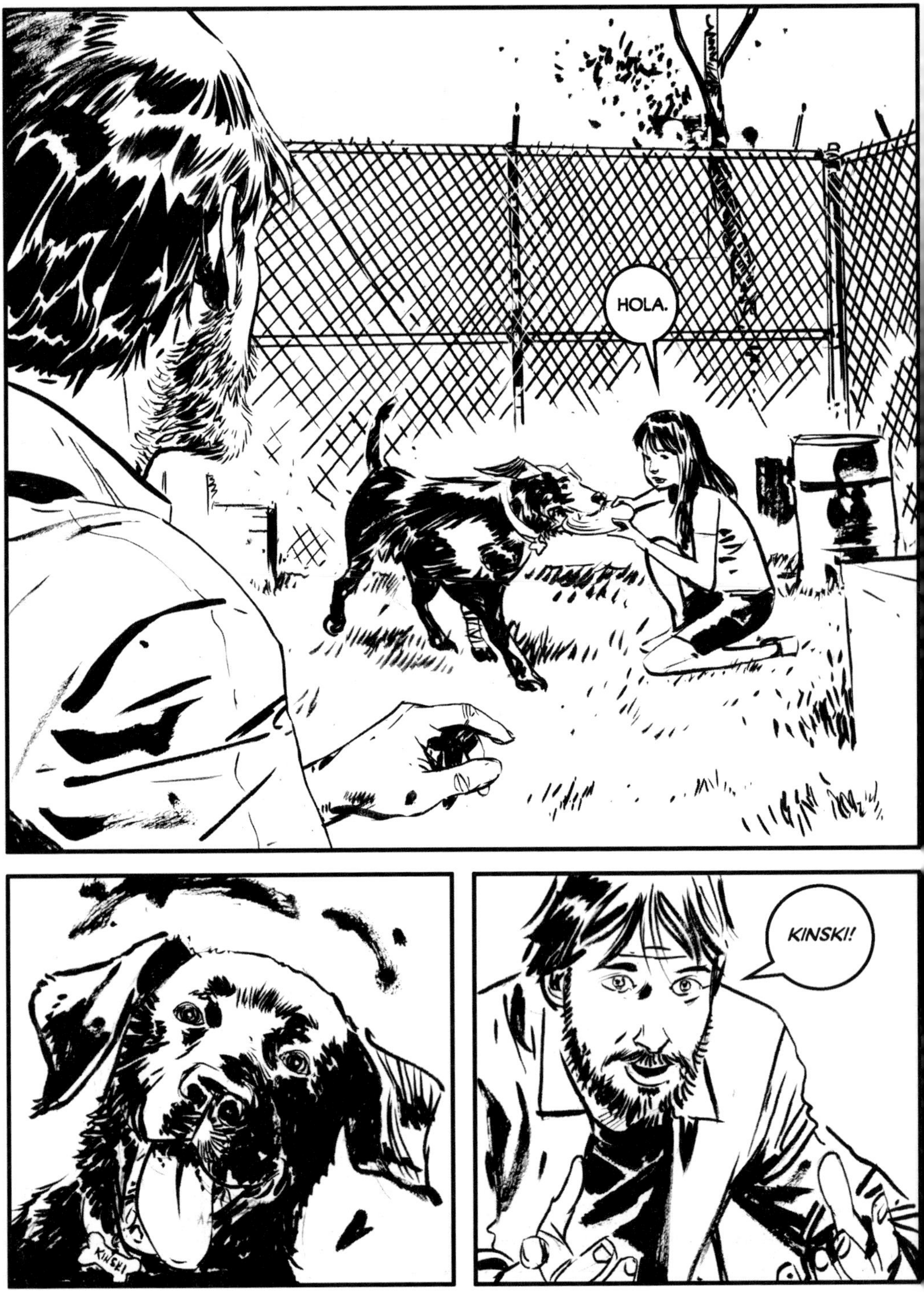
HOLA.
KINSKI
KINSKI!

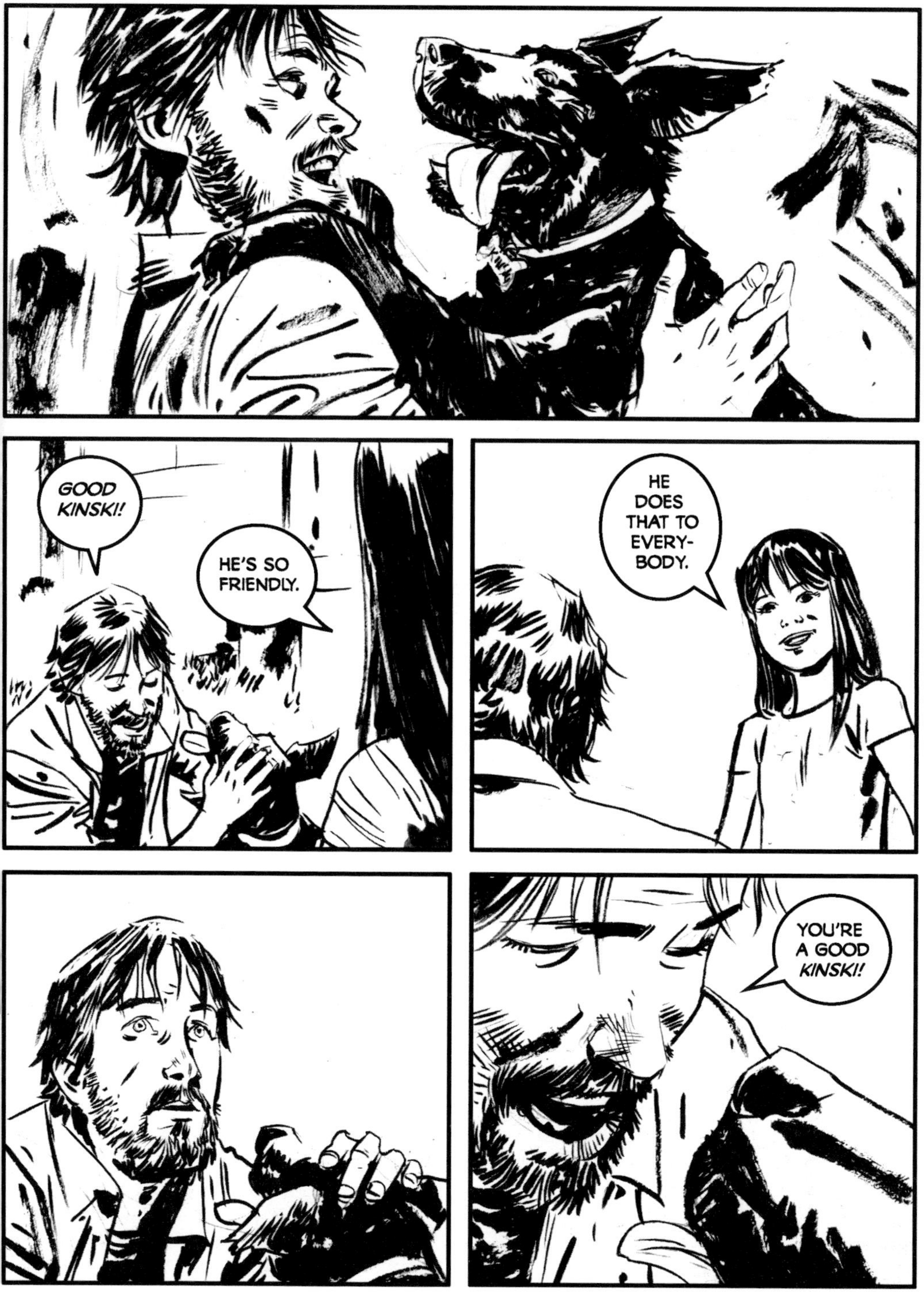
GOOD KINSKI!
HE'S SO FRIENDLY.
HE DOES THAT TO EVERY-BODY.
YOU'RE A GOOD KINSKI!

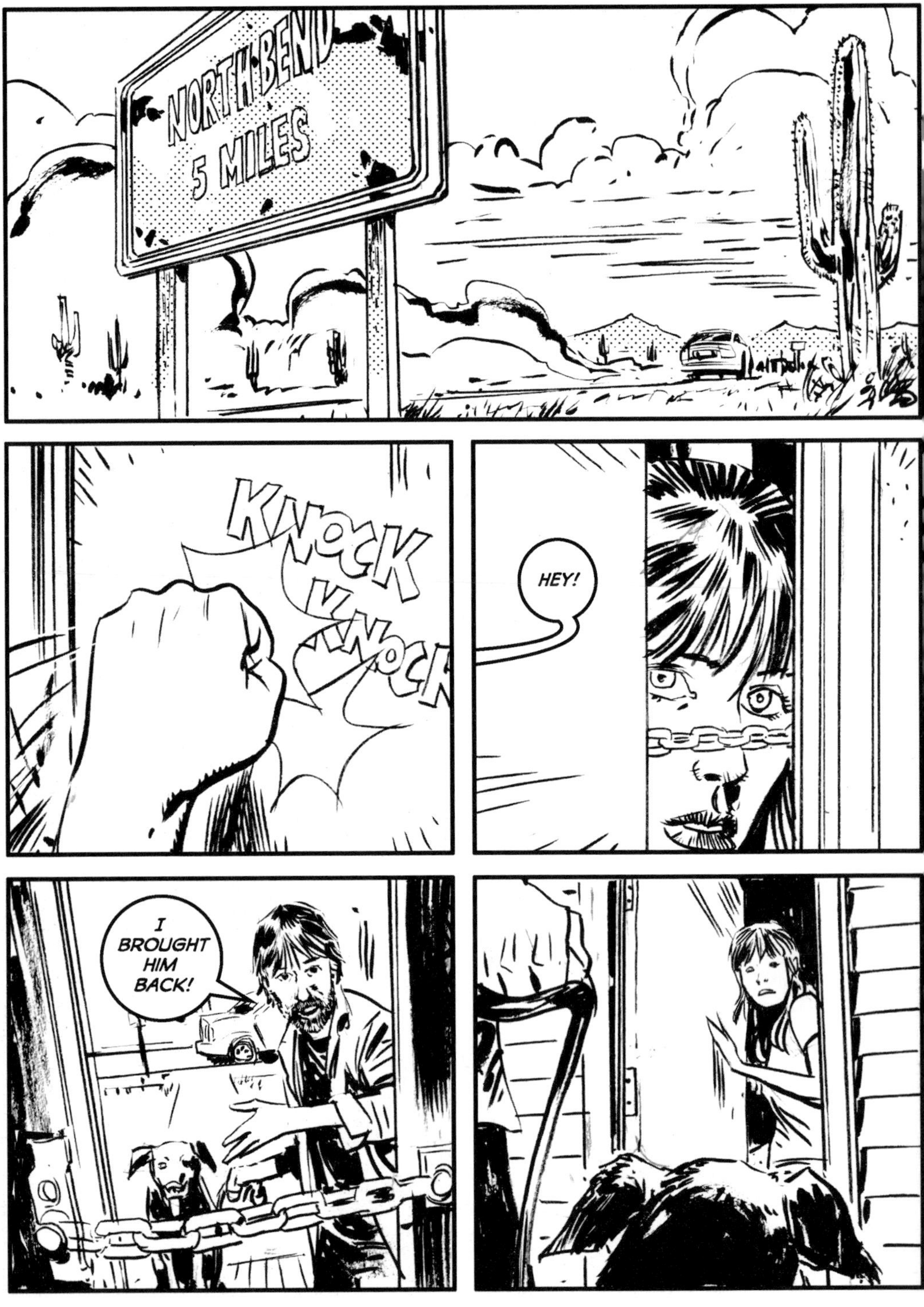
NORTH BEND
5 MILES
KNOCK
KNOCK
HEY!
I BROUGHT HIM BACK!

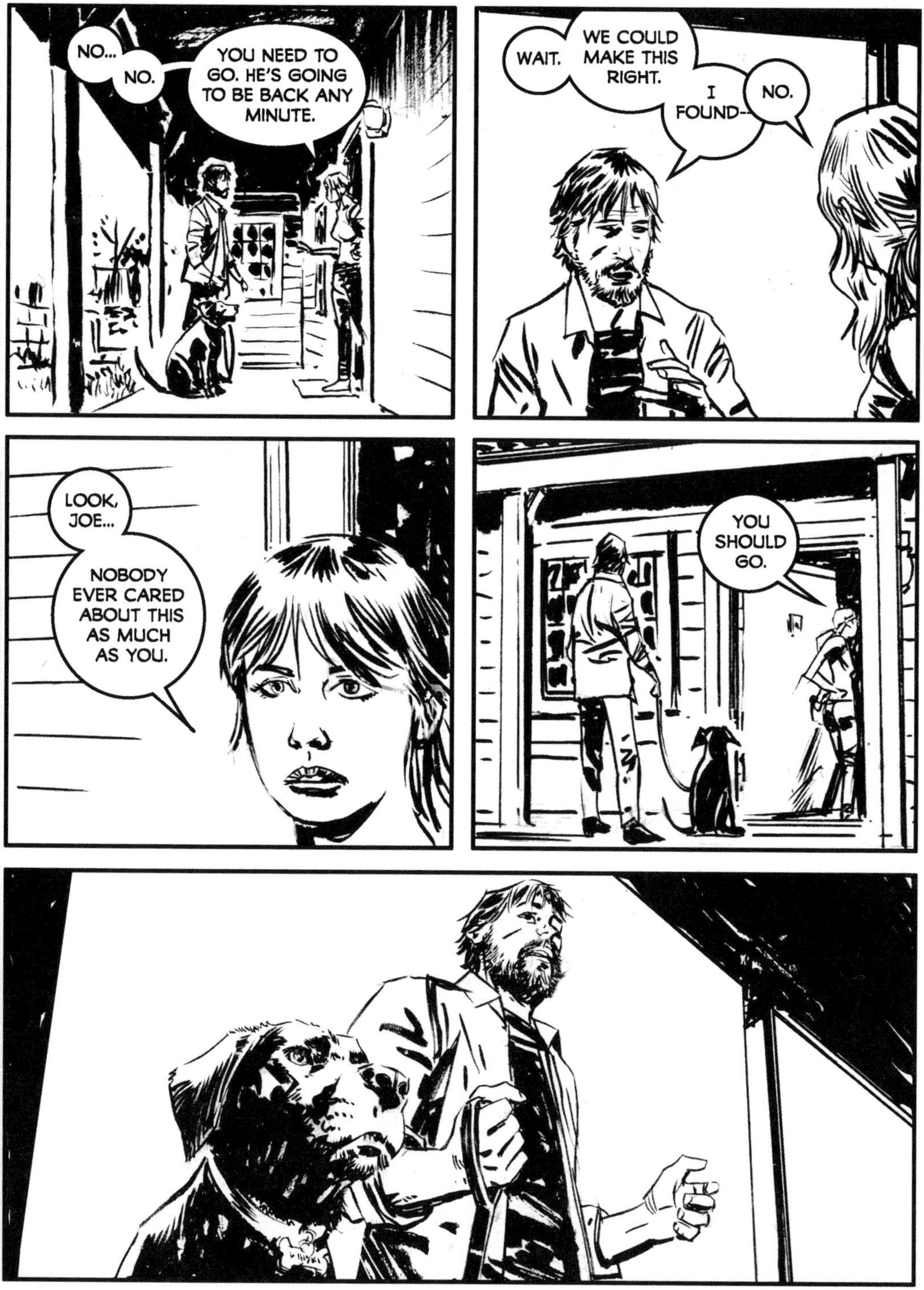
NO...
NO.
YOU NEED TO GO. HE'S GOING TO BE BACK ANY MINUTE.
WAIT.
WE COULD MAKE THIS RIGHT.
I FOUND--
NO.
LOOK, JOE...
NOBODY EVER CARED ABOUT THIS AS MUCH AS YOU.
YOU SHOULD GO.

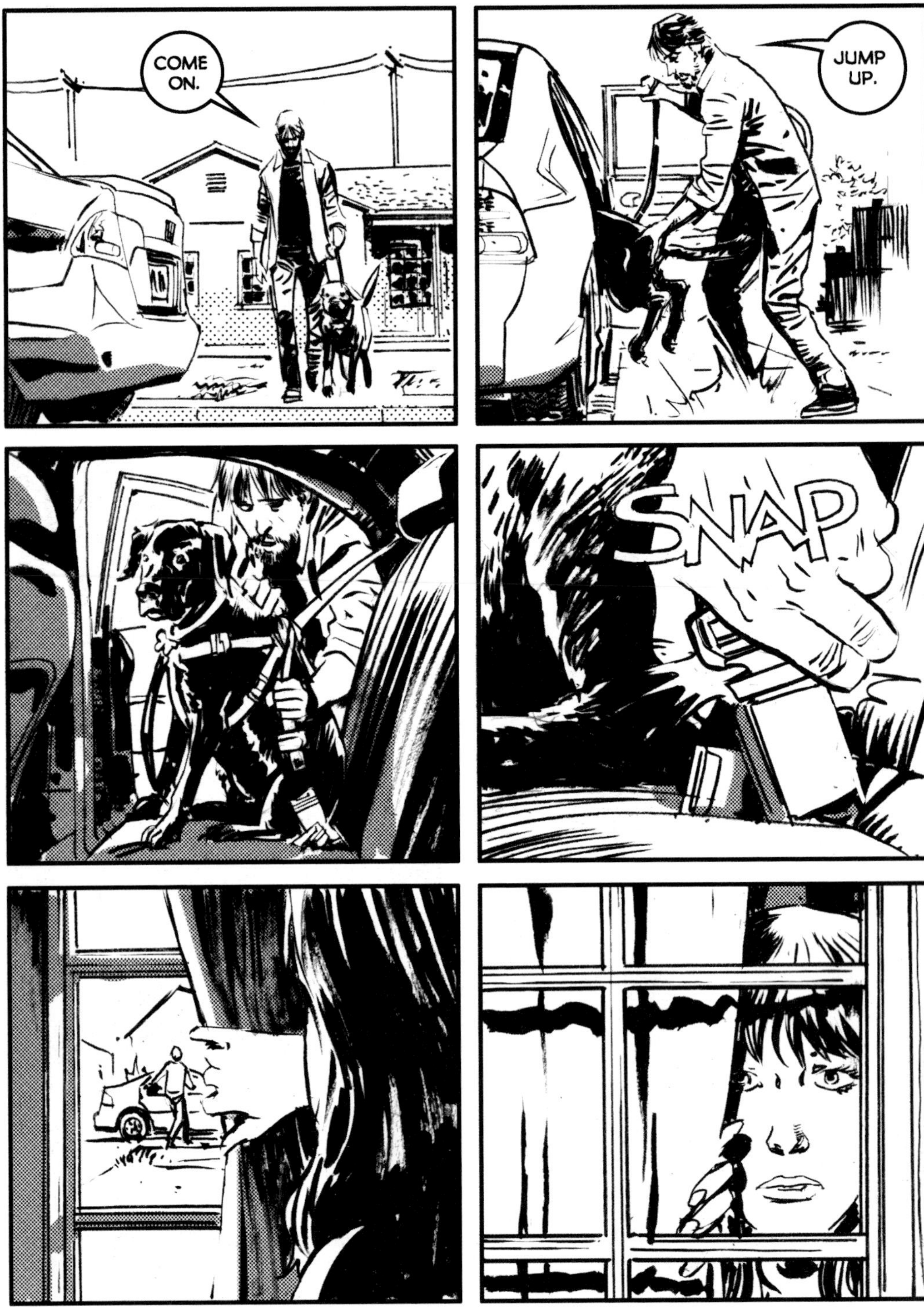
COME ON.
JUMP UP.
SNAP

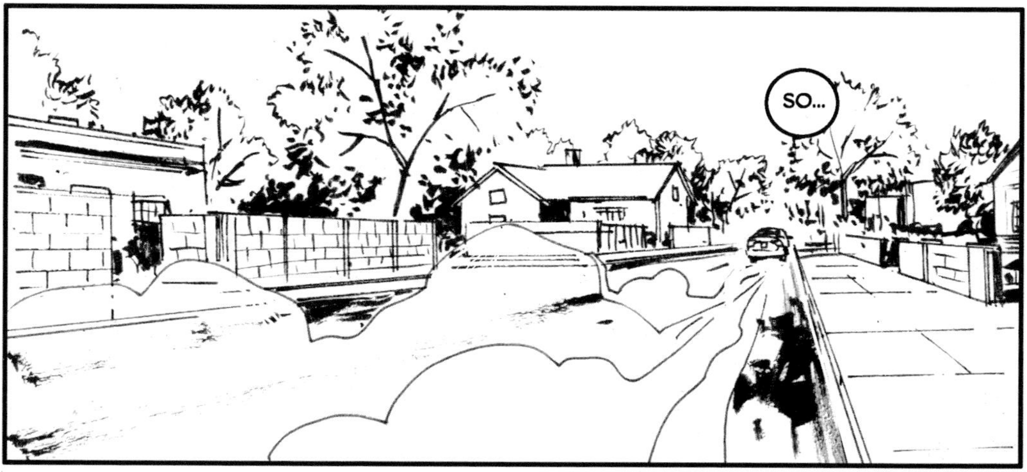
SO...

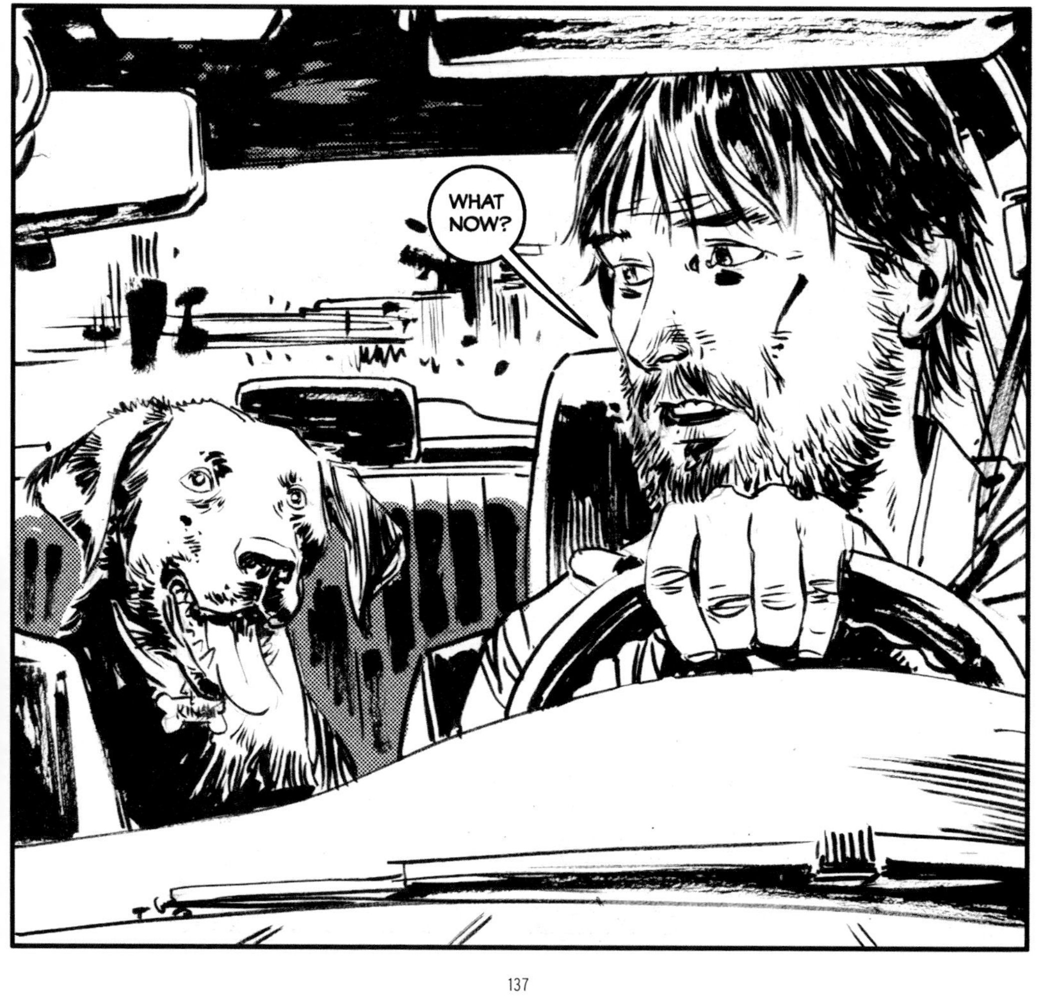
WHAT NOW?

6 MONTHS LATER

STILL IN NORTH BEND

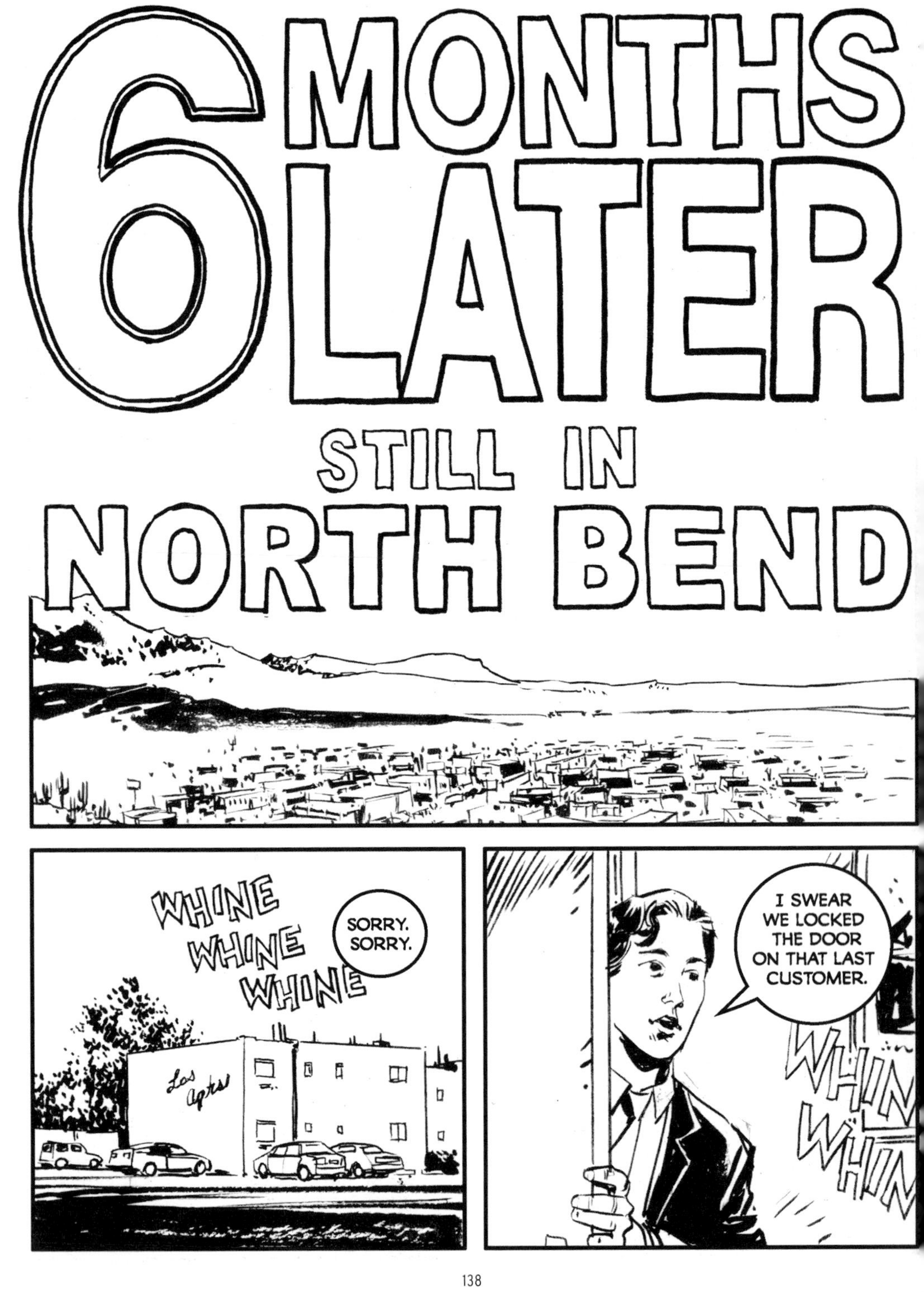
WHINE
WHINE
WHINE
SORRY. SORRY.
Los Apts
I SWEAR WE LOCKED THE DOOR ON THAT LAST CUSTOMER.

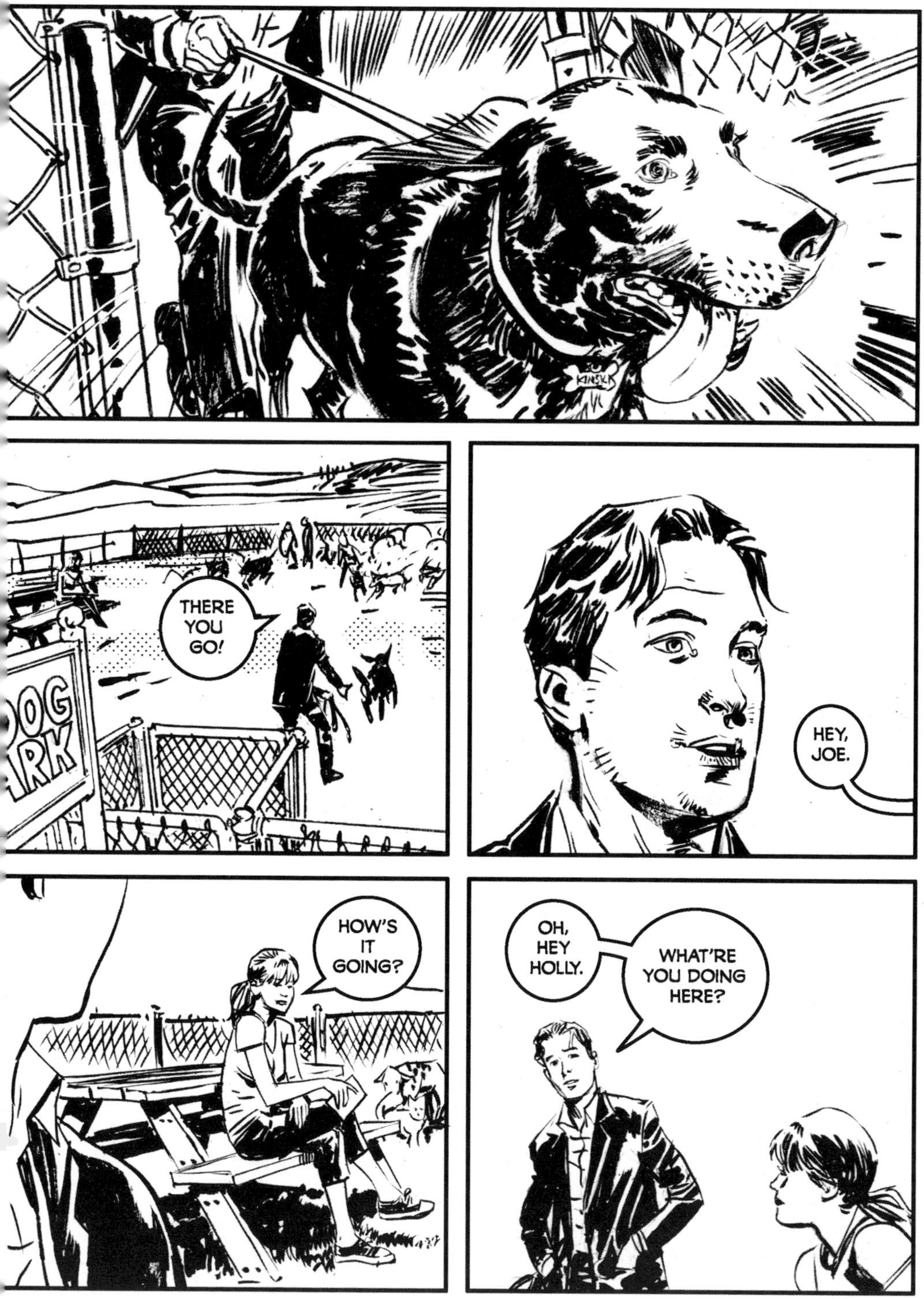
KINSKI
DOG PARK
THERE YOU GO!
HEY, JOE.
HOW'S IT GOING?
OH, HEY HOLLY.
WHAT'RE YOU DOING HERE?

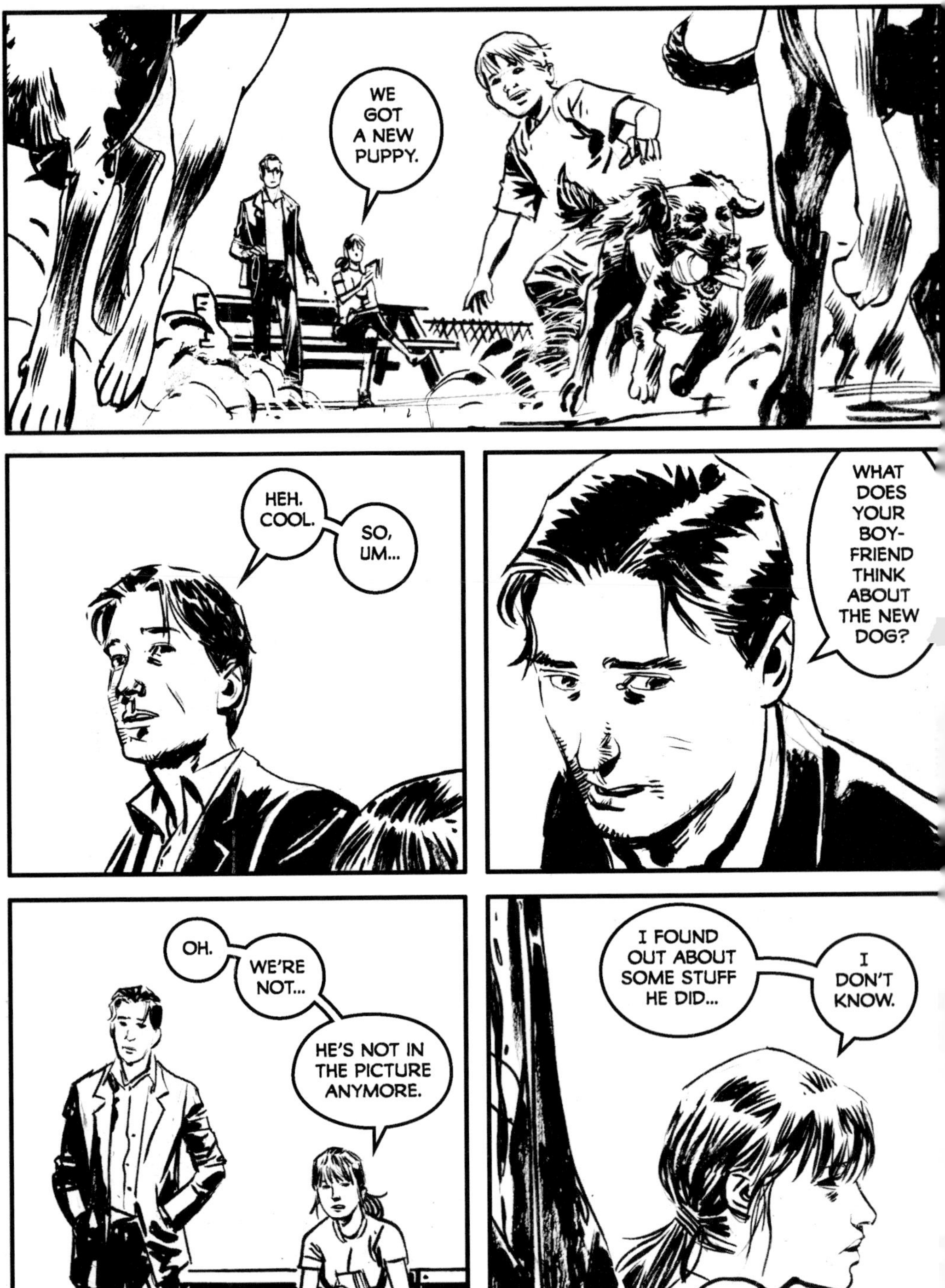

WE GOT A NEW PUPPY.
HEH. COOL.
SO, UM...
WHAT DOES YOUR BOY-FRIEND THINK ABOUT THE NEW DOG?
OH.
WE'RE NOT...
HE'S NOT IN THE PICTURE ANYMORE.
I FOUND OUT ABOUT SOME STUFF HE DID...
I DON'T KNOW.

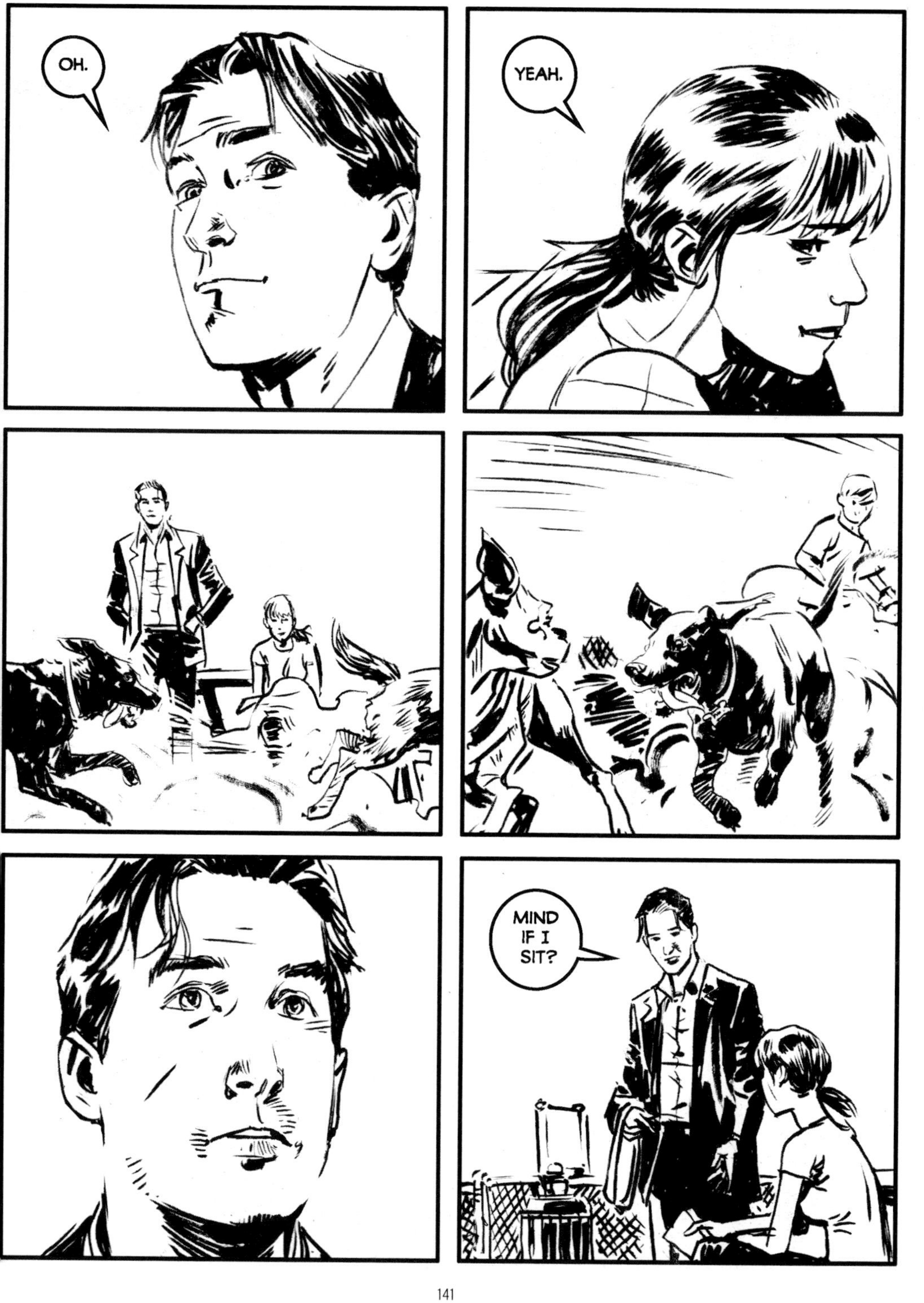
OH.
YEAH.
MIND IF I SIT?

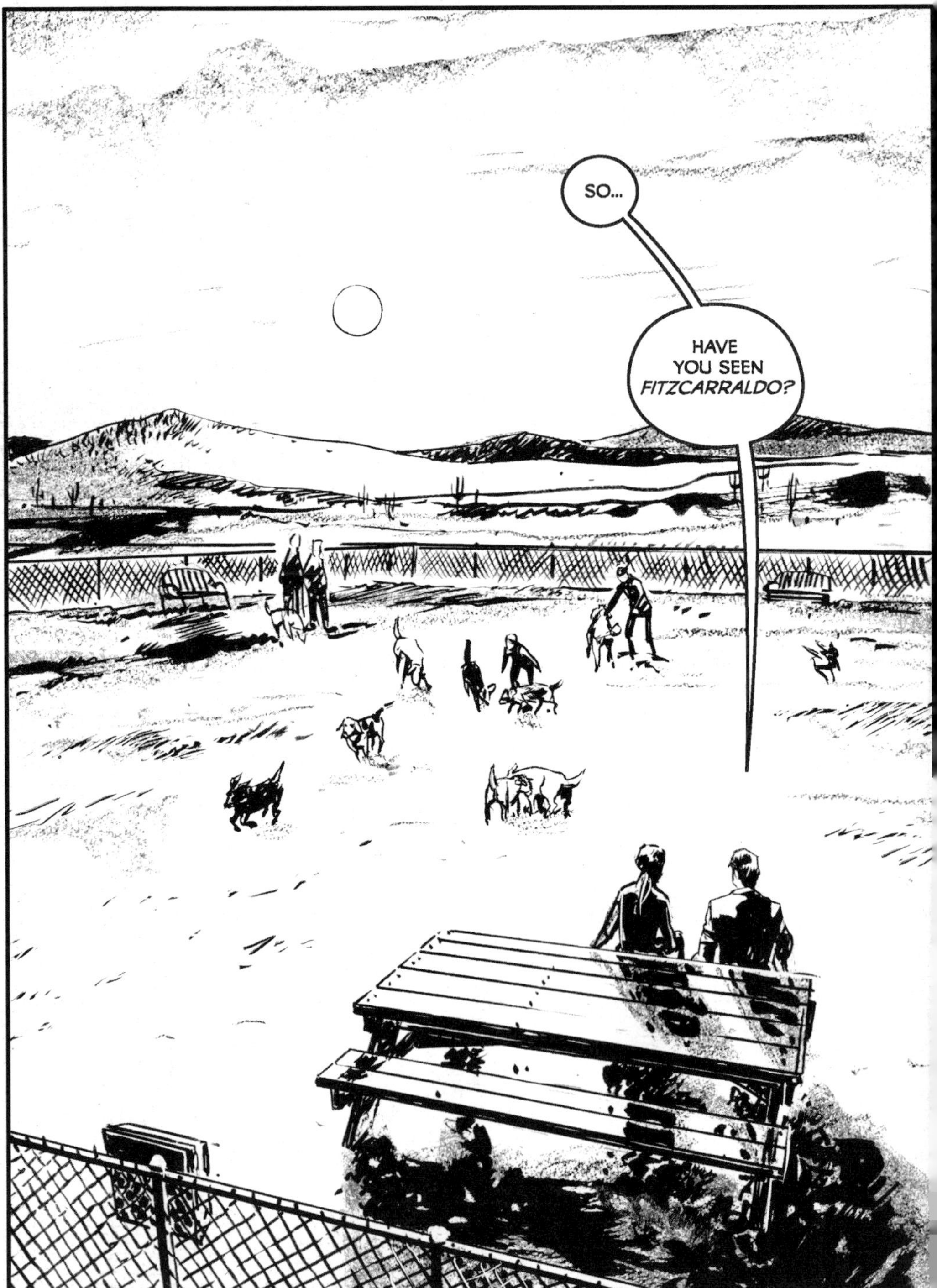
SO...
HAVE YOU SEEN *FITZCARRALDO?*

END

ABOUT THE AUTHOR

GABRIEL HARDMAN is the co-writer and artist of INVISIBLE REPUBLIC from Image Comics. He has written and drawn STAR WARS: LEGACY for Dark Horse Comics and PLANET OF THE APES for Boom! Studios. He has drawn HULK, SECRET AVENGERS and AGENTS OF ATLAS for Marvel and the OGN HEATHENTOWN from Image/Shadowline. He's worked as a Storyboard Artist for films such as INCEPTION, INTERSTELLAR, TROPIC THUNDER and X2.

He lives in Los Angeles with wife and frequent collaborator Corinna Bechko and several animals including their dog. Not Kinski, Camila.